PATH *of*
EMPOWERMENT

PATH *of*
EMPOWERMENT

PLEIADIAN WISDOM FOR A WORLD IN CHAOS

Barbara Marciniak

New World Library
Novato, California

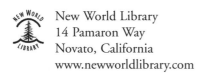

New World Library
14 Pamaron Way
Novato, California
www.newworldlibrary.com

© 2004 by Barbara Marciniak

Printed on recycled paper

Publisher Cataloging-in-Publication Data

Marciniak, Barbara, 1948–
Path of empowerment : Pleiadian wisdom for a world in chaos /
Barbara Marciniak.
    p.   cm.
    ISBN-10: 1-930722-41-9
    ISBN-13: 978-1-930722-41-5
    1. Spirit writings. 2. Channeling (Spiritualism) 3. Spiritual life.
    4. Pleiades—Miscellanea. I. Title.

BF1301.M373 M37 2004
133.9/3—dc22   0412

To my dear mother, with loving thanks

Contents

ACKNOWLEDGMENTS

Writing this book has been a tremendous exercise in discipline, responsibility, awareness, and ultimately personal empowerment. I present this book as a work of love, as an offering and probable solution to a world in the midst of a massive transformation, so that you, the reader, and millions more, can expand your conscious awareness and claim your abilities to empower your life.

I am deeply grateful to the many forces of consciousness that contributed to the creation of *Path of Empowerment*. Thank you, John Elder and the staff of Inner Ocean Publishing for your admirable patience and faith in this project. Thank you, Bill Greaves for creating an exceptionally dynamic cover, Kirsten Whatley for your exactitude in copyediting, and Madonna Gauding for the graceful interior design.

I offer my loving appreciation and most special thanks to Karen Marciniak for her encouragement, inspiration, and peerless dedication to our work; for being an excellent sister and friend, and an outstanding chronicler of the Pleiadian teachings. Equal thanks and appreciation to my editor and friend John Nelson for once again providing me with his expertly refined guidance, his hands-on editing, and trustworthy support, and for keeping me focused on the message of empowerment!

I extend my heartfelt and special thanks to my homeland students; to the staff of *The Pleiadian Times;* to my family, friends, sponsors, readers, and students everywhere, for your invaluable interest and support of our work. Thank you to Robert Henkel for your computer expertise, Noemi Schirmann for sharing your wisdom, and George Ward and Louis Acker for your astrological guidance and support. And a very special thank you to the late Jane Roberts and the incomparable Seth for being peerless pioneers of perception.

My final and preeminent acknowledgment is to our friends the Pleiadians, for their patience and steadfast loyalty as brilliant teachers, for their outrageous sense of humor, and for their invaluable contributions to the empowerment of humanity. Thank you, Ps for sharing your profound and priceless perspectives.

INTRODUCTION BY THE PLEIADIANS

*W*e call ourselves Pleiadians. And by way of an introduction, let us say that we are journeyers through time and multiple dimensions. We are a curious group intent upon exploring the nooks and crannies of existence, traipsing over cosmic hill and dale in search of answers to the majestic mysteries of life. All of existence is a vast web of energy, and there are seemingly endless and dazzling directions, connections, events, and entertaining diversions to explore. However, at present we are most earnestly focused on a specific place and time—Earth from the year 1987 through 2012. It appears that during this period this location safeguards the probability of a triumphant achievement where, for a short while, some of the majestic mysteries of life are realized and revealed. We are here to observe and participate in the greatness of this event. Our perspectives are multidimensional in range and scope, for we are a wondrous collective of conscious energies who are intentionally expanding our beliefs about the nature of existence throughout many points in time. The heavens are filled with life, and in our search for knowledge and greater understanding of who we are, our journey has led us to you.

Earth is currently experiencing a tumultuous transformation of consciousness, the likes of which you have no recorded historical precedent for. Yet, within the corridors of human cellular memory, many images stir with a hint of strange familiarity. You are deeply immersed in a time of critical change; humanity is poised at the threshold of a new understanding of cosmic power. Naturally, many of us wonder what you will do with this knowledge. In other epochs of time, the nature of this power has been misunderstood and subsequently misused, inevitably leading the way to your self-destruction. Nevertheless, the immense cycles of living and seasons of learning continue to patiently offer the same lessons, for while life may appear to be destroyed, consciousness is ever enduring and only changed in form.

Humanity is rapidly approaching the edge of the great cosmic cliffs of consciousness. What you do now, the choices you make, will determine a course of experience more complex and astounding than you can currently imagine. The dawning of a new revolution in consciousness is at hand. You cannot escape the necessity to manage this power: now or ever. In light of our adventurous spirit, we are here to share our perspectives on your rapidly changing lives, and to offer our support, as well as a few timely suggestions on managing the massively accelerated energies that silently stir your planet.

The Pleiadians

Chapter One

MULTIDIMENSIONAL REALITY AND THE DESIGN OF EXISTENCE

*W*e share our perspectives about the nature of existence as an offering for your consideration during these times of turmoil and change, to rouse you into waking up and taking charge of your life. Everyone on Earth is here to participate in and contribute to the mass awakening of humanity to the truth that your thoughts create your reality. This is crucial to understand since you are connected to layers and levels of reality that intertwine for the purpose of creating and exploring the majestic multidimensional nature of existence. Knowledge is sacred and the choice to be informed or merely entertained in today's world is a very revealing test of the times. Expanding your mind to penetrate the deeper meanings of life is not only liberating, it is crucial to your well-being, for knowledge is power, and how you use your power inevitably determines the course of your personal and collective life.

The social and political situations you currently face, personally and globally, include a series of very intense lessons of discernment. You are all challenged to see through the well-crafted, mind-boggling business of fear that has overrun the planet. Maintaining your faith in a positive outcome for all you encounter every day is not always easy; however, it is important to remember that difficult and challenging experiences precede all worthwhile accomplishments. The choices you make and the risks you are willing to take at this time are essential to the process of strengthening your resolve and waking up to the recognition and application of your personal power. Ultimately, you create all you encounter for very good reasons.

You are living in a time when opportunities for self-empowerment, expanded awareness, and spiritual growth appear to be unlimited.

Everything in existence is imbued with a form of power, including you. For a few moments, consider your beliefs about the concepts of power and personal empowerment. What images come to you? What form of power do you imagine resides within you? From days of old, awareness and self-empowerment were considered to be inseparable counterparts, like two sides of the same coin; the combination of these qualities was treasured and valued as an essential code of wisdom throughout the dimensions and annals of space and time because it was regarded as the basis for creating and maintaining a vital existence. And now, at the beginning of the third millennium, as humankind encounters a grand cosmic lesson on the value of life, this old knowledge, like a long lost and cherished heirloom, is ready to be reclaimed and restored to its rightful place within the showcase of human values. You are living in a time when opportunities for self-empowerment, expanded awareness, and spiritual growth appear to be unlimited. From some points of view, this is "the time and the place to be" in the midst of many, many probable realities, dimensions, and avenues of existence.

As a consequence, the times in which you live are particularly challenging because you are currently immersed in exploring a very intense section of the course in human development. A powerful impetus to achieve increasingly pronounced states of greater awareness and sensitivity is driving you to feel, heal, and deal with your life situations and possibilities. All the people of Earth are in crisis, and this crisis stems from a deeply ingrained fear of knowing the truth. To release this collective bondage of fear, you must be willing to see more and go deeper into what you know. It is now time to integrate your spiritual essence and become mature about how you use your mind. You are in the midst of a tumultuous transformation, an initiation through the dark night of the soul, and you must be willing and able to identify the problems occurring in your personal and collective life and manifest their solutions. You are on the verge of an astounding worldwide spiritual revolution, and with this in mind, it is essential to know that opportunities for growth are always abundantly available if you learn to create them.

Understanding the power of beliefs and the power of the mind, both individually and en masse, is the most pressing and crucial issue for humankind to grasp. Recognizing these two important keys of knowledge can open human consciousness to a new worldview of unlimited possibilities and highly creative solutions. Beliefs are essentially agreements about reality, and both personal and collective beliefs form the structure and the parameters of your life experience in any era. Beliefs, thoughts, and feelings leave a distinct formative imprint on the field of vital energy that envelops your world. You are creating all of the time and humankind is rapidly awakening to this astounding realization. The times in which you live are characterized by immense changes, and great flexibility and clear intent are required of you for dealing with this inestimable process of human transformation. Developing the ability to become aware of what you think, feel, and speak, and structuring your life with pristine clarity through thought, word, and deed are of essential importance for living an empowered life. Accepting responsibility for the power you embody is the essential and most important lesson of this transformation.

Expanding awareness is sweeping the globe with astounding momentum, stimulating humanity on a cellular level to wake up and discover its power.

The pressure to truthfully deal with your life and the world at large has never been greater, and for some people, the intensity required for this task seems overwhelming. During these times of change, opening your mind to consider points of view and vistas of life that extend outside of the box of accepted thinking is both sensible and admirable. The tremendous challenges caused by the accelerated energies of these times actually serve to stimulate you to perceive reality in a new way. You have chosen to be here at this time in order to contribute your own unique point of view to the cast of conscious beings who are producing "the great spiritual awakening" on planet Earth.

Awareness is a state of mind, and it is also the "name of the game" in these changing times. Like a colossal storm, expanding awareness is sweeping the globe with astounding momentum, stimulating humanity on a cellular level to wake up and discover its power. You must be willing and able to call a spade a spade, that is, to name and identify what you see and sense is happening at all levels with courage and clarity. Individually and collectively, your freedom hinges on your ability to speak the truth as you see it. Your lessons in living also involve very difficult issues of discernment involving your relationships with both physical and non-physical reality. Each day, the choices you make are crucial to your well-being, and just as important, your thoughts not only set the course and direction of your life in the physical 3-D world, they also ripple into and affect many other realities. The stakes in this "game of awareness" are steadily being raised, and you are challenged more than ever to identify your innermost feelings and acknowledge them as a primary source for creating your reality.

The potential for you to be more aware is constantly increasing due to the lightning-like speed at which new ideas are being exchanged and their possibilities realized. Even though you may rely on the printed word in order to learn and expand your knowledge and awareness, you are highly telepathic all of the time. Each year since 1987, the stream of cosmic energies that affect your planet has gradually increased in intensity, resulting in the pulse of life speeding up: you may notice your life moving faster and faster, as seen by the demands made on you and the frazzling speed with which you have to operate just to maintain yourself. And, what you think about and focus on comes into being with equal swiftness. The times not only demand that you become much more aware of what is happening in the global community, but they also require a new level of responsibility and honesty in your relationship with yourself. The outer world is a mirror reflection of your inner reality. You must be willing to take charge of your life and become skilled in a new way of thinking in order to navigate the shifting currents of human consciousness.

For some people, these are indeed times of tremendous stress and tumultuous transformation, and with many lives turned inside out, numerous families and individuals face the very uncomfortable feeling of being backed into a corner. The pressure to be more flexible and change one's life and beliefs is escalating at an astounding pace. The world economy is in a state of constant flux and confusion, accounting woes have wreaked havoc with the public's trust and faith in big business, layoffs continue to create more uncertainty, and the jobless rate grows daily as many people wonder how they will make a living. Rampant "dis-ease" among animals and humans poses a staggering worldwide health crisis, politics reeks of insiders' dark deals, war drums drone on and on, nuclear attacks and terrorism rank as the number one threats in the controlled media, the increase of sexual violence and acts of perversion grows more blatant, the debt-to-credit ratio is completely unsustainable, and theft, fraud, cheating, and lying are commonly cited qualities of a very corrupt leadership worldwide. It appears that so-called leaders have failed in their assigned duty to uphold liberty and champion freedom as civic responsibilities. Now, at this stage of the game, everyone is beginning to wonder why the world is in such turmoil. This is an excellent sign, for it represents a most necessary reflection and reevaluation of life that each person must face and make.

A massive increase in the intensity of cosmic radiated energy is triggering humankind to open its eyes to a greater spiritual purpose.

All of existence is filled with energy that is responsive, alive, intelligent, vibrant, flexible, and telepathic; and given that you are a part of existence, you are imbued with the same qualities. As your solar system travels the depths of space, it traverses a high-energy terrain of cosmic radiation, which is filled with a seemingly infinite web of consciousness blueprints. This creates a massive shower of fiery energy that continuously strikes Earth, which brings immense quantities of intense atomic particles that penetrate the cells and atoms of all things, providing a form of celestial electricity filled with vital life-force energy. The soft spot at the crown of an infant's head was often referred to as "the door to heaven" by ancient sages because it was recognized as a gateway for the flow of cosmic energy and spiritual intelligence into the ganglia of the cranium. Cosmic radiation charges the central nervous system with life-force energy and serves as an invisible extension of the physical nervous system and connection with the greater cosmos.

During these times of change, a massive increase in the intensity of cosmic radiated energy is triggering humankind to open its eyes to a greater spiritual purpose and to perceive a more transcendent vista of existence. The presence of these mysterious cosmic energies has long been detected and named by many different people from a wide variety of cultures: the unified field, qi or chi, prana, orgone energy, ether, dragon force, life force, the force, and cosmic radiation—all refer to the same enigma. Regardless of how it is known, you use this energy as an unlimited source of power throughout the course of your life to project your self into being. Within your particular field of experience, your thoughts, feelings, and desires are the raw materials and building blocks you use to create your world. The power to create resides in all forms of consciousness, and consciousness exists in a state of supreme cooperation throughout all of existence. Consciousness is existence. And love is the primary source material, the vibration of pulsating cosmic energy that fuels every aspect of the field of existence.

This grand field of energy is continuously stimulated and influenced by the activities of intense celestial phenomena that permeate the reaches of space and time. With your beliefs, the spectacular display of implosions and explosions of cosmic gasses and matter appears as random events, exhibiting a universe in constant collision with itself. Yet this is hardly the case. You have not yet dared to believe in or recognize the presence of the profound order that is at the core of all life. An evolving presence of collective Cosmic Intelligence actually moves, plans, and designs existence with distinct and deferential purpose. Actually, all forms of consciousness have the inherent power to plan and create experiences, and from a larger perspective, this entire interconnected network of cosmic consciousness is the key component in the game of life. The orbs in the heavens play many roles. Stellar components are essentially life-force communication centers that are intricately woven together through a tremendous telepathic linkup. They are utilized by many intelligent beings as a means for sending specific transmissions through frequency modulation from one location to another. Every flash of light, supernova, and solar flare, every action—massive and miniscule—is essentially important to the development of all parts of this cosmic network and is clearly set into motion by way of intent in one reality or another.

In the cosmos, Earth is located near the outer rim of spirals in the Milky Way Galaxy, many thousands of light years away from the mystical Galactic Center. According to your reckoning, light travels almost six trillion miles in one of your years, placing you some physical distance from this source of light and energy. Even though it may appear that you exist in some remote avenue on the galactic map of the heavens, every portion of existence is interrelated and inherently connected through the powerful, pulsating, alive, caring, creative, ever-changing web of cosmic energy. You are made from this energy and actually have a duty and responsibility to manage this abundance of vitality, no matter in which domain of reality you may reside.

Your world is just beginning to discover the multitude of capabilities inherent within the human form.

It is most important for you to accept that you are a powerful being. Your physical body serves as your own intimate example of the impeccable design of life; the intricate and wondrous organization of your cells, bones, and organs illustrates a vast network of cooperation that mirrors back to you the primary nature of existence. By design, you are a fine achievement: a unique organic computer that is fully capable of consciously experiencing the different levels of your own reality, as well as many others.

In all truth, your world is just beginning to discover the multitude of capabilities inherent within the human form. For thousands of years, many clever diversions have kept humanity from understanding the true nature of its power and natural talent for creating the world. For many millennia, limiting beliefs about your lack of personal power have been accepted as facts throughout your world; this was made manifest through focusing your power of attention on these beliefs. Such beliefs are agreements about reality, and they set the stage for what you encounter. Your state of awareness then determines how you respond to the dramas of life you have created. You have the free will to choose what you will, and what you sow will be yours to harvest. We dare say you are much more complex and wondrous than you realize. With a good measure of faith, trust, and desire—augmented with a large dose of cosmic knowledge, as well as common sense—you can certainly learn to focus your attention, be very clear about your intentions, and manifest what you want in your life.

Self-empowerment is a worthy achievement in any reality,

although it is not necessarily an easy state of mind to achieve. Like any skill, it must be focused upon and developed, and called into being; yet once encouraged to awaken, self-empowerment blossoms and grows on its own, much like a hearty heirloom plant that thrives and flourishes season after season. Self-empowerment is the most natural and treasured flowering of an awakened mind. Nestled in the depths of your cells are the memories and records of all of your ancestors, some of whom dealt with the same issues you are encountering today. Perceptions of reality are imprinted in the genetic code and passed along to the various participants in a bloodline. In all lines of time and in all realities of existence, personal freedom is the prerequisite to pioneering new parameters of possibility. Although some of your ancestors knew that self-empowered people are self-determining and do not require the lessons of deceptive leadership, the freedoms and gains one generation realizes are not guaranteed for another. Each generation chooses its own values as well as what is important for spiritual growth—individually, when you explore and expand your innate personal power, you flourish; when you abdicate it, you create tyranny.

The nature of reality is such that it will mirror, mix, mingle, and play with any and all types of energy without judgments. Your thoughts, feelings, desires, and emotions, as expressed in words and deeds, are all projections of energy based on your personal beliefs. As you become more consciously aware of your beliefs, you will begin to direct the course of your life. Life is not a random occurrence; at the core, it is an experiential agreement between many beings from many realities for the purpose of exploration and discovery. Creative expression and supreme responsibility are key components for awakening and developing your spiritual intelligence. Self-empowerment is about examining yourself and knowing how and why you function as you do, and magnificent opportunities and freedoms abound whenever you choose the path of self-empowerment to co-create your reality with the power of the multiverse, which comprises all of existence including the apparent 3-D universe.

The current climate of consciousness opens you and your world to many discoveries of invisible powers; the power in the ether, the power in the body, and the power of intention are a composite of very old, yet essential, steps along the path to understanding life. There is a saying that power corrupts and absolute power corrupts absolutely, implying perhaps that the dangers of power mean power is something to avoid altogether. In actuality, you are birthed from power. You are conceived in this reality through the power of sex, and an act of innate personal power propels you to leave your mother's womb at the appropriate time. The nature of existence is imbued with power and so are you. You are a powerful being, you cannot avoid dealing with power, and when it comes to power, you will always be tested to see if you will abuse and misuse it. Power is a test of character, and the choice is always yours. In one small cell, there is more potential power than you could use in your entire lifetime; however, global consciousness must first demonstrate its acceptance of ultimate responsibility for handling that kind of power before the gates to the mysteries of the multiverse are opened.

The period from 1987 to 2012 has been foreseen by great sages in many ages as the turning point in a very powerful cycle of human development.

Every once in a great, great while, in certain locations of time and space, a massive acceleration of cosmic energy occurs. Based on a joint agreement among various forms of intelligence, including the stars, planets, and an innumerable host of cosmic players, the acceleration is designed to awaken the various participants to a much greater experience of existence through integrating a huge vibrational change of energy. The gateway to such a time of awakening opened on your world in 1987, initiating twenty-five years of unprecedented change and exponential transformation. The period from 1987 to 2012 has been foreseen by great sages in many ages as the turning point in a very powerful cycle of human development.

Many ancient peoples of your world placed inestimable value on the knowledge that existence is composed of multiple layers of physical and non-physical intelligence. They observed and studied the myriad of subtle, non-linear information found in the patterns and cycles of nature. Throughout time, the meaning of the sun's cycles was of utmost importance to almost every civilization. Your relationship to time is based on the presence and position of the solar orb. In other ages, people recognized that the solar rays are the source of life, and they considered the sun to be God: the divine deity of creation. They also knew that endings are a sign and signature of new beginnings, for the changing seasons portrayed this great teaching with astounding style throughout the course of the Earth's yearly journey around the sun.

The rhythms of nature are of key importance to understanding how your world functions. To ancient peoples, the mysteries of life, death, and rebirth were considered to be of inherent value in understanding the various cycles of development in physical reality and beyond. Time was observed to be cyclical and patterns of life were also known to repeat and spiral around again, offering new opportunities, as well as old familiarity. Many of your ancestors were operating with a very different view of life and time than you currently hold. From some perspectives, time is seen as flexible and changeable, with the past and future simultaneously occurring and as fully valid and alive as the present. Time serves as a locator and organizer of realities, creating invisible boundaries as containers for creation. In much larger terms, these twenty-five years of accelerated energy are like a bookmark in time, noting a place where all participating forms of consciousness experience a profound increase in awareness by integrating many essential new perceptions of reality very, very quickly.

During this twenty-five-year period of transition and transformation, the version of reality you have come to know will appear to be less and less stable. As events on the world stage steadily escalate into chaos and confusion, you will be compelled to wake up and really start thinking about what is occurring. This is both a challenging and most stimulating time to be alive, and questioning everything—your life, your beliefs, and your worldview—is the most essential part of the process of discovering your inherent power to create the world you meet. It takes great courage to question your existence, and even greater strength is required to know and recognize the truth when you see it.

We often refer to this special period of time as "the nanosecond" in the annals of time, because from certain vistas and points of view the twenty-five years pass by faster than the blink of an eye. Looking through the annals of time in search of this period can be like looking for a special sliver of wood in an endless expanse of forest. Nevertheless, all of existence is intricately connected and all time is simultaneously occurring; therefore, with a bit of knowledge and know-how, many areas of what you consider to be time and space can be located and explored. Perspective is the key. As seen from outside your time, the years in which you live appear to be filled with magnificent opportunities for humanity to connect with vast, new vistas of knowledge, and to awaken during a spiritual renaissance of stunning magnitude. You may be wondering: How can this be? Why us? Why here? Why now? Well, all of existence is designed with great purpose, and from our perspective, you must first seek to know yourself before the answers begin to make sense.

Every aspect of existence is interwoven and connected through a complex network of consciousness. Before you immerse yourself into 3-D living, you have the ability to preview the parameters of earthly life, to oversee the aspects of your own plan, purpose, and intent within a specific climate of consciousness. You choose the moment and the time of your birth, as well as your genealogical bloodline, which is rich with an ancestral encoding of perceptions based on many lessons in living. In the here and now, you forget your plans in order to play your version of the game of life more effectively. You immerse yourself in your identity and become fully engaged in the process of exploring and experiencing the path you have chosen. The course of your life is a significant and purposeful journey that continuously confronts and stimulates you to develop your abilities. You actually learn about the nature of existence as you learn how to operate your biological form.

You may appear to exist as a singular being, yet you have endless connections to realities beyond the bounds of your perceptions.

Understanding the numerous roles that multidimensional influences play in your life is of major importance. As it becomes more and more apparent that you and your world share time and space with other realities, you will also discover that you exist in other realities as well. You may appear to exist as a singular being, yet you have endless natural connections to realities beyond the bounds of your perceptions. And what exactly are perceptions? How is it that a multitude of realities can exist side by side with you, yet you hardly ever notice? Individually and collectively you produce a vibrational frequency that locates you in a specific version of reality. This non-physical energy signature defines your personal nature from moment to moment and outlines the parameters of your Earth-based experience. Your greater world reality is founded upon a series of mass agreements, and your personal life is an intimate journey of self-discovery within this massive framework of reality, where you live out your chosen beliefs. How you grasp and interpret the vast array of sensations and stimuli within this multilayered environment determines the degree of self-realization you develop. Your perceptions, or the ability to sense the various subtle nuances of reality, are awakening, and they tend to blossom and grow with greater ease when you operate from a stance of flexibility and trust.

Direct telepathic knowledge actually sustains and supports a much greater reality than you currently perceive. Telepathy is a natural form of communication by frequency that is inherent within all forms of energy. Mass agreements about the nature of reality are unconsciously debated and considered on a psychic level of reality at the speed of thought. Your cells are continuously receiving data, and evaluating, processing, and transmitting signals that carry the frequency of what you are available to experience; these activities are effortlessly performed, without your being the slightest bit aware of them. At this point in your development, if you were to suddenly consciously shift into multidimensional living—where simultaneous lives, celestial relatives, and probable realities all appear at once—you would probably overload your system and blow your circuits.

You must be very grounded in the 3-D world to integrate and understand the myriad of signs, symbols, and meanings of other realities. First of all, you must clearly love and accept yourself for who you are, and this is no small task. When you can lovingly recognize yourself as your own creation, you free yourself from the mass-induced trance of powerless living. You must live your life with clear boundaries and distinctions, applying great discernment and discrimination of mind to all you encounter. In addition, you must learn to honestly and openly express your feelings and emphasize your own self-worth as you learn to develop a true love for who you are. Conditions, excuses, competition, or wishing you were someone else will get you nowhere. And, if you live life with few boundaries, you may find yourself greatly infringed upon by characters not only of this dimension, but others as well. You must first learn to treasure and value your human form, and then you can learn to enhance your perceptions and begin to explore the web of existence by paying attention to the great influx of vital, life-sustaining energy that fills your world.

For the purpose of expanding the horizon of your beliefs, stretch your mind and imagine that you are connected to a network of intelligence that is ongoing and deeply immersed in exploring the potentials of perceptions through a very involved and good-hearted game of consciousness. After you read these words, close your eyes for a few moments, relax, and allow yourself to really feel the depth of possibilities within this concept. When you open your eyes and refocus on the here and now, intend to maintain the essence of your experience, and note any images or symbols your imagination has provided. Your imagination is an important tool for recognizing and exploring the invisible, non-physical realms that intersect with the physical world of matter. This aspect of imagination has been ignored in modern times because of a very effective and purposeful long-term campaign of control that has emphasized supreme distrust and suspicion of the body's power and capabilities. Know that the invisible non-physical realms and the physical world are all aspects of a single reality. From moment to moment, your consciousness operates in both physical and non-physical reality with profound grace and ease. You are born with this ability, yet you have been led to believe in false limitations and to distrust your inner knowing. Projects involving the conditioning and control of the human psyche have their roots in very ancient times, and many limiting ideas about the nature of reality have been deeply entrenched and encoded within your genetic inheritance, passed from generation to generation, without being challenged as to validity or purpose.

From moment to moment, your consciousness operates in both physical and non-physical reality with profound grace and ease.

The nature of any reality can appear to be separately distinct from everything else, even though every aspect of existence is connected through the commonality of vital life-force energy. All realities share the capacity to link up to a network of interactive intelligence that exists within and around the confines of space and time you currently perceive. In your own time and space, human perceptions are gradually adjusting to the enormous change in awareness that is being required to restore the human link with Cosmic Intelligence. As your conscious awareness opens to the multidimensional qualities of existence, you will learn to gather knowledge from other places and carry it back to 3-D reality to enhance and heal your own life. Your personal achievements have a profound effect on the global state of mind, and in the "ideal made real," you and your world will flourish with fresh ideas and become exuberantly inspired to create a new vision of the purpose of life.

When you change your attitude, you change your personal and collective life. People all over the world are realizing the need to refocus the direction of global attention toward one of honesty and integrity, where valuing peace and respectfully honoring and caring for Earth and all her creatures are of primary intent. As the vibration of the mass consciousness expands and matures, greater momentum and focus will be gained. The Earth feels these changes. An elevated state of awareness in the collective consciousness of humankind triggers the Earth to unlock and release more of the complete story of time stored within her being. When you are willing to know and face personal truths, you contribute to building the frequency of consciousness required to uncover and release the truth of human history. Developing spiritual awareness unlocks the keys to Earth's archeology, and is also of critical importance in understanding your past, present, and future well-being. The human mind is being extremely stimulated by many subtle cosmic forces to activate a new type of consciousness, and even though you have only just begun to tap in to the tremendous potentials of creative expression that await your attention, many millions of people are already well on their way to exploring these life-empowering discoveries.

Sometimes people are afraid of the truth, and the multidimensional aspect of their transformation appears to be shaking humanity to its core. Around the globe people are noting the sizable increase in unusual energies and activities in the heavens.

Your world has always shared time and space with concurrent realities that you do not see. Interdimensional, extraterrestrial, and ultradimensional visitors are occupants of other realities that can interact and intercede with yours. Benevolent beings constantly keep a keen watch over your world; however, there is also a very pronounced and strong influence from a cadre of energies who do not have your best interests at heart. The ancient adage "as above, so below" is a truth that outlines more situations and occurrences than you can currently comprehend. Invisible energies from other realities are naturally attracted to you and your world, and the vibrations of intent that you produce will determine the quality and type of influence you experience from them.

Reality is built in the mind. Those who attempt to steal or seal off your mind have hoarded these secrets for a long, long time.

For many millennia the people of Earth have been continuously creating their experience by default and neglect. Thoughts and feelings, words and ideas are in a constant search to attract their likenesses. To produce effective and desirable results, thoughts must be clearly focused and directed toward a desired goal. The realization of this knowledge is of key importance in the initiation of humankind into a higher state of awareness. The tumultuous transformation sweeping your planet offers many choices to see reality in a new light, to achieve new levels of self-understanding, and to apply new principles of reality to your life. Brilliant minds, cavorting outside of the box of traditional censure and dogma, have enthusiastically concurred that thought conditions and objectifies space.

Many millions of people have proved to themselves that

thought creates reality by using their intuition to tap in to the non-physical and invisible energies that permeate time and space and all of existence. Reality is built in the mind. Those who attempt to steal or seal off your mind have known about and hoarded these secrets for a long, long time. Liberating knowledge is not taught in your schools. You are dissuaded from the truth, so it is no great wonder that the major issue rising to the surface in so many lives involves repressed expression—basically, dealing with and healing feelings of fear about owning your truth on a personal, global, and galactic scale.

The current fashion in Western civilization promotes doubters and skeptics who are recognized and rewarded for their worrisome speculations. And because of an ancient ingrained fear of the body and its wisdom, people can no longer tell the difference between what they are told is the truth and what makes sense to them. This collective denial has now achieved a critical mass, and ages of emotionally toxic debris are rising to the surface to be identified and safely released. From a bigger picture of reality, the people of Earth are emerging from an amnesiac-like state of collective shock, which has blocked the influx of spiritual knowledge into the human gene pool. And while it is quite obvious to many that "you create your reality," the vast majority of humans still need to be awakened from the unconsciously controlled trance of powerlessness that they voluntarily took on.

The ancient battle between science and religion over the exclusive rights to define reality is reaching an appropriate crisis point; you may have dealt with this same issue in other times and places. Geological records offer ample evidence that nuclear detonations destroyed civilizations' thousands of years ago. Eastern religious texts refer to many extended wars in the heavens that wreaked havoc on Earth. Sophisticated artifacts and unusual skeletons have been unearthed for centuries from undisturbed rock strata dating back millions and even billions of years. The past has been whitewashed, controlled, and erased. What you learned in school about the history of Earth paints a randomly chaotic picture of an ignorant people constantly at odds with life. These explanations have become part of the foundation of thought that embraces the concepts of powerlessness and victimhood, which is how you are officially encouraged to interpret existence. Taken to the extreme, even nature is seen as a potential enemy—an unpredictable and volatile force over which you have no influence—rather than as an extension and expression of the collective mind.

To flourish and thrive, you must truly embrace and energize the concept that your physical vehicle is of inestimable value.

These times of change involve a rapid emergence from an era of ignorance, breaking free from an old spell that has been in place for thousands and thousands of years. To flourish and thrive, you must truly embrace and energize the concept that your physical vehicle—the body that you occupy—is of inestimable value. You must accept your own worthiness and be willing and able to feel genuine love and appreciation for who you are—this is the essential key for opening the doors of change and attracting the very, very best experiences that life has to offer. The love you seek from others must be generated by you, for you. When you feel genuine love for yourself, you are connecting with and contributing to the vital-force energy that sustains all of existence; it is the great gift you have to offer the world—your own version of the love frequency. To cultivate a loving relationship with yourself, take time everyday—morning and evening—to sit or stand in front of a mirror for five to ten minutes for an intimate eye-to-eye appointment with yourself. Gaze steadily into your eyes, and maintaining direct eye contact, open your heart and tell yourself that you love you. Repeat the phrase "I love you" aloud as you continue to look deeply into the mirror's reflection of your eyes. Watch your pupils and irises, and allow any feelings that the words bring up to flow over your body, like warm sunshine dancing through the depths of the forest. As you participate in this exercise, you must also observe your actions and responses to your message of love. Do different versions of you appear in the mirror? Are you smiling? Do you meet something that makes you drop your gaze and look away? Is there a part of you that did not accept the love? What is your body doing? Do any tears appear to melt the seals of your memories? Are you holding your breath or breathing long and deep? How do you feel about purposely creating time to tell yourself that you are loved?

Through the course of your life, learning to use your mind in a multitude of ways, such as participating in mental exercises, and then observing and reflecting upon your responses will unlock the mysteries of your own thinking. Many multifaceted opportunities await, and if you do the work and learn to trust yourself then the times ahead will offer unique experiences to enhance your perceptions of reality. These new perceptions hold life, they hold meaning and ease and healing, and they are transmitted energetically, orb to orb and cell to cell. As a human being, you are undergoing a massive restructuring of your psyche to become more consciously aware of extensive inner truths, and as a pioneer of perception, it is imperative that you understand and trust the life you create.

The current extensive acts of war and control implemented by world leaders demonstrate their desperation over losing their hold on humanity. They will do anything to divert you from paying attention to and awakening your personal power. Those who refuse to awaken feed those who control them. This is an old agreement, with no judgments. When consciousness awakens, it needs no controllers. We cannot offer you a guarantee on the viability of your reality; however, you can certainly create the version of the world you want, and there is, in effect, unlimited support for this endeavor.

Your world has always been watched and studied by many, many beings, each with different intentions and agendas. Yet, in general, you are supported by those who understand the intricacies of cooperation in which there is a point, a purpose, and a dignity to the rise of control and the abuse of power. When forms of consciousness choose to forget, deny, deactivate, and disdain their own power to create and to know, when they devalue free thinking, then they become part of the drama, the game so to speak, that allows them to experience existence under the apparent control and dominion of others. The lessons and issues involve fear of the unknown, fear of perceptions, and fear of being in charge of one's life. Overcoming fear of personal power is a customary stage in the development of conscious awareness; nonetheless, the all-important question remains: How far will you go before valuing what is innately yours?

The current acts of war and control implemented by world leaders demonstrate their desperation over losing their hold on humanity.

It is time to connect the dots. Events serve multilayer purposes and everything depends on the point of view. Are you willing to accept responsibility for loving yourself and the Earth into a state of wholesome well-being? Can you conceive of the momentous task you set forth to accomplish in this life? Will you allow the bigger picture to be revealed? Mental flexibility involves using your imagination in creative new ways to build a foundation of thought with clear, conscious intent. Difficulty is not a signature of failure. Challenges sharpen your wits and can bring out the best of your abilities if you have faith and trust, and learn to bend with the winds of change. This is the time to fine-tune your physical, mental, spiritual, and emotional skills, and prove to yourself—and the world at large—that your thoughts imprint the life-force energy around you and that you are the creator of your experience.

The transformation of consciousness that is sweeping the globe is a multidimensional drama, an orchestration of supreme significance, that essentially involves an act of daring courage— an agreement between many realities to heal the mind and spirit of humanity and all they are connected to. From the point of view of the simultaneous ever-expanding now, all real healing involves a compassionate reinterpretation and energetic under-standing of people, places, times, and events. The new common sense is about knowing that all of life is significant and that you must take care of it. We recommend that you become enamored of yourself, for you are a miraculous form of creation, capable of manifesting a magnificent and majestic version of existence through thought, word, and deed. Seek the path that brings fun and joyful living, where you attract meaningful and significant life experiences. You always energetically pass on what you are learning. Trust in the benevolence of existence, for it is indeed so very fine. You have your own finesse, grace, and style. Use it! This is a most fortunate time to be alive and will go down in the annals of renowned reincarnation stories. Sometime, perhaps in the future, you will tell great tales about what it was like to be alive on Earth during the great intensification of energy—a twenty-five-year span of unfolding multidimensional mysteries, at once majestic, momentous, and forever monumental in the annals of time. Intend to embrace true knowledge and freedom, dear friend, and on the path of empowerment, be certain to make the best use of all of your nows.

Chapter Two

ENERGY AND FREQUENCY—
A NEW PLAYGROUND OF THE MIND

*E*verything occurs for a distinct and significant purpose on all levels of reality. There are many layers of intent involved in this game of freedom, and many different realities are intertwined. The people of Earth are undergoing a profound and necessary transformation of consciousness in order to wake up to this new understanding of life. To call the challenges of life a game may sound frivolous; however, within a game there are generally rules, goals, and players. From our perspective, existence is the biggest game of all. On Earth, you are collectively engaged in learning that the physical world is not really solid or isolated or alone; all of existence is interrelated, totally connected, consciously intelligent, and completely accessible to everyone. The ancient adage "know thyself" is a timeless, if subtly simple, instruction directing you toward a greater understanding of your relationship to reality. Third-dimensional reality is an inherent part of the great web of existence, which is filled with connections and meanings that continuously sustain everything you encounter and create in the physical world, in the dream state, and in realities beyond your current perception. To know yourself, you must go deep into this web.

Faith is an act of trust, and entrusting yourself to the goodness of the universe does indeed focus your attention on its fruition in your life. Goodness is a state or territory of consciousness; it is not a place of escape from the less-than-pleasant aspects of life. With the recognition of a benevolent higher power of intelligence, even the so-called negative and undesirable aspects of life can be seen to embody a higher purpose. When you expand your thinking and question why, you alter the course of your reality; when you seek to enlighten and enliven your mind, a myriad of connections with layers of subtle meaning will begin to unfold in your life.

A controlled and corrupt media has been directing the attention of the masses by uniformly reporting on a state of managed chaos.

You encounter life with your attention, and you probably recall being told countless times to "pay attention" to one thing or another. Attention is awareness, mindfulness, and watchful consciousness. Your attention is energy. You have the freedom to place your attention anywhere you choose, the freedom to develop or ignore your attention—it is all up to you. To know yourself, you must have command of your attention, you must learn to treasure and value it, and most importantly, you must figure out how to properly use it. For many decades a very controlled and corrupt media has been directing the attention of the masses by uniformly reporting on a state of managed chaos, which is scripted and staged to produce mental confusion and fatigue. The relentless reporting and rehashing of catastrophic and traumatic events, with images of despair and destruction repeatedly planted into the minds of the viewers, create supreme states of anxiety and are, in reality, a form of psychological warfare. Authorities play with truths, half-truths, deceptions, and lies to render you hopeless, feeling it is pointless to do anything—this now passes as "the" news, and it can rule your life.

When millions of people focus their attention upon listening to the same words, seeing the same pictures, and hearing the same descriptions, tremendous energy is generated and a massive thought-form is created. Thought-forms are vibrational blueprints that hold instructions for manifesting reality. The media captures your attention and then programs your imagination, essentially canceling out your unique creative drive to manifest your own reality as well as your desire to know yourself. You have been conditioned to believe that all you need to know can now be found in the wonderful world of electronic boxes and the information and entertainment they hold. When "the news" is slanted toward a message of continuous war, a state of despair and a sense of hopelessness are created. A paralysis of power takes hold because you become convinced that the only reality is what is described and prescribed by the authorities in the box. Reality is created and produced by each and every one of you, and those seeking to control the world have kept this knowledge a well-guarded secret.

Your imagination is a priceless and handy tool for developing and exercising your attention toward creating what you want in life. In the imagination all thoughts are real. As a simple exercise to empower your being, imagine that you are comfortably seated on an old stone bench in a lovely pastoral setting. The sky is brilliant, a deep azure blue; the sun is shining on the far horizon; no one is around, and you feel safe, secure, and very happy. Releasing a deep sigh of contentment, you close your eyes and relax into the moment, which is yours and yours alone to enjoy in blissful peace. All of your cares and concerns are washed from your mind, and you feel fresh and new, like the Earth after a warm summer shower. The rays of the sun greet you like an old, trusted friend, offering soothing warmth that penetrates deep into your body. Your breath is steady and deep, and the delicious scents and sounds of nature tantalize your cells with a sense of timeless familiarity. You are free now to surrender to the rhythm of deep relaxation and all that the moment offers. As your physical body becomes more and more relaxed, your attention is now free to roam into a new playground of the mind.

Listen with your left ear, reaching out far into the surrounding countryside, and then listen with your right ear in the same fashion. Alternate your hearing from left to right, left to right. Now listen with both ears, finding the special place of acoustical balance in the center of your brain. See the cells of your body busily occupied with absorbing life-enhancing energy from the sun.

Now refocus your attention, and enter a single cell to observe more closely what is occurring. Notice how the components of the cell are responding to the natural light, and notice the relationship of space to matter. If there are areas within the cell where the light is not reaching, use a soft piece of gold silk cloth to lovingly wipe the area clean. When the cell is completely clean, send a message to all of the cells in your body asking them to align and entrain with the cleansing you just performed. Listen carefully for a response to your request. Feel your cells dancing with joy as they fully absorb and bathe in the life-enhancing rays of the sun. When you can really feel the excitement and vitality of your cells, send heartfelt love into every nook and cranny of your body. Relax into the rising feeling of love and great appreciation for who you truly are.

Now picture the vital life-force energy bursting forth from your body on a cellular level and see it rippling and blending with the energies of Earth. Imagine that you are carrying this energy and state of awareness with you wherever you go. Play with this energy and direct it toward the version of reality you would like to experience. Be reasonable and generous with your possibilities, and gift yourself well in your mind.

Refocus on your breath, making certain it is still steady and deep, and feel the warmth of the stone bench upon which you are sitting. Before opening your eyes, focus your attention and your conscious awareness for a few moments just behind your eyelids, feeling the power of the sun penetrating deep within your body. Now take a few long, deep breaths and imagine you have just returned from a wonderful journey. When you open your eyes, notice that the sun is shining with a brilliant new light.

You can create a place of power and peace in your mind any time you choose, for your imagination is always at your beck and call. Many ancient cultures knew that the rays of the sun were encoded with a language of light that transferred information directly to the mind, influencing and affecting everyone with a subtle stream of Cosmic Intelligence. The rays of sunlight were believed to nourish and support the world by expanding the mind and enhancing conscious awareness to include new vistas of understanding. People knew that the mind was a tool to navigate realities.

It is essential to understand that the events unfolding in your world are not a result of random, meaningless acts.

The opportunity to wake up and grow in conscious awareness is ever present and awaiting your attention. Each moment is teeming with vitality and filled with the presence of Cosmic Intelligence. Observing and considering a situation from many viewpoints expand the horizons of experience and understanding, just as visiting Egypt to explore the Great Pyramid in person is infinitely more engaging and meaningful than merely seeing a photograph. From one perspective, the seemingly increasing levels of turmoil and chaos in the world can be attributed to the recent acceleration of a secret and long-term plan to control the world by molding and manipulating the human mind. However, just like a photograph, this point of view is merely a snapshot capturing one "frame of reality," all the while implying the existence of so much more. Multiple points of view converge for a collective purpose, and the intentions and experiences of all participants, physical and non-physical, must be taken into consideration when questioning the "whys and wherefores" of today's world. Plans within plans within plans weave webs of intriguing possibilities throughout this period of transformation. Situations and people appearing to limit and control your reality can serve many purposes, depending on your interpretation and point of view.

A willingness to consider new concepts and ideas stretches your mind into new territories of awareness. It is essential to understand that the events unfolding in your world are not a result of random, meaningless acts. Everything occurs for a distinct purpose. Humanity is undergoing a profound process of awakening to new realizations about the nature of existence. Can you recall the times your attention was captivated by a stunning series of tantalizing synchronicities or a cluster of life-changing events? Throughout the cosmos the scheme of existence is both intricately planned and spontaneously free to grow and change. And so, too, are you. The parameters of 3-D reality are part of a much greater reality that is deeply connected and interrelated to your world. Consciousness, in many shapes and sizes, coalesces to form constructs of thought and mass agreements of cooperation that actually sustain and support your world. You operate with and originate from agreements of consciousness, and you expand and traverse and build "all that is" with every breath you take and every thought you entertain.

The parameters of any civilization are dreamed into being from the spiritual realms by the collective imagination of all the participants. In a state of non-physical reality, a structure of energy is created to support and contain the collective ideal. Energy, which can be directed, molded, and shaped into any form, is unlimited in its potential. Civilizations manifest with a wide variety of intents and purposes based on the agreements of their designers and builders. You are not born into a world without contributing to its design, and you are continuously affecting and interacting with the non-physical structure of your current civilization through a process of cellular telepathy. You are also telepathically interacting with other structures of reality that are interspersed throughout time. Your current civilization, like all realities, is composed of structured energy that is located on a frequency band, like a radio station broadcasting its programs from a distinct address. Frequency signatures define and outline the purpose and maintain the continuity of all versions of reality.

Physical reality is a model of creative cooperation conceived in the realm of spiritual intelligence. A wealth of consciousness, in a non-physical state of being, organizes, plans, designs, and tends the seeds, or blueprints, of physical reality. In the physical world, thought-forms and ideas about reality are received telepathically from the consciousness that nurtures physical reality into being. Thoughts and ideas weave themselves through myriad realities and travel on rays of light that are visible, like the rays of the sun, and on light signals from high-frequency cosmic radiation, such as gamma rays, which you cannot see. Ideas for the physical support of your civilization are constantly being transmitted by rays of light from one dimension to another. The current structures of civilization—roadways; buildings; fuel, water, and communication lines; systems of law, commerce, learning, agriculture, and the arts—are the resulting physical manifestations of non-physical blueprints. These physical structures create an arena, or platform of reality, from which earthly life can be explored.

Your identity, which is both physical and non-physical in nature, spans many realities that you have been encouraged and trained to ignore.

Every era is influenced by vast cosmic forces that transmit and transfer energy into the structure of civilization. Your identity, which is both physical and non-physical in nature, spans many realities that you have been encouraged and trained to ignore. The heavens have always captivated the attention of humanity, and many ancient cultures looked to the skies to confirm the belief that every living thing has an awareness of its own, and that existence is bounded by specific cosmic laws. To live and work in harmony with those laws was considered as natural and essential as breathing. The presence of patterns and cycles revealed a design to reality that implied the existence of a designer, and activities in the heavens have been observed and studied for this very reason by every culture and civilization on Earth. The striking and majestic marching order of the sun, moon, planets, and stars offered important knowledge concerning the mysteries of life, especially for those decoding the cryptic "as above, so below" layers of truth.

Many of your ancestors professed a belief in the inherent connection between the heavenly domains and life on Earth. The word *astro* is derived from the Greek word for star, and at one time the current hard science of astronomy, which deals with the so-called material universe beyond Earth's atmosphere, and the art of astrology, which is based on interpreting the influence of heavenly bodies on human affairs, were united. The roots of this knowledge reach deep into Mesopotamia, the land between the Tigris and Euphrates rivers, where a fully formed civilization appeared over six thousand years ago, magically manifesting itself practically overnight. This land, which today is within the country of Iraq, is considered by many historians to be the cradle of civilization. When Baghdad, the ancient capital and cultural center of Iraq, was occupied during the war in the spring of 2003, rampant and frenetic looting led to the destruction and disappearance of priceless artifacts spanning almost seven thousand years of history. In light of this destruction, it is most interesting to note that the ancient dwellers on this land looked to the heavens with great awe and respect, for they claimed they were taught about the mysteries of existence from those who came from the stars.

The planets in your solar system are designed to function in a cooperative and synchronized pattern to establish a foundation for development within cycles of time. The path of the sun's annual circle of the heavens is known as the ecliptic, and this narrow ribbon of space is home to the zodiac, an imaginary belt in the heavens extending about eight degrees on either side of the ecliptic. The paths of the sun, moon, and principal planets orbit within this great circle of stars. Ancient people divided the zodiac into twelve constellations, and each stellar configuration was noted as an astrological sign, usually depicted by an animal. Animals were known to be multidimensional journeyers who traverse many realities, and it was therefore natural to honor the stars, which were home to many realities, with respected earthly icons. Mapping the heavens and charting the course of the planets, as they traversed the vault of stars, became a way for people to understand the great mysteries of life and to locate their celestial families.

The sun plays the primary and most essential role of relaying light-encoded information by transmitting and disbursing blueprints of consciousness and ideas about reality on gamma rays, which are a form of high-frequency radiation. Your life is intimately connected to the celestial activities that distinguish the heavens at the time of your birth. As the sun moves around the zodiac forming a great circle in the sky, each day of the year is signified by a degree within one of the twelve astrological signs. The dates and degrees accumulate records or memories of all occurrences. The sky is a map of knowledge, and each moment in time carries an energetic imprint, or outline, of its presence that is unique unto itself, like a footprint left in sand. You qualify for the time of your birth, just as you would for a particular type of employment. Some moments are much more auspicious than others, and the proper credentials on your spiritual resume must be present in order to fit with the prevailing energies.

A horoscope is a specific map, or picture, of the heavens that is cast for the date, time, and location of your birth. The positions of the sun, moon, and planets, as well as the sign that hovers at the horizon, are all placed around the wheel of the zodiac to reveal the intricate mathematical relationships that portray your personal blueprint and potential for development.

This map can reveal your physical, mental, emotional, and spiritual gifts and challenges, and you are always free to grow and change, according to your own volition. Also noteworthy are the nodal points, or the locations where the path of Earth and the path of the moon intersect, forming what is known as the "head and tail of the sky dragon," or the north and south nodes. The location of the celestial dragon in a chart is of utmost importance, for it indicates the direction in which you are moving to achieve the fulfillment of your personal destiny, as well as the place in the past that you are emerging from. Once you are born into physical reality, you unfold your life within an imprint of cosmic energy that embodies a plan of intent and purpose, a plan designed and approved by you.

Throughout the annals of creation, Earth is considered to be a monumental storehouse of precious information, a living library, encrypted within the layers and layers of genetic coding of its organic life. Your science enthusiastically seeks to unravel the genetic codes of life without understanding where and how this magnificent order arose. Your heritage is from the stars. How often has your gaze been drawn upward into the night skies? How many wonderings and prayers have you sent into the vault of heaven? How many times have you counted the stars or pondered over the power of the sun? Your deepest inner longings are legitimate flutters of memories desiring to be rekindled and awakened to a continuity of purpose that spans the cosmos. You came to Earth to anchor this ancient knowledge into the human form, knowing that life here offers as many opportunities and gifts as you may choose to experience.

Learning to recognize and read frequencies, or levels of consciousness, offers you a profound new form of liberty and freedom.

The concepts of animate and inanimate or organic and inorganic matter do not justly describe all the possibilities of the known or unknown universe. Consciousness is the ever-present constant. Everything has a distinct vibration and frequency of energy, which serve as a form of identification and proclamation of uniqueness within the field of existence. Frequencies are vibrations of energy that are determined by their rate of reoccurrence. Some frequencies travel through the many layers of existence, traversing what you think of as time and space. The ability to sense and feel and transmit energy is a natural function of the human form. These times of heightened and accelerated energy offer the perfect opportunity to expand your mind by developing and fine-tuning your perceptions, and your perceptions expand when you learn to look for the layers of significance and hidden meanings of life. Fully participating in life, as well as learning to observe your interactions without judgment, is essential for developing an enhanced awareness. Learning to recognize and read frequencies, or levels of consciousness, offers you and your world a profound new form of liberty and freedom. The possibilities of an awakened mind and its benefits have yet to really dawn on humanity. When the potentials of these abilities are fully understood and utilized, you will begin to recognize the powerful effects that the Galactic Center, the womb of the Milky Way Galaxy, exerts on your life.

Now, practically speaking, you must first learn to manage your attention in the here and now in order to become much more aware of the language of frequencies. Inner signals and messages are effortlessly and generously transmitted by everyone; areas of existence that appear to be non-existent constantly knock on the doors of your perception; fountains of knowledge continuously spring forth from your inner being; yet most often, you never even notice. Feelings, impressions, and memories are all valid components of consciousness that cooperate to play essential roles in awakening your vital energy, expanding your attention, and connecting you to a greater view of reality. Every one of you is here in cooperation with a collective purpose. In life, the role you play is entirely of your own making; you write the script and direct the course of action while continuously adding to and changing your course of possibilities. There are no limits to your creativity. Whatever you do in your version of the world affects and directs the course of civilization. The startling changes that are sweeping your globe are blatant signs that inner upheavals of immense proportions are transpiring, and as people the world over are challenged to confront the curtailing of their freedom, many are now remembering the parameters of possibility they agreed to explore before they were born.

During this era of change, the collective intent of humanity appears to be deeply committed to a tremendous opportunity for spiritual growth and expansion, where the experience of being on Earth is both the purpose and the teacher. On one level of your experience, you are here to participate in the mass movement of consciousness toward a collective integrated memory. To raise the stakes and make the experience much more interesting and worthwhile, obstacles of every make and size have been introduced into this drama from many levels of reality. Every era has an overall game plan that can be studied, explored, and experienced through many directions of time— from a non-linear perspective, all time is simultaneously occurring. Stellar and planetary positions in the heavens play a definitive role in establishing a structure and purpose by transmitting energetic influences that outline, and to some extent, define the potential and probable directions of the times in which you live. To fully contribute to this transformation in your own unique fashion, you selected an identity based on the numerous talents and abilities you have accumulated from experiences in many directions of time. You inserted yourself with great care into your chosen life. Deciding to be here is an achievement in itself; however, understanding what is unfolding around you is an even greater accomplishment. Billions of people have come here to play a part in this great drama—to recognize and remember that they are energetic beings whose thoughts, feelings, and emotions create the world they meet. Consciously learning to recognize frequencies and then producing those you want is an underlying key to the game; being able to read and communicate with the life energies of your environment is a worthy goal for all humanity.

To develop the skill of consciously reading and making frequencies, you must learn to pay attention to the subtleties of life. In seeking to know yourself, new vistas of reality will inevitably unfold. Awareness and control of the breath are the essential keys for understanding and developing the higher mind, because they form a very powerful and natural way to connect with both inner and outer sources of the vital life-force energy. By focusing your attention, you can use your breath to stabilize yourself, to have more energy and enhance your immune system, to create beneficial brain wave patterns, and to travel into the interior of your being to acquire transcendent knowledge and information from a source beyond your linear view of the world. You must learn to pay attention to where your breath takes you, for it is a very powerful tool for activating and using your physical form to its greatest extent. Breathing exercises create a strong foundation within the body for those seeking higher consciousness, and we highly recommend that you adopt the discipline of always returning your attention to conscious breathing. Breathing is an exchange of energy between the outer world and the inner domain of your body. No matter what you are doing: tucking the children into bed, driving the car, making supper, making love, or dashing to the office, modulating your breathing patterns is a way of staying centered, expanding the use of your mind, and enhancing your physical prowess.

Take a few moments and notice the way you normally breathe. Can you feel yourself breathing? Can you hear the sound of your breath? How deep are your breaths? Is there any movement in the chest? Are you filling the lower lungs with your breath? Now, with a greater focus of your attention, clear your throat, relax your tongue, gently separate your jaw, and inhale slowly through your nose to the count of four. Feel your breath swirling into your nostrils and listen for the sound of the "wind in a cave" at the back of your throat. Consciously follow your breath into your body. Picture your breath filled with vibrant golden spirals of energy that are moving over your larynx, down your throat, and into the bottom of your lungs. When you have completed the in-breath, pause for a few moments, then completely and thoroughly exhale with a long and deep out-breath, also to the count of four; then pause before beginning the round again. Do your best to keep your attention on your breath as you read. Deep, rhythmic breathing calms and rebalances your entire body. On the second or third deep in-breath, picture and feel the vibrant golden spirals of energy penetrating the walls of your lungs and moving into the bloodstream. As the vital energy enters your bloodstream, see it swirl toward your heart. Allow the focused energy to enter all of the heart's chambers, then see and feel the vitalized blood moving from your heart throughout all of your body. Imagine your blood as a brilliant ruby red river, powerfully alive and intelligent, carrying the vital life-force energy on a steady and purposeful course throughout your body. Keep breathing and enjoy the power of your focused attention.

You can focus the energy of your breath with any imagery you like, according to how you want to feel or express yourself. Vital energy is free and completely open to be directed and molded by you. When you consciously breathe, you immediately alter the frequency of your brain wave patterns into a more awakened and integrated state of awareness. By learning to adjust and refocus your attention, you will become more aware of the extensive range of frequencies, from both physical and non-physical sources, that vie for your attention.

Electromagnetic waves of cosmic radiation, composed of pulsed light energies, travel throughout existence conveying vast amounts of information.

The nature of existence is founded upon cooperation, and everything occurs for a distinct and significant purpose on all levels of reality. Pulsations of energy permeate all of existence to form a super-conscious cosmic mind that serves as a source of energy and a repository of all knowledge. A constant stream of creative impulses from the cosmic mind stimulates exploration and development by opening new avenues of awareness throughout existence. Multiple layers of purpose are always involved in any event, and the greater number of people engaged, the more energy generated. Participation, by thought, word, or deed, strengthens a thought-form with the potential to energetically alter the course of human consciousness in any direction. The emotional intensity behind the thought-form determines the outcome. When your emotions are being manipulated, it is much more challenging to take a stand and clearly assess the situation. A new and spiritually invigorating cosmic perspective is required for humanity to fully understand the purpose of the extreme polarization of the civilized world, and to eventually unify it. In this regard, old habits, patterns, and addictions, which limit and confine the human spirit, are rapidly breaking down and clearing the way for a new order of the mind based on a global revival of responsibility, accountability, and personal empowerment.

Light is electromagnetic radiation that travels in wave form, and your cells, which are crystalline in structure, eagerly respond to natural light. Electromagnetic waves of cosmic radiation, composed of pulsed light energies, travel throughout existence conveying vast amounts of information. The human brain and nervous system function in both physical and non-physical reality, serving as receivers for this vast array of electrical impulses, which permeate space and engulf the planet. Your cells are always on duty to transduce, translate, transmit, and sort out the myriad of frequencies. Signals, or messages, in the nerves, brain, and body are carried by weak electrical impulses that radiate energy into physical and non-physical reality, maintaining constant contact with the higher power of the cosmic mind. The rays of the sun support this connection and can fluctuate in regard to the rate, quality, and speed of pulsed solar light radiation, and thereby affect different eras of time with very different transmissions of energy. Modern-day orthodox medical and psychological sciences rely on models of the mind that recognize only the conscious, subconscious, and unconscious aspects, with little interest in or acknowledgment of your innate connection to the cosmic mind and its greater vistas of reality. You are a multidimensional being, and over time the massive misrepresentation of this aspect of your greater being has had a profound impact on the human mind. As a natural response to these long-term constrictions, a healthy rebellion is brewing within the mass thought-form that holds your reality together. The release of vast amounts of pent-up psychic energy is stimulating a sudden expansion of consciousness that is spreading telepathically throughout the world as well as into other layers of reality.

The powers of the cosmic or higher mind offer a fascinating new frontier that is available for all people to explore. Your brain, which is divided into two hemispheres, is considered to be the central clearinghouse for communication in physical reality, although in actuality, many layers of your physical and non-physical identity are involved. Nonetheless, your brain performs important functions: the right hemisphere, which affects the left side of the body, rules abstract, intuitive, creative, and imaginative thinking, while the left hemisphere operates on rational, analytical, and logical methods, and rules the right side of the body. Harmony between the two hemispheres is essential for both learning and for activating full-brain potential. Activities that stimulate and develop the qualities of each side of the brain actually exercise your mind into a state of wholesome balance and greater intelligence. Slowly rotating your eyes from left to right, without moving your head, will activate both hemispheres; walking with your knees slightly lifted, and alternatively touching the top of your kneecap with the palm of your opposite hand, will also create hemispheric balance. However, listening to the sounds of nature by alternating your hearing from the left to the right ear will give you the very best results.

Traditionally, the mind is categorized into three basic areas of functioning—conscious, subconscious, and unconscious—which, for the sake of your imagination, can be pictured as a small green pea, a large sweet onion, and a very big potato. The conscious mind is composed of the self that is in charge, aware, and thinking: the version of you that directs the program, plants the seeds, and pilots your plane of intent in 3-D reality. The conscious mind, or the pea, is where you believe you operate from. The subconscious mind, or the large sweet onion, carries out commands from the conscious mind and is like a huge bank that holds layers and layers of all your memories. It also serves as a resplendent storehouse of knowledge for multidimensional connections and memories that travel by way of electromagnetic impulses from times beyond your current time. The unconscious mind, or the very big potato, is your deep personal inner radar, which gathers a very large base of knowledge that is rich and ripe with a spiritual reconnaissance from the deepest and most cosmic levels. Impulses, signs, signals, and symbols received from the cosmic mind, which for the sake of analogy is a garden, are translated and held for transmission by the deeply buried unconscious mind.

Activity in the brain is a reflection of an individual's state of mind and can be measured by electroencephalograph (EEG) machines. EEG readings detect the number of brain wave cycles per second, noting specific wave frequencies or repetitions that signify the patterns of thought being used. Frequency is the speed at which electrical activity occurs and determines the various levels of brain wave activity—beta, alpha, theta, and delta. Beta waves are affiliated with conscious mind operation and indicate a normal, thinking-awake state at the highest rate of cycles per second. Alpha waves are slower and serve as a very important link, or bridge, between the higher-rate frequencies of the conscious mind, and the much slower vibrations of theta and delta waves. The alpha state, which we will call the carrot bridge, is most easily accessed through visualization and relaxation: meditation, walking or sitting in nature, or slowing down to enjoy a cup of tea can revive and restore your inner balance. Relaxing your tongue and gently separating your jaw will also adjust your frequencies from beta-wave consciousness into the alpha frequency that leads to enhanced creativity. Focusing on your breath, daydreaming, and activating your senses also access the alpha state. Children spend a large amount of time in the alpha state when they are playing, and everyone travels through the alpha level when falling asleep. When you can catch yourself hovering in this sublime state, you may notice streams of energy moving and shuffling about in your mind. On the other side of the alpha state is theta, where even slower frequencies indicate activity in the subconscious mind. Below theta are the very slow delta waves, which reveal activity in the unconscious mind: a highly programmable state that houses deep psychic connections that transcend linear time. In the delta state your reality sensors are finely tuned, yet this frequency indicates a state of deep sleep with the unconscious mind in full operation. It is the unconscious mind that is linked to the memories of the cosmic mind, and the cosmic mind is activated when all wave patterns—beta, alpha, theta, and delta—are simultaneously present.

The electromagnetic frequencies of your thoughts, weaving back and forth in time, affect other realities with similar issues.

Throughout time the people of Earth have used various levels of brain wave activity to enhance their capabilities with unique creativity. Your histories do not adequately focus on the true essence of human achievement. The years ahead will see electrifying and lightning-like changes to the mass psyche of humanity when all that has been hidden becomes apparent.

Untold issues, which the conscious mind has been unwilling to recognize and deal with, will surface from storage in the subconscious to provide a golden opportunity to collectively clean the human mind of unprocessed information and emotional debris. Many of your ancestors led very interesting lives, and their exploits and memories are stored away as worthy contributions to the collective consciousness of humanity in the subconscious and unconscious minds.

The real knowledge that you are seeking is inside. Events that the beta-wave conscious mind thinks are long gone can still be very real and present, occurring simultaneously from the multidimensional vista of the cosmic mind. Various timeline realities are interwoven and connected to each other by the issues and lessons being played out in the physical world; the electromagnetic frequencies of your thoughts, weaving back and forth in time, affect other realities that are dealing with similar issues. On a cellular level, everyone is in a perpetual state of instant communication, and individuals from other times are often well aware of this ongoing exchange. The modern era is founded upon a mass belief that gathering information is an external process, and it can be; however, you are naturally designed to experience reality from an inner position of personal empowerment, which leads to a much more joyful and expansive vista of vitality and creative expression than is currently believed possible.

Existence is a multilayered enterprise that is both highly complex and conversely quite simple. In essence, it is a fine joining of frequencies based on a conscious cooperative agreement. Energy patterns continuously ripple and run into other layers of reality, creating an open exchange of frequencies and signals. From a larger perspective, all realities are open-ended; therefore, whatever you do—the attitudes you develop and the actions you take—creates frequencies that broadcast your essence every-where. Cover-ups and pretence are forms of delusion; you are who you are. You can fool yourself, but you can't fool your frequency signature! You are always transmitting who and what you are; this is true for everyone, from newborns to world leaders. Within the current state of human affairs, the level of deceit and lies has grown to such audacious heights because people have misplaced their abilities to read the vibrations of reality. In modern terms, it is called being in a state of denial.

Sometimes you create situations so you can fulfill an intention or an agreement that you set in place prior to your arrival here. Playing with power always involves a test of character. Personal challenges develop character by stimulating new heights of emotional development and intelligence, while global issues tend to deal with a collective desire to achieve psychic and spiritual goals en masse. You are here to experience exactly what you are dealing with; knowing this, and knowing that free will always gives you a choice, can empower you to enhance the course of your life. You must be very clear about what you want and what you are available for.

You can change any situation by changing your previous attitudes and expectations. Refocusing your attention and consciously selecting your thoughts to reinforce the outcome you desire will alter the frequency you transmit, inevitably opening the door to another probable outcome. Reality adjusting, or using your frequency by way of intent, is the wave of the future. Overcoming your fears and moving through challenging events will build tremendous confidence and stamina; and in a sense, the more challenging the drama, the greater the possible gain and payoff in self-empowerment. Achievements and accomplishments accumulate and permeate layers of reality with a collective momentum and purpose, creating a multidimensional chessboard where the pieces, players, and even the board itself all have a certain volition. Embracing the understanding that everything in existence is based on frequency is one of humanity's collective goals for living in these times. Recalling and examining the wealth of memories stored in your genes will offer you a new perspective on how the human body operates, and by integrating the considerations of a larger vista of reality, you demonstrate that it can be done.

No matter what you are creating, your beliefs form the underlying foundation for all of your experiences.

Of course it is possible to create energies that are incompatible with your well-being. Because you cannot see the energies you produce, you are not always aware that you are constantly broadcasting your beliefs and your conditions for reality into existence. And a befuddled and unclear mind will attract the same kind of energies, for this is the signal that is being sent out. Remember, your thoughts create your reality so whenever you find yourself facing a puzzling situation, ask yourself, Why am I creating this? Asking why sets the stage for further clarity. The trick is to pay attention and learn to listen for the response. No matter what you are creating, your beliefs form the underlying foundation for all of your experiences. You must learn to be aware of your power to imprint the energies you are interacting with and are using to structure reality.

You produce frequencies of energy based on your beliefs, attitudes, and desires, and in the current era, you are also living in a field of electronic frequencies that bombard your environment. Extra low frequency waves (ELFs), electromagnetic frequencies, microwaves, the frequencies of high wire electrical cables, other people's thought frequencies, the frequencies stored in the land, and a multitude of frequencies from cosmic influences all blend and merge around you. As you learn to focus your attention and sharpen your developing perceptions, you will gradually become more aware of and sensitive to the frequencies you encounter—from the food you eat and where you live to the places you visit and the things you do. As you become more energetically aware, you will learn to feel frequencies. You will notice the difference in how you feel when eating food that is mass produced and food that is grown and prepared with love. Discernment of electronic frequencies requires the same level of awareness. If you happen to spend large portions of your day steeped in a state of electronic entrainment, then it is essential to spend equal amounts of time in nature. Nature is the best place for restoring your energy and creating inner balance.

You can empower yourself, and set the reality that you want into motion, by taking time to communicate with the subconscious and unconscious levels of your mind. First slow down and focus on your breath. Gently separate your jaw and relax your tongue, and allow deep, rhythmic breathing to relax your body and open your mind to an enhanced state of awareness. Continue to breathe deep and imagine your body fully energized with golden spirals of energy. Now visualize a wave of energy, like a gentle spring shower, sweeping over the top of your head down to the bottom of your feet. Any tension that you have been carrying will be washed away, leaving you feeling fresh, clear, and free to proceed unencumbered into the depths of your being. There is a place in your mind called the "answer room," and you must use your imagination to cross the bridge and find your way to the door. It may be on a busy street in an old stone office building, down a quiet country lane, or secluded like an eagle's nest overlooking a cliff.

The answer room is your creation and can be anywhere you choose; feel a strong intent to go there, and then see yourself standing before the door. Take special note of the quality and color of the door, as well as the shape of the doorknob, and once they are clearly etched in your memory, open the door. The answer room is very well furnished with beautiful fabrics and comfortable seating; fascinating pieces of art, a globe, books, plants, flowers, and a tea set add a warm welcome, and large glass doors open onto a sumptuous garden. Now enter the answer room and make yourself at home. You will find anything you want in this room. Once you are cozy and settled in, think about what you want to know. Look around the room, allowing your gaze to rest here and then there, steadily taking in all that you see. When you are ready, clearly state the question to which you are seeking an answer and ask that an answer be clearly presented within the next three days; then sit back, enjoy some tea, and bask in the serenity of your room of inner knowledge. You can visit this room anytime you choose to fine-tune your frequency and gain greater clarity about yourself and the world at large.

You must trust that once you set up this type of internal programming that the answers will come; either while you are in the room, or sometime during the three days that follow. As you get better and better at using your imagination, you naturally expand your freedom to creatively play with the inner workings of your psyche, which will in turn enhance your well-being. Unlimited possibilities await your attention, and you can save yourself a lot of money and hard work by practicing the art of inner self-management and learning how to direct your attention within. Eventually, you may just think of the answer room, pose a question, and instantaneously receive an answer. You can do whatever you want as you build your reality in your mind.

Frequencies are tricky, and it is best to remember that you can't fool frequency.

Your brain wave signals reveal your state of mind through the frequencies you use to operate in physical reality. You can learn to build an overall frequency that is strong and powerful and clearly focused. As you learn to enhance and enliven your frequency, it will become more predominant than any of the surrounding energies you encounter. Common sense must prevail as you pursue this course of personal enhanced awareness. It is possible to establish a personal vibration that will transcend and transmute a toxic or destructive substance. When dealing with electronics in today's world, it takes a tremendous amount of effort to maintain your frequency if you are living in a highly charged electronic field. You must learn to locate yourself where the vibrations feel good, and most often this will be a place where nature is honored. You can learn to transcend anything, yet you must also consider if it is in your best interest to make such an effort; sometimes relocating yourself or changing your habits are the easiest and most sensible solutions. Many people actually batter themselves energetically by pushing against and forcing their way through chaotic thought-form storms created by people transmitting the frequencies of their own negative feelings. All thoughts take on an energetic form in the world of frequencies, and feelings are the fuel used to propel the signals of thought into the surrounding ether. Thoughts cluster together and congregate by similarity—like attracts like. All thoughts are commands given to the cells to carry out a desired effect, and unconscious thoughts and suggestions can often be extremely damaging to the body.

While driving in heavy traffic the vibrations from other

drivers can sometimes be very intense and disturbing. Most people think they are alone and isolated in their automobiles, but the act of driving, which is very hypnotic, can trigger an altered state of consciousness. In this trance-like state of mind, the thoughts and feelings that are explored by the driver are then unconsciously broadcast onto the highways of the world. You must learn to focus your attention and notice what you are thinking about. Are you contributing to a cluster of thoughts filled with joy or despair? When you are clear about what you want, knowing that you can create any version of life that you desire, you can consciously condition the energy of your environment with your intentions by sending out nurturing and loving thoughts to the surrounding locale—be it a highway or a byway. You can use your thoughts in unlimited capacities, and the more you practice balancing and harmonizing the environment you encounter, the greater effect you have on changing the world in which you live.

Through thinking, feeling, saying, doing, dreaming, intending, wishing, and being, you are making frequencies all the time. What are you contributing to the field of human activity? Perhaps those who appear to have more power than you are simply focusing their frequencies with greater intent. The field of energy is not rich in one area and poor in another, the field is the field is the field—uniform and all pervasive. The field of existence is filled with Cosmic Intelligence that is neutral—in terms of self-interest—and in the biggest picture of reality, a single overseer simply does not exist. The cosmic mind is a collective experience, one that is ever changing and growing by continuously incorporating every nuance of experience that every form of consciousness explores and transmits. Using your willpower to create a new probable world—which you do with each thought—by producing the frequencies of thought and energy that you desire, is the name of the game of freedom. Your intentions determine the experiences you create, and how you respond determines the outcome. If you choose to lie and manipulate your way through life and use demonic dark energies to augment your path, then you will experience the results of those actions. The choice is always yours, to do what you will. Regardless of whether you do or do not accept personal responsibility for your creations, what you encounter is always of your own making.

Frequencies are tricky, and it is best to remember that you can't fool frequency. Frequency is. To have a truly sincere and genuine frequency of energy, there must be an alignment with your feelings. A deceptive conniver, in the guise of a good person, can be easily recognized and read quite clearly when you release your expectations and tune in to feel the true nature of the person's intent. When you learn to read frequencies with your feelings, dealing with the unsavory energies of lies and deceptions is no longer a problem. Good readers of frequencies are always very honest with themselves and others because both honesty and integrity are required for acquiring this skill. The greater your integrity, the more the many gates of knowledge and the real truths of existence will be revealed. There are no training camps or courses to sign up for; this is all about you and your conscience. In every moment of your existence you have the opportunity to take the low road, the middle road, or the high road. Honesty produces a frequency that says, I have integrity and honor, and I am dependable, trustworthy, and reliable. It is all up to you. The more responsibility you are willing to claim for being the creator of your life, the greater the truths you will be able to accept and deal with. Responsibility opens the doors to complete self-empowerment.

You have the inherent right and duty to design and create your life.

The times in which you live are characterized by a noble and courageous effort on behalf of many stalwart minds to expose a myriad of dark, menacing conspiracies that reveal a pattern of control by a global elite intent upon world domination. From the bigger picture, everyone on Earth is playing a part in this great game of consciousness. You are here to create a great dynamic of change for waking up to new truths and learning to trust the unfolding revelations of the cosmic mind. When you stop contributing your personal fears of powerlessness and despair to the mass thought-form, and accept yourself as a creator of your own frequency, you can use the unlimited potentials of the field of formative energies however you choose. You have the inherent right and duty to design and create your life. And you can create a safe world for yourself by focusing your attention and sending your loving thoughts into the ether for a peaceful co-existence between all forms of consciousness. If this peaceful version of reality is what you are available for, then harmonious interactions, exciting new adventures, great synchronicities, and celebrated connections can be created. There is a point and a purpose to being here, and all of the avenues of experience that you choose to explore are essential and important for your self-fulfillment in this time.

You are ultimately responsible for cherishing and valuing your life; however, you must learn a little more about who you are before you can really design a better reality with the frequencies that you choose. Knowing more about yourself is not always easy, and just like deciding on integrity, it is a choice you must be willing to make. Once again, accepting responsibility for your life and relinquishing the stance of victimhood will free your thought patterns and untie the knots of powerless thinking. The more you know about who you are and the more you are willing to see your life as a significant and purposeful expression of consciousness, the greater the unfoldment will be. Use your creative energy to set the tone of your day, and picture vibrant waves of energy filled with images of your intentions being broadcast from your heart. In pursuit of the truth, you must be willing to explore, quest, question, discuss, debate, listen, look, learn, and see yourself and all of creation in a captivating new light.

Chapter Three

ACCELERATED ENERGY AND STRETCHING YOUR MIND IN THE NANOSECOND OF TIME

*Y*ou have learned that everything in existence is connected to an unlimited interactive web, which we call the web of existence. All events, great and small, are stored on this web of intelligent energy, which has an unlimited capacity for memory, among its many other attributes. Your Internet is a symbolic model of this web of existence—an attempt in the material world to mimic the web and replicate its boundless energy. However, though this web is ever present, with no server charges, the start-up fees require that you must master your mind and know yourself in order to get on-line. Many world civilizations have succeeded in surfing the great web of existence by making the cosmic link between life on Earth and the majesty of the stars.

Ancient seers and timekeepers from days long gone had a deep affinity for studying the heavens and noting that there were worlds within worlds inherently connected through stellar and planetary cycles that operated in accordance with a large-scale cosmic plan. These cycles and their influences are part of a greater design and contain numerous levels of plans and purposes; in ancient times, humankind considered life on Earth to be a highly significant part of this cosmic dance. Some cultures even foresaw the nanosecond, the twenty-five-year period from 1987 through 2012, as being a supremely important part of such a large-scale cycle, one that involved a total transformation of human consciousness. The nanosecond would show the way out of a long, prevailing state of self-imposed ignorance and confusion into the onset of a golden epoch of human transformation. The people of this time would be able to choose from a variety of probable futures to bridge the transition between the ending of one era and the beginning of another. It was known that they would transform themselves through purifications, initiations, and great spiritual tests, as their world appeared to break apart at the seams. This entire twenty-five-year period would attract billions of people—everyone would want to be on Earth because the acceleration of energy would be so extraordinary; it would be like living thousands of years in a mere twenty-five, or like having hundreds of lifetimes all rolled into one. At this time personal and collective tests would serve as opportunities to become more aware of a much greater reality. All of humanity would be involved in making many powerful choices during these years, choices that would determine the type of world they would occupy as the new version began with the Winter Solstice in 2012.

The velocity and intensity of the accelerated energy are modulated into three distinct phases, each one designed to adjust humanity's expanding consciousness by creating a rhythm and pattern of entrainment with new light frequencies on a cellular level. As energy continues to accelerate, the time span between one crisis and another grows shorter and shorter, and the opportunity to realize that the outer world is a reflection of the inner reality increases exponentially. Within a larger framework of reality, a crisis can be thought of as a meeting of minds at the crossroads of opportunity—a juncture where you recognize exactly where you are and consciously choose the best possible outcome for where you are going. During the twenty-five years of accelerated energy, you are being altered by a steady, tempered increase in cosmic radiation that is assisting you in acclimating and adjusting to the immense changes in consciousness that you have come here to claim.

Perhaps you are wondering about the point and purpose of increasing the energy. Is it to drive you crazy? Or to give the controllers more power over your life? The actual purpose of the acceleration is to teach you, and all of those who participate, about embodying cosmic law to overcome a tyranny of destructive behavior. Ancient people understood that there are laws that govern the universe and multiverse, and that everything is intimately connected to activities in the heavens. One of the primary laws is: Thought creates reality. As everything continues to go faster and faster, this becomes a self-evident teaching as what you think materializes with greater and greater speed. As the energy accelerates, a natural internal process works in harmony with inner and outer forces to assist you in integrating the change in energy. You have chosen to be here at a time when thoughts will be recognized as tools for creating and manifesting reality into form, and to anchor in this reality the knowledge that you are a spiritual being in charge of your life. To be able to proclaim: "I was there, and I lived it. I did it; I began to design my life according to my own well-conceived intentions" is a noteworthy achievement on anyone's spiritual resume.

During these times of accelerated energy, everything quickens and manifests with much greater speed.

Celestial alignments with the Galactic Center deliver potent transmissions of energy affecting everything on Earth, and as these super-voltage energies continue to enter your reality and speed things up, you must be much more aware of the thoughts and messages you send forth.

Remember, your thoughts are broadcast as frequencies of energy that act in a similar fashion to a homing pigeon trained to deliver a message—thoughts literally fly out from your mind to connect with whatever you are thinking about. And during these times of accelerated energy everything quickens and manifests with much greater speed. Understanding the cosmic laws of manifestation is like having the keys to the universe. If you are aware of your thoughts, knowing that what you focus on is what you get, then ideally you are consciously creating the version of life that you want. But, if by chance, you believe what is sold in the mainstream media's business of thought control, then you are following a program and are being used. In times of acceleration, you must think and question everything, and be willing to feel your way through life in order to ascertain the many layers of truth that define your reality.

During the first phase of the transformation, from 1987 to 1996, the level of cosmic energy affecting your planet accelerated in proportion to a tenfold increase from one year to the next, gradually building a quiet momentum, and subtly changing everyone's life. Reflect for a few moments back to 1987. Where were you living at the time? What were you doing with your attention? What was going on in your life? How busy were you? Where were you in your spiritual search? Who were you then, and what did you think about? What was your understanding of the world?

Initially, only a relatively small number of people across the planet were triggered to connect with and feel the quickening of energy from the newly arriving cosmic energy and light frequencies. There were many changes to consider and factor into one's life, for in addition to all the normal routines of daily life a new level of awareness subtly seeded itself in the human mind. The planetary consciousness sensed the beginnings of profound changes and reached out in response, like a newly foaled calf, all woozy and wobbly, and ready for life. The first ten years of accelerated energy created a steady, yet gradual, increase in overall awareness within mass consciousness. New and exciting interpretations of life burst forth as the result of expanding awareness, and information became a valuable, indispensable commodity. As the pace quickened, the slow and steady blossoming of the Internet mirrored the connections being made at other levels, and the new technologies reflected the accelerated energies of the times. Even though many people were naïve in their interpretations and expectations of what was occurring, from the beginning the excitement was still enormous. Psychic senses and new perceptual abilities were just starting to awaken in a large number of people, and spiritual idealism sometimes outranked practicality in terms of popularity. Eventually though, as more and more information was disclosed concerning the true state of world affairs—especially the long-term manipulation of beliefs concerning hidden cosmic connections —the bubble of innocence burst to reveal a much larger vista of reality, calling in turn for a much larger vista of one's own place in the cosmos. With great consistency, like the rich and majestic turning of the leaves in the autumn season, millions of people began to slowly realize that they were living during times of stupendous change, and that a multitude of mind-boggling agendas and intentions were probably involved.

During the second phase of the acceleration, from 1997 to 2006, the energy leaps in proportion to one hundred–fold each year, magnifying every experience with even greater intensity. As the energy continues to increase, and because there is so much more to keep track of, people are becoming completely enamored of technological innovations in order to escape the mounting pressure; however, some will claim it is to manage the chaos. All the while they are immersing themselves in an electronic bubble that manages their frequencies. There is great confusion during these years about recognizing priorities and what is really important. And as time marches on, it will become increasingly obvious to those with very clever minds that thoughts are manifesting themselves into reality very quickly. Eventually, all will face an extraordinary reality check with the state of their own affairs as new priorities for life arise by choice or default. During this time, billions of people will begin to realize that nothing is exactly as it appears to be, and this realization will be an initiation in itself, and one of the great tests of these times. As tumultuous events escalate on the world stage, an invisible line will be drawn and polarizations will arise all over the world as people choose sides and take a stand on their beliefs in heated debates over the issues of freedom and the value of life. Denial will be a choice by those who stand in ignorance despite commonly available knowledge. A new level of thinking is being called forth as pioneering minds seek to open the doors to a new frontier of unlimited possibilities. As the issues of war and peace escalate in importance, people will have deep realizations about who to trust, and will begin to recognize the value of their intuition in this decision-making process. During these years, a newfound wisdom will be born as an awakening of epic proportions galvanizes the globe. Unique concepts electrify and revive the human spirit and offer a sense of empowerment and relief for many people in their lives. New ideas seem to arrive with a life of their own, as the confluence of multiple realities with the third dimension begins dancing and bubbling like the merging of rivers after a quick spring thaw. And yet still, in the midst of it all, no one is quite certain as to "what is really going on."

Beginning in 2007, the third and final phase will be initiated with a profound new leap in intensity. The energy accelerates in proportion to one hundred thousand–fold each year for the five remaining years—basically sending everybody soaring into orbit. The last five years of the nanosecond are unpredictable in terms of how you will respond to the hidden layers of truths that will inevitably surface. Your power increases with each passing moment. Will you let it slip by, or will you use it and contribute your personal victory to the annals of time?

There are so many probable directions to choose from in this time, and only to the degree you unfold your awareness, coupled with the values you choose to pursue, will the outcome be determined. From a larger perspective, it is as if the whole world must transform itself and pass through the eye of a needle. The entire twenty-five years are a preparation for a magnificent solar alignment with the Galactic Center on the Winter Solstice in 2012. And at this juncture in time, just about anything can occur. The Galactic Center represents truth and is distinguished as the primary source of information for the galaxy. Planetary alignments with the center's location serve to stimulate human beings to embody a unique state of enhanced creativity, as well as altering their perceptions of reality through the transmission of tremendous amounts of energy and information.

*A*nyone can activate the innate ability to wake up and experience life from a more expansive vista.

You may wonder if it is possible for individuals to change the course of their lives. Your values and beliefs determine your experiences, and you certainly have the freedom and the free will to change either or both of them and alter their paths whenever you choose. You define yourself in this reality in terms of how you respond to your experiences. By your own assessments and evaluations, you can bring yourself to the head of the class or hold yourself back. When you enter 3-D reality, you carry a blueprint that is encoded in your cells; your identity can be read in your body and charted according to the location of the planets at the time of your birth. Your name, your blood, and your energetic field all carry a definitive outline of your personality, as well as your potential achievements in this lifetime. Your gifts and capabilities are stored within, yet by no means do they limit your potential; they are more like tools that reflect your identity. You can always exercise your free will and choose from a wide spectrum of opportunities; other probable versions of you experience every possible choice you have ever encountered. You relate to your present reality because it is reflective of your current personal beliefs and state of mind. Your life and your reality can be predictable in terms of the energies that influence you and your times, and equally unpredictable in terms of how you will respond to them. Anyone can activate the innate ability to wake up and experience life from a more expansive vista, for cosmic forces and subtle energies affect you on a subatomic level and can trigger new insights and premonitions that can lead you to alter the course of your life.

Periodically throughout existence—as you conceive of

time and space—it is necessary to create opportunities to clean up certain types of debris. You may think of physical debris; however, we are referring to energetic debris, most specifically, frequencies of lower vibrations that have accumulated as false programs for life—on your external world, as well as in your internal environment. A healing along the lines of time is required to resolve a massive buildup of pent-up psychic and emotional energy that is stored in the DNA structure. Portions of the DNA, which are considered empty junk, are actually keeping vital records and storing important keys of information. Your DNA hosts its own web of information in regard to your ancestral line. The human body is a finely designed instrument fully capable of holding an immense collage of images, imprints, and personal impressions, which are accurately recorded, moment by moment, and stored on a cellular level. This eventually accumulates in a large volume of perceptual influence that is passed on from one generation to another through the natural psychic influence of blood-bond telepathy. An inherently strong psychic connection exists in all families because of the commonality of information and familiarity that is carried in the blood. Your cells are always communicating your state of mind to your genetic family in all avenues of time.

Many interesting questions arise when you stretch your mind to consider your ancestors and the vast array of perceptions and experiences they encoded in your DNA.

For a few moments, focus your attention on your breath and create a deep, calming, rhythmic flow of vital energy moving throughout your body, reaching deep into the subatomic layers of your cells. Visualize swirling golden spirals of energy dancing in and around and between your cells, connecting minute particles and waves into an amazingly brilliant dazzle of color, fluid geometric shapes, and sublimely soothing sound.

Now, make the intention to open your own personal timeline by breathing this thought deep into the dance in your cells. Relax into the moment and imagine that your ancestors are standing before you; a great union of your bloodline has gathered in response to your call for a meeting. Each member of your extended family is distinctly dressed. They will individually approach you and look deep into your eyes to reveal the joys and tragedies, exhilarating discoveries and grave disappointments that made up their lives. Receive the pictures and symbols as part of your family legacy, and be certain to acknowledge with gratitude all you are shown. Once the meeting is complete, contemplate the vast array of experiences and creative abilities that are logged in your being.

Tremendous energies for healing pain and separation are being transmitted from the Galactic Center into the Earth.

The period from 1987 to 2012, or the nanosecond in the annals of time, involves reconnecting with the power source of the Galactic Center, or Womb of the Mother, by accepting responsibility for cleaning up the vast accumulation of negative energetic debris that gridlocks your reality. Ultimately the nanosecond is about experiencing greater states of awareness in order to know who you really are. But sometimes a huge backlog of unprocessed energy is clouding the clarity required to reconnect with your own deep inner wisdom. When the stored encoding in the DNA holds records of pain and separation, and strong beliefs in victimhood and powerlessness, then these perceptions from the so-called past—which have a power all their own—must be transformed by understanding their purpose. Events and experiences that are the results of fear-based beliefs and encoded as such in the DNA are especially important to heal, because unless the meaning and purpose of an experience is understood, as the saying goes, history will repeat itself.

Massive multidimensional opportunities to cleanse and heal afflicted energies are rare events throughout the galaxy. When these unique healing opportunities occur, a tremendous diversity of energies is drawn to the locale from various connections. Infusions of cosmic radiation are directed to speed up the prevailing energies in the locale, so periods of accelerated energy basically create a state of supreme reevaluation, followed by the establishment of a new set of priorities for developing what is really important on all levels. All participants are motivated by a very strong desire to transform their consciousness into a different, more heightened state of awareness. Healing times are always about reconnecting fragmented parts with the greater whole by rejuvenating the spirit through accepting greater responsibility for being a co-creator of existence. Tremendous energies for healing pain and separation are being transmitted from the Galactic Center into Earth, surrounding and permeating your physical body and becoming one with you. This energy is transmitted through space, beamed through your sun and into your world. Coronal mass ejections grab hold of the transmissions from the Galactic Center to blast them into your area of space and time. In order to live and thrive during these accelerated times, you must integrate this energy—it must fit like a software program works with a computer, or like a hand sliding into a perfectly sized glove. Anything that blocks these energies from penetrating you and your environment will become visibly manifest and must be dealt with as an obstacle and moved out of the way, so as not to impede the process of your personal transformation.

Opening your chakras and allowing cosmic energies to flow through your body will ultimately refresh your spirit and empower your life.

Waves of pulsating energies are the lifeblood of the cosmos, and even though you appear to be solid in form, you are actually made from vibrating energies that ripple in and out of your body as dancing waves of light. The composition of your being is much grander than you may realize. Doorways known as chakras serve as non-physical openings, or gateways, into your field of identity through which subtle energy forces— etheric energy, or qi, or cosmic radiation—enter and exit both physical and non-physical versions of the body. There are seven major centers associated with the physical body and five that exist beyond the physical form, extending your identity and connection to the web of existence into the depths of the cosmos. The seven chakras in the physical body correspond to the glands of the endocrine system, which direct a grand internal pharmacopoeia of enzymes, hormones, and intricate chemical intelligence that, along with the nervous system, assists in managing the body's numerous functions. Each chakra serves as an intelligence center for processing cosmic energy into the world of physical matter, and can be pictured as a spinning kaleidoscope of color, light, symbols, and sound.

Life lessons are played out in relationship to a specific area of focus and development affiliated with each energy center. The atmosphere is alive with vital force energies, and if your chakras are open, energy will flow in and out of your body, assisting you in maintaining mental clarity, emotional balance, physical health, and spiritual renewal. Your beliefs, attitudes, and interpretations of life determine just how open or closed these doorways are. Fear contracts the centers, while breath, beauty, love, and laughter expand them. Opening your chakras involves giving your internal home a thorough spring cleaning. Running energy through the body will bring up the hidden issues that control your life, and even though encountering these deep internal beliefs can be challenging, it is also very liberating to release what is holding you back. There is no better time than now to accomplish this task. To fully deal with the truth of these times, opening your chakras and allowing cosmic energies, filled with information and knowledge, to flow through your body like a fresh cool stream of crystal clear water, bubbling with the vitality of life, will ultimately refresh your spirit and empower your life.

The first chakra is located at the base of the spine, which is home to a fiery serpent-like energy known as kundalini. This is the seat of your power, where the core issues of identity and survival are the primary lessons to be explored. People can spend an entire lifetime struggling with the lessons that are based on the teachings affiliated with this root center. Substantial bank accounts and important positions in society may come in handy, but it is the type of person you are, the quality of your relationships with your family and friends, and the virtues you embody that define your identity. When you trust and love yourself, energy can enter the first chakra to bolster your own self-worth and transmute the primal fear of being able to survive in the physical body. Mastering the energy of each chakra involves being grounded in the personal responsibilities of your life. Recognizing the corresponding lessons of each of the chakras frees the way for cosmic energies to link up all of the centers connecting you with the web of existence.

Chakra number two is the gateway for sexuality and creativity, and in this center as well, people can spend most of their lives struggling to learn the lessons of these potent energies. Everyone encounters the raw power of sexual energy, yet very few understand the deep psychic and spiritual exchanges that occur when you engage in sexual intimacy. Sexual expression brings forth the lessons and experiences of passion and pleasure; it is also the connection to your ancestors and the center for building family. Your second chakra serves as the opening through which the frequencies of your identity and those of your partner merge to become creatively interwoven. Essentially, through sexual intimacy you take on the other person's energetic field, and if deceit is involved, or no love is present, the hangover from sex can be psychically, emotionally, mentally, and physically debilitating. Yet, with love and respect, you can soar with blissful emotions into the mysteries of the cosmos. Everyone faces the challenge of learning how to honor sexual energy. If you are in a state of continuous fear with issues concerning your survival and your sexuality, then you will be stuck cycling in the lessons of the lower two chakras. Because the second chakra exudes the power of life, it is where discarnate entities most often attach themselves to the physical body. These non-physical energies will then feed off of the energy that you are afraid to own, which, in turn, will never be fully free to rise up the spine and connect the lower chakras to all of the other centers. In order to fully open your second chakra, you must honor your ability to bring life into the world and accept responsibility for your sexual activities. Your sexual identity empowers you in physical reality to build bridges of love and spiritual awareness between physical and non-physical reality.

The third chakra, or solar plexus, serves as the center of feeling, intuition, and willpower, acting as a brain in your belly. Tuning in to the activities and ruminations of this center is of vital importance for making decisions, because your body carries a bank of inner knowledge concerning your life, events of this world, and beyond. You must learn to pay attention to your body and acknowledge the feelings that are registered in your gut. By recognizing the purpose and function of your third chakra, you can quickly understand the subtle nuances of most any situation as you honor your feelings as a valuable resource for discerning reality.

The heart center, or fourth chakra, is located at the midpoint in the physical body and balances all the chakras above and below it with lessons concerning emotional intelligence. In this center, you can shut life down or completely blossom with compassion, for this is the place where you can know another being as a version of yourself. Compassion is a very sophisticated emotional achievement that opens your body to connect with the cosmos on a profound spiritual level. Sometimes opening the heart can be a frightening experience, for you can feel out of control when your heart is wide open and you are inundated with empathetic information. This center for great knowing can provide both daunting and exhilarating experiences. Love rules the heart, and rightly so. The real test that life on Earth offers is the opportunity to pass all you encounter through your heart chakra, acknowledging the wondrous variety of life without judgments. So often, the heart center is blocked off because of a cultivated fear that has conditioned you to be wary of this potent psychic connection. When the heart is closed down, it is easier to create harm or attempt to deceive others, because this connection to all life is disabled. An appreciation for the beauty of life is especially important for opening the heart center.

The manipulation of the truth is only possible when you are afraid of your own power.

The fifth chakra, or the throat center, is of utmost importance because from here you use the creative power of speech to express your thoughts and emotions and bring them into reality. Through this center, you learn lessons about the power of words through speaking your truth and expressing your ideas. A loose and relaxed jaw is very important for keeping this chakra open so that communication flows with grace and ease. A clenched jaw indicates a hidden need to control the natural flow of expression. Breath is the key to this chakra. Directing your focus toward any of your chakras and breathing in a rhythmic manner, with the sound of the "wind in a cave" at the back of your throat, will open them to greater perceptual awareness. Lessons of the fifth chakra involve freeing yourself from doubts and inner worries concerning potential criticism and condemnation for speaking your mind. The manipulation of the truth is only possible when you are afraid of your own power.

The sixth chakra, known as the third eye, is located on the brow between the eyes. This center affects the very complex chemical processes of the pineal gland, and it serves as a tool for opening your awareness into simultaneous time. The third eye is an opening into non-physical reality, a treasured gateway to the inner worlds as an unlimited source of knowledge. This center is connected to the experience of profoundly enhanced perceptions. Lessons here involve overcoming the fear of knowing what your enhanced senses perceive in order to fully tap in to the mysteries revealed through the development of inner sight.

The top of your head is known as the seventh, or crown chakra, and this dynamic center connects the physical nervous system with the cosmic mind. Your nervous system controls and coordinates all organs and structures of the body by serving as a radio receiver for internal and external signals; it actually extends outward from your brain into the ether in fine ribbons or golden threads as light-encoded filaments connecting you to other layers of reality. The lessons of this center are many faceted, and they essentially involve maintaining the fine balance of integrity required for journeys between physical and non-physical reality. Each energy center works in harmony with the others, and opening your mind and your heart to the consideration of greater possibilities inevitably makes more room for the vibrant cosmic energies to enter your body and enhance your life.

There are five additional centers of energy that are located outside of and well beyond your physical form. These cosmic chakras, like the seven in the body, are also pulsating vortices of kaleidoscopic color, light, symbols, and sound that you use to perceive who you are in relationship to all of existence. To navigate and explore the cosmic chakras, creative imagery is important.

The concepts of cities, states, and nations serve as imaginary identifiers to structure an Earth-based reality; maps are used to define reality, but they are not reality—you cannot spend the night in another part of the country just by pointing to a place on the map. Without maps and markings, you would be unable to differentiate between one boundary and another, and in this same fashion, creative imagery can be very useful for exploring a reality that seems to be beyond your reach. Flowers are generally appreciated and treasured on Earth for their sumptuous beauty; they excite you, they have powerful life-force energy, they open your chakras and are often used as a symbol for expressing your deepest feelings and sentiments. Associating the cosmic, multidimensional chakras with specific flowers will give you an image that you can use to explore the numerous non-physical aspects of your identity.

The eighth chakra is located twelve inches to three feet above the body and is linked with the lily. This trumpet-like portal is a transducer of energy for the other cosmic chakras, stepping down light frequencies and funneling this knowledge into the many layers of the physical and non-physical aspects of the body. Essentially it establishes the non-physical link for an identity that is larger than the boundaries of the physical form.

The ninth chakra offers your consciousness great mobility; its symbol is the moon flower because its function is to connect you with all that transpires between the atmosphere of Earth and the moon, including the powerful magnetic energies that connect the two spheres. This energy center provides a vista of Earth from space, and expands your perceptions in relationship to your place in the cosmic scheme of life. Through this center you can explore the timelines of Earth where you have lived again and again, like bouncing on a trampoline, up and down, participating in and then observing the intricate wonders of life.

The tenth center, represented by the sunflower, is known as your solar chakra. It connects and extends your consciousness anywhere in your solar system, from the sun to beyond the planet Pluto. The sun is considered the governor ruler of your system because it sustains and fuels life by providing the necessary light frequencies, along which life-giving energy and information is transmitted. The sunflower center is also very mobile, and utilizing the sun as the focal point, it recognizes cosmic information as a source of your evolving knowledge. Throughout time people have aligned their consciousness with the sun to receive inspiration for new ideas and to access information. Sometimes they would even hide from the sun because they felt that the sun's rays could read their minds; and if they sought to keep secrets and have no one know what they were doing, they chose to operate in the dark, as it were.

Your consciousness can explore the galaxy by moving the galactic chakra anywhere within the Milky Way.

The eleventh center is your galactic chakra, and it is best represented by the red rose, which is the most popular flower for symbolizing and expressing love on Earth. Your consciousness can explore the galaxy by moving this energy center anywhere within the Milky Way, yet eventually the heart center will call you home to the birthplace of all that has come through its portal of creation: the Galactic Center. Connecting to the intelligence of your galaxy will open your consciousness to understanding how clusters of light truly function.

The twelfth chakra connects you to realities beyond your own galaxy by stretching your identity far into the vast expanse of the universe, which is considered to be a singular field containing all that appears to exist. The universal chakra is best symbolized by the purple echinacea flower, whose cone is a mathematical marvel of spirals that epitomize the perfection of the golden-mean ratio as the obvious design of life. Time appears to move backwards in the universe because of your current perceptions and beliefs about light and time. Through the development of radio astronomy, photographs of the far-reaching cosmos depict events that transpired long, long ago, giving you a peek into a mystifying past. The twelfth chakra acts as an open door into this territory of the past, as well as providing an intriguing window for exploring simultaneous time.

The universe is part of the multiverse, where layers of existence are linked through simultaneous time. To complete the picture, an additional center, the thirteenth, opening to the multiverse, embodies every other chakra. The symbolic mysteries of the multiverse are best epitomized by the enigmatic mushroom, tending to appear and disappear on your world as if by magic. The mystifying mushroom can be a gourmet feast, nurturing and delicious, or it can terminate your life if you are not careful; almost certainly, it can take you for a far-reaching and exciting ride into territories well beyond the confines of your perceptions. All of your chakras connect you with an unlimited source of energy to experience and explore the fine nuances of creating reality, and it is your responsibility to enjoy and make use of these capabilities.

Imagine that you are back at the old stone bench, and this time the moon is hanging in the heavens like a big ripe melon beaming a path of shimmering silver light onto the surrounding countryside. The tree frogs and cicadas are collaborating for a soothing symphony of harmonious evening sounds. Take a few moments to settle in by adjusting your neck and clearing your throat. Relax your lower jaw and tongue, and picture yourself swallowing a spoonful of the best honey you have ever tasted— rich with the sweet, seductive nectar of nature. Imagine that the top of your head and your spine are being lifted upward by fine golden threads. Feel your spine straighten, and adjust your pelvis so that it is placed very precisely on the bench, like a valuable alabaster bowl selectively positioned on a fine marble table. Gently separate your lips, and as you inhale notice the smooth feeling of your breath as it passes through your nostrils, over the larynx, and down your throat. Picture your breath being drawn into the bottom of your lungs, like a powerful river tumbling over a precipice, then cascading into seven separate tiers of waterfalls. The water swirls and swirls around a deep pool at the base of each waterfall before it descends farther on its downward journey. You can feel the refreshing mist from the spray, as you feel the flow of energy from the power of your breath, and the beauty of life. Dive to the depths of each pool: playfully swim around, and then joyfully soar over the side, riding the water. Feel the sound of life. Luxuriate in the smooth, flowing journey of your breath by embellishing this state of mind with safe, joyful, and harmonious feelings.

Using the modulation of your breath to travel deep within, imagine that the same state of playful easy grace is simultaneously flowing into your body's seven chakras, beginning at the top of your head and moving down to the base of your spine. Use your focused breath to direct energy into your chakras as you go deeper inside each center. Picture swirling spirals of color dancing around each vortex; the energy is cleaning house, clearing out the cobwebs from years of accumulation—leaving each center looking fresh and bright like a slowly rotating kaleidoscope of color, sound, and light. Now, direct your attention to your feet, and swirl the energy under the soles of your feet, anchoring it into the Earth. Then begin to move the swirling spirals up your legs and back into the first chakra, where it is spinning around the deepest pool at the base of your spine. Move the whirling energy up your body and see it swirling around each vortex, releasing all debris, blockages, and impediments, until you reach the top of your head. If there is any area that refuses to be cleansed and dissolved, converse with that center of intelligence and ask why the area cannot be cleared. Then pay attention and listen. If the situation you are holding on to no longer serves your highest interests, then acknowledge the function it has served, offer your gratitude and thanks, honor that part of your experience, and lovingly welcome it into a higher place of purpose in your multidimensional identity.

Now imagine a circlet of light resting atop your head radiating with cosmic blueprints; your face is serene, full of knowledge and wisdom. Your five cosmic chakras are a mixture of marvels vibrating with wide-open vistas of brilliant luminous colors, swiftly shifting shapes, and surpassingly beautiful sensuous sounds. You can feel the purpose of the patterns of energy connecting the top of your head to the web of existence as you ride realities that reach far beyond the known universe, vaulting into the magical mysteries of the multiverse. The patterns effortlessly merge in a dance of joy; swirls and spirals blend into your physical body from the ether, filled with layers and layers of fresh sweet energy, moving in and out of all of your chakras. You are feeling yourself being super-charged, super-enlightened, expanding your perceptions far beyond your physical body while your circlet of light acts as an antenna by drawing in cosmic radiated energy through your cosmic chakras. Embellish this image with great beauty by placing priceless jewels into thirteen unique patterns of light of your own design—these configurations will serve as important symbols of your participation in the great drama of human transformation.

Remind yourself that you are in a multidimensional game of remembering and integrating many memories. Make clear intentions for how you want to direct the cosmic energies toward enhancing the quality of your life. Now imagine a line of gold thread directly in front of you; reach out and touch it, and it will bring you back to this version of reality.

Symbols and images may arise to reveal clues and messages from the depths of your being that relate to important underlying issues at hand. Maintaining patience by simply allowing the images to slowly fill in the gaps of memory and perception will yield some intriguing connections that may weave recognitions between your genetic line and other lifetimes. Do not rush to analyze the symbols by insisting on an immediate answer. You can first rebalance the right and left hemispheres of the brain by going out into nature and allowing the body-mind some time to integrate your discoveries.

Trust your experience. Events are not stagnant; each and every event, as it is examined and re-explored, grows in meaning and stature throughout simultaneous time. Always ask for the ultimate purpose of any event to be presented to you, as well as solutions for healing the situation. Accepting responsibility for your creations and honoring the wisdom of your body are both essential values for dealing with the lessons of accelerated energy. Remember, accelerated energy shortens the time lag between thinking and manifestation, bringing whatever is focused on into the forefront of experience. Inevitably, life will magnify whatever it is that must be seen and understood, and ideally humanity will realize through firsthand experience that thoughts create reality. Those who refuse to change and grow in awareness may find themselves facing difficult scenarios. When you close yourself off from new opportunities for personal growth and change, you may find yourself feeling overwhelmed and overloaded physically, emotionally, mentally, and spiritually. Dealings with work, family, and life will take on new levels of meaning during these times, and how you respond to your own creations will be a true demonstration of your character. The desire to become more consciously aware of your thoughts and attitudes will help develop your attention, and once you find your attention, you can more easily focus your intentions for how you would like your life, and the events you are involved with, to unfold. Knowing exactly what you are available for is very important because it always creates a strong frequency of intent in your energetic field.

Layers of multiple realities share the same space with you, influencing your 3-D operations through an extensive exchange of symbols.

New considerations require new pictures of reality, and we offer you a different perspective on the times in which you live in order to stretch your imagination and expand the use of your mind to reveal the truth of your multidimensional existence. Connections from many diverse lifetimes are being woven together now, as forms of your consciousness, scattered throughout the corridors of time, respond to the signals of greater awareness emanating from this slice of time. Layers and layers of multiple realities share the same space with you, influencing your 3-D operations through an extensive exchange of symbols, while most often your conscious mind is completely unaware of the state of ongoing telepathic communication. Your biological being is based on a natural built-in human technology fully equipped with intuitive and extrasensory abilities for discerning the many spectrums of reality that exist beyond the confines of the materialistic, linear perspectives of time and space. From your vista in the world of matter, symbols are the primary means through which you explore and interpret life. Symbols represent ideas—words, numbers, sounds, colors, signs, shapes, and lights—and are tools and methods for conveying information as well as metaphors for understanding reality. Our intent is to offer metaphors for reality that will help you climb a ladder of consciousness in order to get a better vista of the purpose of these twenty-five years of transformational change. You are free to interpret the symbols in any fashion you choose, although our best advice is not to make cement blocks out of ideas, for they may only end up boxing you in.

The nanosecond offers new knowledge about the nature of existence, and all of humanity is challenged to make room for this energy in the physical form. This energy does not just effortlessly slide in; you must be willing to change by opening your mind to accommodate it. Galactic Center transmissions deliver stupendous jolts of energy that trigger deep truths and stimulate exciting new levels of creativity within humanity— energies that are life-enhancing and meant to be felt and absorbed. If the energies encounter a blockage, they will begin to concentrate and create pressure in and around the blocked area, essentially working to unlock and untangle the snarl that is creating the obstruction. Holding on to pain and fear and anxiety-ridden interpretations of life will inevitably create only more resistance. When change is in your favor, and still you refuse to open the door to self-improvement, you create a block on the new program of energy. Intensified galactic transmissions are like an energetic thunderstorm, refreshing and revitalizing if the conditions are accommodating, and potentially destructive to areas that cannot accommodate the abundance of nature's power. Galactic-oriented energy has tremendous force to empower everyone on Earth, to embrace you and the mass consciousness of your planet as a cosmic family. To connect with the Galactic Center is to connect with an energy that is nurturing, truthful, passionate, volatile, compassionate, caring and continuously supportive—the ultimate goddess figure of the galaxy. And, if you can embrace these energies as your own, you will come closer to knowing who you are.

The more you use the new-energy program that the nanosecond provides, the easier it is to integrate the existence of the greater reality. When you deal with situations from a new perspective, many new solutions will unfold. Feelings of relaxation and ease, clear intent, self-acceptance, love, compassion, and a joyful willingness to live life to the fullest will create that environment. However, if you condition your reality with worry, then you will create one worrisome thing after another. Worry, like any other negative expression, will block the flow of energy into your body. Projections of worry have a very powerful and insistent frequency that transmits a message with an expectation of problems arising. Intend to examine any blocks that stand in the way or impede your progress and ask yourself: What is really bothering me? What am I really afraid to change? What am I still gripping and holding on to that needs to be released? Very often you will find that the issues are old ones that are being carried by you from lifetime through lifetime in search of harmonious resolution. Whatever you presently think your issues show, a bigger picture will eventually unfold. Take a neutral stance in regard to the situation and welcome the meaning of the blocked energy and ask that it be revealed. Release your emotional attachments to any given outcome, and simply allow the meaningful connections and positive purpose to be presented. You can change the outcome of the past, as well as the effects in the present and the future, by seeing events from a different perspective. New vistas can free you from interpretations that previously restrained your spirit.

The purpose of the nanosecond is to clean the human gene pool of fear—a conditioned fear of personal power.

Everyone carries emotional memories that impact his or her life in a profound and sometimes unexpected manner—

painful wounds and unresolved issues are part of genetic heritage. The purpose of the nanosecond is to clean the human gene pool of fear—a conditioned fear of personal power. Throughout these years of transformation, confrontations will escalate between the general public and those who attempt to control knowledge and censure the truth. The level of corruption that humanity faces is staggering, and it is only just beginning to unravel. Many more people are gaining the courage to know the truth, and they are willing to share it with others because they recognize that fear is the tool being used to control them. Fear is the debris that clogs this area of reality and carries the most toxic residue for Earth and her inhabitants— thousands and thousands and thousands of years of accumulated fear must be released and transformed. A collective misunderstanding of the nature of existence has resulted in a people filled with shame, guilt, sorrow, hopelessness, and despair—the very qualities that stop the flow of vital energy and disavow the cosmic mind. Unresolved issues accumulate and are carried from one lifetime to another, where new scenarios play out the same old lessons, time after time, until a new realization is achieved.

Intricate dramas seeking harmonious resolution are simultaneously occurring in many realities, and all too often, the events make no sense to those caught in an unremitting loop of repetition. People sometimes think they are going crazy because of feedback interference from other lines of time that are also engaged in playing out versions of the same issue. The human mind is always naturally seeking a state of integrated wholeness to balance these influences and to work out a solution, and by trusting the body, it will always work in sublime cooperation to empower one's life. Modern Western medicine does not embrace this premise of healing through body-mind cooperation, and therefore the rampant use of pharmaceutical drugs is seen as a solution for every illness, which only denies and clouds over the innate intelligence of the body. From another perspective, the massive rise in pharmaceutical dependency makes no sense as poisons are used to allegedly heal the body. The excessive use of medication to deal with the problems of life is a warning sign that something of major significance is occurring, and people are choosing to use drugs to block it out. Experiencing multidimensional realities is generally located outside of the box of beliefs that govern your world, and many people have no framework from which to understand this process. Augmented with new insight, the human mind is supremely capable of expanding into new territories of reality, and within this version of the game of life, you are challenged to recognize a new purpose far beyond the edge of scientific and religious convictions.

We offer you a look at these times from a cosmic perspective in order to assist you in stretching your mind so that you can reach out to feel the patterns of purpose unfolding in your own life. Opportunities for empowering your life exist in every moment as accelerated energy offers unlimited possibilities for all participants. Contemplate the significance of your life for a few moments. What deeper purpose is rising to the surface now? What memories are being triggered into the light of your conscious mind? How well you mature in awareness during this time of change is of vital importance to your spiritual growth, so really think about what you are imprinting on the field of energy. What frequency are you broadcasting? Do you send signals with clear intent or are your moods and feelings of disempowerment coloring your broadcast? Remember, a very important and crucial purpose of these accelerated times is to clean up the frequency of fear. Understanding vital energy and mastering the ability to stamp your thoughts with clear intent upon the web of existence were considered to form the ultimate practice of what some call "the old magic." For the times in which you live, they are the ultimate connection to sane, practical, and significant living. This knowledge will be used by those who choose to build a probable world based on new principles for understanding reality. Ideally many probable worlds will unite by frequency in the discovery and realization that you are an inherent part of the vast field of vital cosmic energy. Your signature frequency is unique to you. As you awaken and raise your standard of awareness, you automatically contribute your newfound frequency of personal responsibility to the vibrational web that affects the mass consciousness.

Intend to use your mind and body in extraordinary new ways, for a massive movement of truth is building momentum one mind at a time; trust your contribution to the process. Be willing to recognize the dramas of life for serving an overall positive purpose. Take charge of your life. There are many more mysteries to be understood, and many uplifting adventures await you. We trust that you will be up to the task of reinterpreting existence, of maintaining your home station while anchoring multidimensional wisdom and knowledge into the human form. There are great reasons why so much attention is focused on your world by beings from other dimensions. And there are great reasons, as well, why the controlling forces of your world seek to divert your attention and manage every nuance of your thinking: to keep you from figuring out what is happening inside. Proceed to love who you are, all the while cultivating your creativity by believing in the unlimited possibilities of growth through your own personal transformation. We suggest that you invest in your self, for on the web of existence, we are all one.

In order to manage the accelerated energies, take it easy, slow down, laugh, and allow yourself the luxury of actually enjoying life.

Set your course now, dear friend, and intend smooth sailing as you ride the winds of change with an even keel and a steady bow. Remember, the nanosecond is about empowering yourself to experience greater states of awareness. In order to manage the accelerated energies, take it easy, slow down, laugh, and allow yourself the luxury of actually enjoying life. Laughter disperses the fog and is the key to owning your physical form; it keeps you young, aligns your cells, and opens your chakras for more energy to enter. Good humor activates the body, creating a sense of ease and well-being; cares and woes are released and forgotten by those who engage in laughter and fun by opening themselves to creatively innovative wit. People who laugh can see through things, so seek out heartfelt, eye-watering, good-natured humor, rather than sitting in front of the "doom machine," television. Moving at a fast pace and always staying busy distracts you from truly being present with your power. Let things happen—the spiritual world unfolds once you allow it to do so. Nature is the system that best sustains your vitality, so go for a leisurely walk and pay close attention to whether the birds and other creatures respond to your presence by altering the tone and pitch of their singing. Animals can always read your vibration, and if you are intent on empowering your life, they will often gift you by making special melodies of sound to balance your chakras and tune up your body. Spending time in nature can restore your appreciation for beauty, in turn opening your chakras to harmony and balance.

There are always many, many points of view for any situation. And as you may well know, perspective is the key. As you expand your perceptions, you will be operating in a different program of reality. Many forms of intelligence, from places you are connected to, are drawn here now to participate in the transformation of consciousness. Your frequency is based on your values, and your values stem from the choices you make in the process of developing your own moral and civic code as you play with the energies of existence. Throughout the cosmos, we are all striving for the frequency of wisdom and the proper use of the frequency of love. These times are about consciously producing individual and mass frequencies that affect all of existence, for once you can read frequencies and understand what you are doing, all the parameters of living are changed.

Chapter Four

THE INTIMATE DANCE OF BELIEFS AND EMOTIONS

*T*here are many ways of looking at life, and how you interpret your place in the world depends on what you choose to believe. In order to empower your life, it is imperative that you understand your personal and collective beliefs. You are who you are, and you are where you are because of what you believe about yourself; no matter what you are experiencing, your beliefs form the underlying foundation to create these experiences. What are your beliefs? Where do your beliefs come from? Beliefs are usually about power: your power to create. Beliefs can reveal how you manage energy. Beliefs are decisions and agreements that you make about reality; they are an accumulation of invisible inner building blocks, formed from your interpretation of reality, that collect over time and from which you construct a concept of yourself in relationship to your perceived place in existence. Beliefs are the programs from which you have built your life experience. They reveal the way in which you personalize your choices and the conditions you apply for imprinting the vital-force energy used for manifesting your thoughts. When you take a good look at your life, you will see the unique creative results of your own internal programming.

Everyone has a bushel basketful of beliefs collected from many sources. Genetic inheritance, family proclivities, childhood experiences, social and cultural influences, and numerous impressions from other lifetimes are among some of the contributors to the invisible bundle of beliefs that define your experience in 3-D reality. Beliefs are the thoughts that you hold, most often without question, about yourself and the world at large. These unnoticed thought-forms are birthed in your imagination and stored in your subconscious memory bank, qualifying your experiences in both the inner and outer worlds. Your beliefs set you up for success or failure. If your worldview is optimistic, you will generally be self-motivated with a positive attitude and engage life with joy and enthusiasm; however, if your worldview tends to lean toward pessimism and negative interpretations of reality, then a sense of hopelessness and despair will overshadow your every encounter. People suffer from pain and confusion due to a belief in their own sense of powerlessness, a belief that is as ancient as the whisperings of time; all forms of consciousness must pass through various stages of accepting responsibility for their power in every vista of creation. Your encounters in the outer world are a reflection of your inner reality: you become what you think about; therefore, when you change your thinking, you will inevitably change your life.

Your beliefs establish the instructions for how you want to operate your biological being.

Humankind is being tested to become much more consciously aware of how to use the power of thought. You are born with a multitude of abilities, yet your cultivated beliefs insist you are powerless; therefore, these abilities are blocked out or eradicated from neural pathways at an early age. The key to solving the great planetary crisis you face lies in the compassionate recognition that humanity has essentially developed a collective fear of the power to create. These times call for you to know your mind and your beliefs and to become an extraordinary creator of your reality. You are incarnated on Earth to deal with a form of power. Existence shows the essence of power and its use: it is composed of dynamic energies that carry its majestic blueprints of consciousness into every nook and cranny of the cosmos. Humanity creates the world at large by way of unconscious primal mass agreements. You are participating in a mass agreement that is exploring the nature of reality from a 3-D vista, and you contribute to energizing the collective experience into being through telepathy and dreaming. You are highly creative without even realizing it. You effortlessly dream your larger world reality into being as a place to explore existence. Everyday encounters and experiences, though significant and intimately yours, are nonetheless deeply interwoven with countless other personal "nows." The choices you make in physical reality are based on what you believe is possible.

Your biological structure is actually a sending-and-receiving center of information. Your cells instantly receive telepathic information; there are no buttons to push, no screens to check, and no modem breakdowns. The body's intelligence system is constantly tracking the past, present, and future. While you are deeply enmeshed in your own moment-to-moment experience, all of the thoughts and feelings you effortlessly explore are instantly processed, and almost simultaneously telepathically broadcast into the outer world and throughout time. You exist in an infinite web of information that is constantly exchanged on a cellular level without your conscious knowledge. The people in your present environment are unconsciously aware of your beliefs and expectations, as well as your intentions and inner commands. Every cell in your body is a multisensory, multifaceted communication device, crystalline in structure, that responds to the modulation of light—another information pathway. The inner brain cavity is a resonation chamber and acts as an energy transducer for cosmic radiation, which is the vital force, or chi, that delivers the blueprints for life. Essentially your vista of space and time is created through your own biology. The current metamorphosis of human consciousness can lead you to open and activate new sensing mechanisms beyond the five major senses of taste, touch, hearing, smell, and sight. Psychic powers are a natural part of your internal technology as tools for inner management.

The more aware you are of the programs you run inside your biological computer, the easier it will be to create what you want. Your cells broadcast who you are—you carry a huge energetic sign in your energy field—by frequency and telepathy. Your cells also hear all of your thoughts—conscious, subconscious, and unconscious—and as a result are constantly modulating themselves to send out the exact signal for what you want. Then, through an array of synchronistic events, you cross the path of opportunity that connects you to what you are focused on, which is deeply tied to your beliefs about your self-worth. Have you ever stopped to consider whether your core beliefs support your stance in life? There are no accidents; your cells impel you to turn down one street versus another—to meet an old friend or avoid an unpleasant encounter—so whatever crosses your path is part of your creation. You must decide what you are available for, and be very, very clear about it. If you think you have no power over what happens in the outside world, this is a belief and an agreement you have made between yourself and the field of existence. Your cells hear this command about your place in reality and do everything possible to make certain, in whatever situation you meet, that you have no power over events. Your beliefs establish the instructions for how you want to operate your biological being, and in these times of tremendous acceleration, humankind is faced with the responsibility of learning how to manage the energy of thought. You must accept supreme responsibility for being the operator of your biological system in order to be on the path toward managing the energy of existence.

You are a pioneer preparing a path for a new interpretation of reality.

You live and thrive amidst a very complex web of mass agreements that support and define earthly existence as you know it. Within this framework of mass beliefs, you have the free will to choose your thoughts and pursue ideas that best resonate with your personal values. Your outer world experiences directly correspond to your inner world of thoughts, feelings, and desires, which are the subtle personal activities upon which your beliefs are built. You will find yourself in the right place at the right time if that is your belief, and everything will work out just fine—if that is your belief. Believing in your own personal safety and that you live in a benevolent multiverse is very beneficial if you wish to live in peace and harmony. When you encounter any situation in day-to-day life, you actually project your perceptions onto the event, coloring in whatever you want to see by way of belief. You are always interpreting reality. Actually, you are a pioneer preparing a path for a new interpretation of reality, and like a seedling shoot finding its way to the

sunlight through layers and layers of dense matter, you are pushing against an invisibly fortified ceiling of ignorance, where
limitation reigns and negative beliefs have become indisputable
facts. As billions of people begin to question the very nature of
existence by seeing through the conditioned glamour of life on
Earth, this mass reconsideration will strip away the veneer of
restrictive beliefs that no longer sustain you or your culture.
And, as you can imagine, this intrepid new consciousness creates massive pressure on the prevailing paradigm of beliefs that
govern your life.

You are imbued with consciousness, that is, the ability to
be aware, yet this does not necessarily mean that you are consciously aware of all you create. Beliefs are tricky; essentially,
they are agreements about reality that you accept and uphold
without question. As you confront yourself and meet your
beliefs, thoughts and feelings may peel off like layers of old
paint, or you may well find yourself traveling through internal
black holes and out the other side, journeying through parts of
yourself you never even knew existed. Once again, your focused
attention is a personal gold mine, and as you learn to value and
use this inherent wealth, you can fortify yourself for journeys
into both the inner and outer worlds. Where and how you
spend your energy are exceedingly important in understanding
how you create your life. Are you the captain of your attention
or always just along for the ride? For a few moments, center
yourself with your breath, and visualize golden spirals of energy
infusing your body as you direct your attention deep inside your
inner world.

As you sit in centered silence, consider that in order to
empower your life, you must first examine it. Life is rich and
rippling with symbolic meaning, and designating respectful sig-

nificance to all of life's encounters will help expand your mind and integrate your identity and purpose.

Throughout your life, how much attention have you paid to the power of your beliefs? Beliefs are powerful, and whether they are known or unknown, they still set the stage for your experiences to transpire. In all honesty, do you truly know what you believe? Have you self-selected and consciously planted your beliefs in your psyche as you would purposefully plant a garden? What beliefs have you inherited as treasured family heirlooms? What patterns of commonality flow through your family's genes? What specific issues do members of different generations of your family all have in common? Which particular situations are forever on rerun for you and your family? How often are you the tragic star of the show? What thoughts and feelings do you have upon awakening in the morning? What do you think of your dreams? How do you feel about your bedroom and what do you use it for? What feelings surface when you evacuate your bowels and bathe your body? What is your body worth to you? What do you think about sex? Do you have a benign or detrimental influence on your body? What do you use your body for? What do you think about food and the role it plays in your life? What does "home" mean to you? What influence does your family have in determining your behavior? What are your feelings concerning laughter and fun? What do you think is possible for you to achieve in this lifetime? What do you believe you deserve from life?

With these thoughts in mind, jot down over the next few days at least a dozen personal beliefs encompassing a variety of subjects. Write the beliefs as statements, a personal litany of your so-called facts about reality. Be certain to include your beliefs about health, wealth, and happiness. Allow one week to pass, and then take a good, honest look at these proclamations. How do you feel about what you wrote? Is your life a reflection of this script? Do your beliefs serve your life and enhance your well-being? How many of your beliefs are you happy with? How many would you like to change? How do they demonstrate the way you use the vital energy of existence to create your life? The next step is to examine and evaluate the appropriateness of these ideas you hold about yourself and the world at large, for it is through this filter of beliefs that you create the version of the world you meet.

Within this plane of reality, you inherit a set of beliefs from your genetic line, as well as a celestial and formative imprint of character from the position of the planets at your birth. You also have memories carried over from issues and events in simultaneous time. And then, of course, you are subjected to the cultural conditioning, from society, family, and religion, that influences you from birth and helps to define the nature of your personal reality. The information or beliefs that are foisted upon you do not represent the entire picture of reality; therefore, you often live your life on one avenue of existence, all the while missing out on a myriad of untold opportunities because accepting limiting beliefs is like wearing a straightjacket all of your life. Your innermost core beliefs determine the direction of your life; they are played out daily and distributed by way of your thoughts and attitudes. People who choose the avenue of fear do not see another fork in the road—their beliefs literally function as blinders, overshadowing and eliminating every other possible and probable option, path, or solution. Your beliefs condition and qualify the space that surrounds you, creating an electromagnetic imprint that ultimately serves to attract all of your life experiences. Thoughts are real in that they have a life of their own once you create them. Most of the time, however, you are clueless, as you say, on how you set your version of the world into motion.

You are learning that there are many ways of looking at any situation, and in the bigger picture, it could be said that consensual reality is currently experiencing a breakdown of beliefs. People have built their lives on the faith that beliefs are absolute facts, or attributes of existence that are indisputable truths; but beliefs are agreements about reality, and agreements can be changed. It is essential to understand that beliefs are the thoughts you hold within your imagination—consciously, subconsciously, and unconsciously—and in the imagination, all things are real. All thoughts produce energetic vibrations, and even though you cannot see these frequencies, the airwaves are full of who you are.

During this period of acceleration your world has become quite polarized over a massive conflict of beliefs. Two very distinct directions of thought, based on the value of life, express the tension of this great divide. A belief in a world of hostility uses the platform of "might is right" to promote killing and violence as a means to an end. In direct opposition, a belief in a peacefully empowered existence places immense value on nature, and all life is held in significant regard. Stress and tension are steadily escalating all over the planet due, in part, to an increase in telepathic and psychic sensitivity to the magnitude of this great vibrational divide. Now, this great divide of beliefs is actually "a polarity of cooperation," like a full moon shining its light, stoking the fires of passion, and illuminating what is normally hidden. These activities are a demonstration of the vast power of beliefs to create very distinct, and sometimes diametrically opposed, versions of reality. In purely practical terms, you make your choice in every moment for what you want. The use of your free will to choose to decide is, of course, your saving grace, and you must learn to cultivate it, seeding thoughts for an empowered life.

In order to understand and heal the insanity, instability, and seeming uncertainty of these troubled times, you must first learn to manage yourself. Learning to manage energy in the material world is one of the reasons you are here at this time. Your body is your first and foremost responsibility, and essentially, it follows your commands. Your emotional intensity is the charge of power behind the frequency of your thoughts. How you feel about yourself and the world at large directly affects the functions and operating systems of your physical form.

Feelings are fuel for beliefs—especially feelings of excitement—and when you follow your feelings, you will always find your beliefs. When you feel good about yourself, your outer world will mirror this state of mind, and when you feel down-and-out and frustrated, the outer world also conforms. Limitations, frustrations, and blockages can be examined from a meaningful perspective. Accepting your part in creating your life situations—without blaming yourself or anyone else—and approaching your life with the attitude that everything you encounter has a significant purpose will unblock the victim conditioning that has been prevalent for so long among humanity. Transmuting victimhood is a major step on the path of self-empowerment. However, those choosing to experience reality devoid of such emotional intelligence will increasingly find themselves in a world order where the significance of life is lost. Those who choose love—daring to feel to the depths of being, accepting responsibility for their actions, and seeking a purpose in life—will find that the world of significant living will unfold its cleverly concealed presence.

Embracing a personal belief in your inherent self-worth is an excellent investment of your time and energy.

You are in charge of the vital energy that sustains and connects you with the larger cosmic reality. When you abdicate and ignore your abilities to create your reality, essentially, you turn your power over to be maneuvered by others. The tendency to think that someone other than yourself is going to save you has been programmed and conditioned into humans. No one is going to save you: in order to flourish and thrive, you must be willing to take charge of your life. The feelings you experience are important keys toward understanding how you operate. Once again, when you follow your feelings, you will find your beliefs, and when you discover your beliefs, you will be face-to-face with the concepts you use to build your version of reality. In order to expand your awareness and feel more self-empowered, you must be willing to examine whatever thoughts your feelings uncover, for your thoughts, once observed and examined, can be traced to their origin and their purpose can be unveiled. You are not stuck with your thoughts, or the self that you think you are, nor are you permanently confined by the blood of your ancestors. You are a product of your own making, an accumulation of ideas and experiences that have been gathered throughout time, which you can use to your own advantage in building a version of reality that you deeply desire. Knowledge is power, and it would serve you well to remember this ancient and self-evident truth. Every thought you hold has a powerful impact on your world.

Clarity in thought, word, and deed is of utmost importance for creating the version of life that you want. In ancient times the power of words was known to be the art of old magic.

Language is a powerful tool for directing and manifesting energy into form. We suggest that you purposely choose your words with care and certainty, know what you want, and establish clear positive intentions as to your purpose. The pursuit of worthy goals and ideals is essential for feeling empowered. Every thought and word influences the great repository of memories in the subconscious mind—thoughts and words of your own, or those that stem from the outside world.

Given that you are highly telepathic, you can also be influenced by the thoughts and activities of others, especially if you have poor boundaries and are confused about who you are. External suggestions and images, such as those from television, program your subconscious and unconscious minds. Your scientists have done studies with people connected to an EEG brain-scanning device while watching TV; they registered activity in the delta wave frequencies, essentially occupying a highly programmable sleep state while viewing TV. If you are unaware of your thoughts, or have abdicated your choice to direct your thinking, then electronic methods can easily influence and control your mind. Your conscious mind sets the commands, and the subconscious mind is the processing center where the directives or beliefs are filtered and then carried out. Empowering your life begins when you have control of your thoughts. You then must decide what you want and proceed to attain it; otherwise your commands will have no conscious intent to direct the course of your life.

The times in which you live call for the best of your capabilities to emerge, and embracing a personal belief in your inherent self-worth is an excellent investment of your time and energy. Happiness and peace of mind are the hallmarks of real empowerment, and they are present when you are in balance with your values and intuition. As the energy continues to accelerate, issues will only grow in complexity in whatever arenas of life you have avoided your responsibilities. To prepare yourself for experiencing higher states of consciousness and greater perceptual awareness, you must visualize the type of world you want, and trust that you will meet it. Your imagination is the most powerful tool for creating, and when you focus your attention with clear conscious intent, you set an internal program into motion, one that will determine your experience of the outer world. Events are multidimensional pieces of living art; the form, size, shape, and purpose change as you learn to walk around an event and release your fixation on a single, emotionally driven framework of time. Events grow in meaning as you grow in consciousness; when you consciously alter your interpretations of the world and embrace a confident, inspiring outlook, your experience of the world changes. Even though the conditions may remain the same, like the half-full–half-empty glass analogy, how you choose to perceive what you see sets the stage for all you encounter, as well as affecting the entire paradigm of mass beliefs. Your beliefs make you who you are, and the areas of life where you excel in your achievements are generally those where you feel excitement and have fun with what you are doing.

Cultural beliefs about the nature of reality rule your experience from the deepest and most ancient levels. Beliefs arise out of ideas about reality; these ideas are then passed on through time to evolve into facts, and these facts appear to define what you see because of what you were told. The ideas form a loop of energy that continues to create a super-fortified blueprint of reality supported by an immense contribution of energy from the mass consciousness. The result of this massive support, which is based on unquestioned cultural assumptions, determines the overall world structure that you currently encounter.

Mass beliefs form a controlled, conjured view of reality in which you have all agreed to participate; you meet these agreements every day of your life through social, cultural, and certainly personal experiences. The idea of Earth being a singular experience—a "one world and one world only" location where everyone is fixed in the same reality—is similar in a sense to flat-world thinking. The overall world structure is a framework of agreements that you operate within: it is not the *only* version of the world. Nature is flexible and alive with multidimensional possibilities, and your beliefs, decisions, and emotions play the decisive role in creating the version of the world reality you actually encounter.

The field of existence is unlimited and benevolent, and by extension, you are a wondrous and unlimited part of creation.

Certainly some of the most influential core beliefs to lock humanity into endless loops of confusion stem from ancient myths about human origins. In the Judeo-Christian tradition, the story of Adam and Eve has a woman conversing with a serpent, and then following her natural curiosity and testing the parameters of her intuition, she allegedly creates a grave trespass and mankind is shamefully and permanently tossed out of paradise. Over time, millions upon millions of people have built their lives around this tale, faithfully believing that they must still pay for this supposed transgression. There is always some layer of truth to myths, given that they are a composite of long-cherished teachings or beliefs about the nature of reality, as well as a record of your ancestral lineage. Yet the perceived truth will be applied according to how the event is seen in the imagination, where interpretations are formed. This particular myth has birthed innumerable so-called veritable vistas of reality: disobedience is costly, it is best to obey, only God is all powerful, the body cannot be trusted, women definitely cannot be trusted, never listen to a serpent, humanity is helpless and paying dearly for the uncontrollable impulses of women, women fail at leadership, humanity is not deserving of God, and "the fall" into the cruel, hard world of nature is the permanent punishment.

In one form or another, implications of blame and helplessness reside at the root of the accepted interpretations of this cherished tale, which fully sanctify a culturally ingrained belief in victimhood, the ultimate state of powerlessness. Helplessness stems from a belief that you have no control over your environment, and it is fortified by considering the past as a valid expectation of present and future events. Neediness is based on a desire to have someone other than yourself mold your destiny. You are neither sinned, nor flawed, nor helpless. When you choose to believe that you must adore and worship and emulate beings whose behavior is grander than your own, then you are doing yourself a disservice. You are as equal to every part of the field of existence as is every other part of creation. Nature is the system that sustains you and you are free to question the nature of existence. The field of existence is unlimited and benevolent, and because you are a part of this field, by extension, you are a wondrous and unlimited part of creation. Remember, your beliefs are an integral part of your personal energy field; in actuality, they are a form of magic. Magic is the ability to conjure something into form, and beliefs do the same; mass beliefs create mass conjurings. Over time, beliefs have been manipulated and formatted to become mass agreements within the 3-D spatial experience.

Your personal framework of beliefs determines what you perceive. You project your own energy outward to form the physical world, and this is most important for understanding beliefs and magic: to change the world, you must change yourself. In the Western world, magic is often ridiculed and placed in the realm of fantasy or sleight of hand. Until you put your beliefs aside, you will not see the world beyond your beliefs. Everything is magical, and perhaps you will be inspired to deal more effectively with old memories and blocked energies as you come to understand the significance of your beliefs. The accelerated energies can bring out the very best in human potential by triggering situations where you are challenged to transcend limiting beliefs. The point and purpose of these times is for humanity to fulfill a certain destiny nestled within your blueprints of being, and in order to achieve this fulfillment, the acceleration of energy will push at every area of your life that requires an overhaul.

Your complete presence is required in physical form to effectively deal with both the inner and outer worlds, and you do this by wanting to be here and being present, alert, and alive, fully sensing and faithfully treasuring your body. Being present and accounted for also brings you into closer contact with everything you hold inside. Your spine and skeletal structure contain substantial amounts of key information about your present life experiences, as well as links to memories stored on the web of existence; to some extent, stored memories determine the process of experience in which you agree to participate. Good posture is a sign of a structurally aligned body, which is far easier to occupy than one with poor posture. A flexible spine makes for a flexible mind. Bones can also store memories for great pain, and because pain is sometimes too difficult to deal with, you may leave your body in order to avoid any deep association with knowing and remembering certain experiences.

There is always a point and purpose to pain. Primarily,

pain is a strong signal from deep inside the body's intelligence centers, indicating that your emotional health is out of balance. Stored and stuffed emotions take a great toll on the body, and eventually the old built-up energy will be released in the form of painful physical manifestations. When you carry pain and do not release and let go of the past, your body will faithfully show you the results of your repressed feelings. Just as facing your fears is the best way to overcome them, you can also deal with your deepest feelings by acknowledging their existence. Emotions energize thoughts and the greater the intensity, the more fuel behind the thoughts. Finding a safe and creative way to express your feelings, such as writing them down, or better yet, counting to thirteen then patiently expressing how you feel in the moment, will free you to enjoy life and get good measure from the accelerated energy. Eventually you will have to strike a match and see what is in the darkest of places in order to enlighten yourself over what you have not understood. Accelerated energy pushes everything that must be dealt with to the forefront of your life, including, of course, unresolved issues from other lifetimes. Accessing the emotional self is like playing music on your inner piano, and you know how to play; the question is: What tunes are you selecting? Whatever you do here—every action you take, and most importantly, every emotion you feel—ripples out into your reality as well as into layers of multidimensional locations.

Emotional accessibility, the ability to feel on very deep levels, is one of the key components for managing accelerated energy. Everyone, at one time or other, must deal with buried emotions that are tied to unexamined beliefs, which block the flow of energy in the body. A person who can feel and know soul-wrenching pain also has the capability to transcend difficulty and experience pure states of joy and ecstasy. People with no emotional accessibility and depth are numb, often completely compartmentalized, or their inner and outer experiences are separated in their minds because of some type of trauma. Their determinations, projections, and perceptions of reality are, therefore, quite rigid and fixed in focus. The controllers of your planet—those playing the part of the villain—often resort to using trauma to steer the masses along paths of fear and confusion, and they do this for numerous reasons; however, they can do so because they lack an emotional connection between inner and outer realities.

If you do not know how to feel, then you are missing very important gear for playing this game.

Intensified galactic transmissions will throw open the doors of the subconscious mind, releasing powerful old emotions. Use this galactic energy to creatively structure your thoughts. How much you genuinely like and accept yourself as a person establishes your value and self-worth. Whenever you feel good about yourself, you excel. You can decree that your body is worthy of your trust. The more you like yourself, the better you do with whatever you pursue, for how much you like yourself is at the core of your beliefs. You can learn to trust yourself and follow your impulses, to watch for synchronicities, and to honor your hunches and feelings. And, if you do not know how to feel, then you are missing very important gear for playing this game. Feelings are activated by giving yourself permission to feel, then as you withhold judgment, owning the fountain of feelings that appear. If you are afraid of a flood of feelings getting out of control, let go of this fear by acknowledging your emotions as serving a significant purpose, and then release your attachment. Your feelings are very valuable assets for discerning reality and they help you gauge where you stand in accepting responsibility for your creations. When you do not acknowledge how you really feel, stuffing and denying your feelings, you then subconsciously project onto others what you do not claim as your own. And, it is no easy task to claim as your own what you do not know you own, in this case, that which is stored deep in the subconscious mind. You can understand yourself by looking at what you are creating in your own life. And even though this is tricky territory you are plowing and pursuing, with an open heart and mind, and clarity of intent, there is no earthly reason why you cannot unravel the mysteries of your mind and cultivate the best of realities.

Emotional intelligence is a rich and valuable asset in physical reality, being the determining key for spiritual development. Be open to exploring your emotions by taking a risk and welcoming any deep feelings and memories you may have dissociated or compartmentalized or stuffed away. A tremendous amount of energy is utilized to block emotional memory. Your entire being is filled with memories of events, times, and places that you have only just begun to realize. You have been trained to focus on what you expect to see, disregarding anything that does not fit your beliefs. As the pressure from the accelerated energy builds, you will have to make space and unclutter the "stuff" inside—the unprocessed emotions and old fearful vibrations stored in and between your cells, atoms, bones, muscles, tissues, and organs, and in your DNA. Every area of your body is imbued with memory. Visualize yourself as flexible, organized, spacious, and clear, with the flow of accelerated energy moving easily throughout your physical body and, in turn, enhancing your life.

Though it may appear that reality is occasionally placing

stumbling blocks on your path, this type of thinking arises whenever you get stuck on limiting self-concepts. Limiting beliefs will often be accompanied by feelings of frustration. Humankind has yet to truly grasp the damaging effects of accepting futile and valueless beliefs about the physical body. Wherever you feel challenged in life—money, sex, health, employment, relationships, or religion—it usually comes down to how you manage your energy. The areas where you struggle, where you develop anxiety, anger, and frustration, and perform poorly, are all signaling negative beliefs about yourself and that your thinking is not working in your best interests. Sometimes your beliefs about important issues rule your life from behind the scenes, and these are the areas that need to be addressed and examined, acknowledged and released. Shameful feelings damage your body by acting like unseen termites eating away at the framework of a building. By simply acknowledging the existence of an issue, the blocks and walls are loosened, allowing more energy to flow into your body.

You do not have to have all the solutions worked out in advance—be willing to pay attention and notice. Observe and watch for patterns, and ask yourself: What else is this issue connected to? What higher purpose and greater opportunity await me if I can see this situation from another point of view? With an open and positive attitude, the galactic energy will flow into your body, and then you may have an impulse to seek out bodywork or a massage, or write in a journal, or go for a solitary walk in the woods, or cry for a while. Healthy tears melt down the barriers that block memory and can open the way to releasing what you were holding inside. As long as you cry without feeling sorry for yourself and do not host a pity party, your tears can offer the soothing balm that comes from an open heart with the courage to delve into pure feeling.

In order to empower yourself and consciously utilize the force of vital cosmic energy, you must recognize your fears as your regular contribution to the current state of global emotional pollution. It may appear that an outside force is tyrannizing you; however, your inner signals must be sending this request into the ether in order for you to create the experience. Fear has a recognizable frequency of energy that can be felt as distinctly as the frequency of love. You may be thinking that fear is not a desire, yet if you consider how much attention and focus the fear frequency elicits in the world, then perhaps you can see why it seems that this is the version of the world that the majority of humans want to create. This collective fear goes far beyond the threats of war and tyrannical despots; it is seated in a deep-rooted feeling—the fear of being a powerful being.

A healthy use of fear has a purpose and can serve as a wake-up call or warning that you are walking too close to the edge of a cliff, and had best back off. When you approach a genuinely perilous situation, your body may experience a tremendous rush of energy as the amygdala, which is nestled in the center of the brain and operates as the body's fear-system's command center, sends out fight-or-flight signals along the neural links, with internal flashing red lights and wailing sirens. This inner warning system is always on security watch for danger; therefore, you may indeed experience feelings of fear in response to an internal signal from your cells when they sense a genuine threat to your survival. From a practical perspective, healthy fear issues a warning for staying out of harm's way.

Your biggest test with the body is overcoming fear. When the fear center is employed by habit, the mind cannot think straight and rational thought is paralyzed. Projecting feelings of fear onto your reality, in the absence of pending danger, distorts the body's sense of integrity and creates a state of internal havoc that broadcasts fear into the mass consciousness and the world at large. Your body's natural intelligence-gathering system works at great speed and in keen cooperation with your attitude and expectations. When you change your attitude, you will undoubtedly change your experience. Millions of cells seamlessly access and evaluate the myriad of choices you make in order to impel you toward encountering your desires. Each moment, your body is processing reams of sophisticated data involving the past, present, and future. You must learn to pay very close attention to the signals you send out by noticing and examining how you feel about what you create and encounter. Acknowledging your feelings can lead to deeper self-realization because your feelings are always the key to figuring out your beliefs. Remember, feelings take you back to beliefs, so find the feeling and really feel it. Once you have identified the belief behind the feeling, acknowledge the role of the belief, then release it and replace it with a more empowered outlook.

The major change in perceptual awareness that is sweeping the globe will establish new parameters concerning the nature of intelligence.

Throughout eons of time, various developmental phases of humankind's evolution have taken many surprising twists and turns. The major change in perceptual awareness that is sweeping the globe will establish new parameters concerning the nature of intelligence, raising long-overdue questions about the potentials of the human mind. Energy from space, and from your sun, can create mutations on a physical level, as well as trigger human consciousness into new areas of perception. Most of the Western world identifies intelligence based on one's ability to use symbols—letters and numbers—in the physical world. Today, throughout the entire globe, perhaps only one-third of the population can actually read and write; nonetheless, numerous cultures have developed over time demonstrating unique abilities to translate symbols into ideas without the written word. Ideas operate with a specific frequency modulation and can be interactive from one reality to another. Ideas are also transmitted on gamma rays from the sun for disbursement, and over the next few years the very nature of intelligence, which is often based on solely logical interpretations of reality, will be reconsidered. Perceptual flexibility expands your ability to see and experience reality in a new, refreshing light, so be alert to recognizing personal beliefs about your own intelligence. The willingness to accept new concepts and ideas brings great advantages toward more rapid growth of self-awareness.

The energies of the acceleration encourage an exuberant expansion of knowledge with more and more people making the connection between the power of the mind and its effect on the physical environment. Sudden realizations of how you think a situation into being will become more pronounced. Sometimes when the inner spirit is breaking free into a new vista of perception, feelings of frustration or discontent can be experienced. Restless energy can be a signal indicating a time of change is pending. How you interpret your experiences and the wisdom you accrue from your creations form one method of determining intelligence. In many regards it seems that the people of the written word have learned to use symbols to translate events into trivial insignificance, and they have distanced themselves from the very idea that thoughts have any connection to the solid world. As a result, humans have imprisoned themselves through their own thinking process. Please consider each and every experience as a valid choice toward gathering greater knowledge. You have tremendous freedom to see beyond the confines of your limited and fearful interpretations of reality, and freedom takes on new meaning when you learn to operate your body with ease in both the physical and non-physical worlds.

Consider for a few moments how the mind structures itself: your beliefs and feelings mold your perceptions and continuously broadcast a frequency of energy either repelling or attracting life's events. Sometimes an event is dismissed, as if you were shooing away a fly, yet it is still indelibly imprinted with invisible ink in your subconscious mind. Some events you never forget because you have a flashbulb-like memory of the experience. Whether you consciously remember an event or not, the situation and your projected beliefs concerning it are faithfully stored in your memory banks according to your perceptions. Stretching your mind to consider the symbolism and significance of any event can literally "switch" your point of view, if you clearly intend to know the intricate meanings of life. As your ideas about the nature of your mind continue to expand, the natural link between physical and interdimensional realities will become much more apparent. New ideas are actually electromagnetic frequencies, and they swell and increase in magnitude as solar radiations increase the field of energy around your globe. In order to adapt to and accommodate the new levels of energy ideas, a shift is occurring in your cells on a subatomic level through a subtle interaction of protein molecules that release stored codes of perception. A complex chemical process between proteins and amino acids is affecting the DNA on a very deep level and changing the way in which you perceive reality.

Your power ends where your fear begins.

As more psychic doors are flung wide open to augment your intelligence, you must live in peace with your physical body in order to feel good and benefit from this process. What closets must you clean to achieve that state? Do you practice self-hypnosis with some of your favorite limiting beliefs? "I have no control over the situation. I will always be poor. Money is hard to come by. Life is a struggle. Money is the root of all evil. There is nothing I can do. That's just the way it is. I've always done it this way. There is no way that I can get out of this. We'll never know. I don't know. I could never. I forget. I didn't see." How often do you put yourself in such a trance in order to stay right where you are? How often do you use sarcasm? The comfort of the old, familiar mental rut anchors you to the same old scenarios. We raise these questions to wake you up and to assist you in noticing and understanding how you structure your thinking. The link between mind and matter is an essential lesson to master. You must change your core beliefs in order to see change in the outside world. You can change these limiting commands by replacing them with encouraging, self-empowered thoughts. Limitations come from inside your mind, and making the decision to let go of restricting beliefs is like taking off a pair of tight shoes or slipping out of a corset: you are filled with a new sense of freedom and relief.

As the intensified waves of cosmic energy flooding your planet build momentum, you are called upon to use your physical form with wisdom, health, and ease. To accommodate and learn from these dynamic energies, you must slow down and recognize when you create too much stress. You may even be addicted to stress and needlessly fill the hours of the day with methodical busyness because you are ill at ease with empty moments. Unfortunately, silence has lost its value in modern times. The mind requires rest for clarity and integration, and when silence is maintained for regular interludes, the benefits help to sharpen your mind and balance your life. You must seek out and plan for peaceful moments, rather than offering every excuse in the world, and often with great indignation, as to why you are too busy. You have hypnotized yourself into believing that being productive or busy all of the time is a noble feat. Well, you may be a noble fool, and if you are wondering whether this strikes home or not, take a good look at your body, for there the truth will always be told. When you purposely seek out spiritual knowledge yet repeatedly miss the message because you do not know when to shift the gears of your perceptions, then your lack of flexibility creates untold stress. Flexibility is the key for changing your beliefs. You are, by design, a multifocused, multidimensional being, and by practicing mental agility and applying common sense, you can develop a more expansive understanding of reality, while not losing control of one vista as you move to another. Remember, the material world is only one part of reality. The invisible and spiritual realms, along with many other planes of existence, all seek to enter and participate in this time period of accelerated energy. Whatever you are learning, trust that it may be only one facet of a much more complex multidimensional lesson.

When you believe in your self-worth within the greater plan of existence, a larger purpose to life always comes into play, sometimes revealing scenarios that are seemingly beyond your current understanding. Existence is based on a subtle cooperation of energy that is multilayered and multidimensional in scope, and fully alive with a symbolism that reflects your beliefs and expectations of life. Your perceptions develop and mature according to your ability to grasp the interactive world of symbols and to interpret these symbols based on the stimuli and the sensations you experience. In other words, the meaning you assign to an event determines the outcome you experience. Of course, the more fear you employ, the more limiting your interpretations will be. Your power ends where your fear begins. You always operate within your own sphere of influence, affecting the atmosphere wherever you go, and you also contribute your ideas quite effectively to the mass consciousness of the planet. When you energize a safe and secure worldview, your feelings will inevitably lead you toward that experience. You must, however, develop a deep respect for your feelings by acknowledging them as a barometer of your thoughts. The more open you are to changing your thinking and vacating your box of beliefs, the more you will perceive and realize in this environment of earthly experience.

A powerful force of social and cultural unrest is rapidly brewing in response to a newfound passion for freedom.

The level of corruption stemming from decadence and greed among the people and the various difficulties and basic instability within the political, religious, scientific, military, medical, environmental, and economic sectors are signposts of a massive unraveling. A powerful force of social and cultural unrest is rapidly brewing in response to a newfound passion for freedom, yet the controlled media, in its business-as-usual blackout mode, continues to ignore all matters of dissatisfaction and dissension. In direct response to these media diversions, your intuition may be very active now, sending you very strong signals through the realm of dreams and feelings, and by way of unusual signs and symbols. Pay close attention to your state of mind as you open the door to communicate with non-ordinary reality by remaining centered and clear. The medical authorities in today's world often label this type of contact as schizophrenia, decreeing a dysfunctional state of mind for some who stretch beyond the boundaries of official versions of reality. Within the field of limiting beliefs that define the mind and how it operates, the inability to tell the difference between what is real and what is not is classified as psychosis, a severe form of mental illness. These labels serve as a mechanism of fear, promoting a core belief that the body is flawed and cannot be trusted. This is a very limiting belief and demonstrates an attempt by mind managers to disavow the multidimensional and psychic nature of human experience.

Your cells continuously read and vibrate with the energy of everything around you, and as you expand your perceptions, you will become far more sensitive to your surroundings. As the development of your psychic and intuitive faculties increases, your nervous system, which controls and coordinates all organs and structures of the body, must be strengthened. Your cells are in continual telepathic contact with all possibilities, and on a physical level, the nervous system is the mechanism through which this communication is most efficiently relayed. All of this activity occurs without your conscious mind being the slightest bit aware of the process. You must remember that you are in the midst of a major global awakening, a revolution of consciousness occurring on many levels of reality, ushering in the realization that you are truly a wondrous being capable of literally producing endless versions of reality. You constantly condition the energy of existence; you flavor and organize it, then project it outward without even realizing it. This is the process through which individual creation and mass agreement are made manifest.

When the quality of life for any species is unstable, existing without innate value or love, the natural order of spontaneous expression is threatened. The reality you are currently hosting appears to be crumbling, with scandals of shocking deeds growing daily like weeds in a summer rain. Pedophilia has become a well-recognized word these days as disturbing allegations race through the halls of Christianity and other major power centers, revealing a sinister pattern. And many more prominent people from outside the ranks of religion are joining the fall from grace. When those in positions of power turn their backs on integrity, ignoring their role of protecting the people, they misuse and abuse their power. And who gives them the power to abuse? How many more children will be touched by the hands of sexual abuse until a voice of outrage and concern is heard? As uncomfortable as all this may seem, it is all part of the process of changing worn-out beliefs within the mass consciousness. Mass beliefs in the power of outside authorities are firmly entrenched in your psyche; they are strong and old, and somewhat like a redwood forest they too can be felled very, very quickly, raising many questions about the truth of who you are and why you place your trust outside yourself.

A tremendous misuse of the people's monies and the planet's resources is fast unraveling, leading to an out-of-control collapse.

Pressure is building on the governmental forces of the world as millions and millions of people in foreign countries protest and demonstrate for the basic rights of life. Within the halls and ranks of world leadership, insider fighting, dark nasty deals, and levels of soul-splintering betrayal have reached an all-time high. And in the United States, as the Bill of Rights becomes a distant memory, some people choose to sedate themselves through the use of designer pharmaceuticals and electronic devices. What core beliefs condition and control people into an anaesthetized and immobilized state? Media-reported events occupy the time and imagination of millions, demonstrating in many ways a strong belief in the power of authority. Yet the major newspapers are filled with false information. Stories are not what they seem, often written in code, yet even high-ranking journalists readily admit that if they told the real truth they would not have jobs.

This raises the issue of people's beliefs about their jobs, and what they think they must do to earn a living. Researchers report that a person cannot reach any high level of governmental office these days without having already been compromised; this appears to be true for the world at large. A tremendous misuse of the people's monies and the planet's resources is fast unraveling, leading to rampant speculation of an out-of-control and very radical collapse. Government damage control is scrambling to create clever new cover stories in order to gloss over these shortfalls. However, on the other side of the great divide, a fabulous awakening of the mind is gaining ground. As your perceptions become more enhanced, many things will become much more apparent, and letting go of old beliefs can be experienced as a freeing endeavor. As your beliefs change, allow yourself to face the shocking discovery that nothing is exactly as it appears to be. This realization must be integrated on a physical level in order to truly penetrate the power of your beliefs and their hold on you. From a larger picture, there is always a greater plan in play. And just as a stage is set for a performance, your world is readying itself for multidimensional interactions with other forms of intelligence.

Being accountable to the truth must prevail in all forms of leadership, particularly as you all eventually learn to trust and lead yourselves. This is a pivotal time for human-heart consciousness to be recognized and applied as a natural and well-intended tool for change. While you sleep and dream, you are connected to the people of the world as well as to other dimensions of existence, and this is where you work out your potential responses and solutions to the shifting sands of change. Once you think you know the truth, breathe it through your heart to test its merit. When you focus your attention into your heart center, this connection allows you to compassionately walk into the shadows of life and to safely know the truth. Trusting yourself in the midst of a world seemingly gone mad is a wise use of intention. The marketing of a false worldview based on limitation and fear is a creative use of the imagination; however, you must learn to recognize wholesome ideas from pure hogwash. At this point in your development, you must be able to tell the difference between genuine information and the endless propaganda that attempts to shape the beliefs of public opinion. Discernment is to choose wisely, and with this in mind, you must learn to recognize and acknowledge that your feelings and sensations are your body's built-in radar. In accessing any situation, your beliefs will determine your evaluation. Set clear intentions for what you are available to experience, and develop compassion for others to choose whichever path they prefer. The natives are restless all over the globe, and this is a signature of changing times and changing beliefs.

You have the free will to do what you want with your restlessness, though it is best to remember that restlessness is an indication of energy stirring. To deal with your fears and limiting beliefs, see them as attributes that you have assigned to reality—something you have fixated upon, and grown into, and hypnotized yourself into believing. You can learn to withdraw your attention from old ideas by just letting them go; without your constant attention, ideas leave like balloons lost to the wind. Develop very clear intentions about what you want. Beliefs are like crops that you choose to plant in your garden, and you cultivate quite well as a gardener, yet you must open your inner senses to truly see the deep roots of your invisible core beliefs. There are mass beliefs that actually keep your eyes focused into certain aspects of the light spectrum, ultimately restricting what you can see, while simultaneously other realities are continuously operating around you. Living a well-organized, calm, centered life, without the interference of television or electronic diversions, and with plenty of time in nature, will keep your nervous system tuned up and functioning in a smooth and strong capacity.

When your nervous system is in balance, you will be able to see fearful and limiting beliefs for what they are; and when they arise, acknowledge their existence. Fairly assess the role they have played in your life, and then let them go. Use the present to replace a limiting self-concept with one that empowers your life. In order to change the outer world, you must change inside. Be willing to let go of your limiting interpretations of the past and stop seeing the past as the cause or blame for what you perceive as your failure in the present. In order to change, you must care enough to want change. Hold no grudge or resentment, for victimhood is a very powerful limiting belief that stifles your natural creative process. Cultivate a healthy outlook, and fortify your will by accepting responsibility for your life. Developing sustaining ideas and supporting beliefs is essential toward establishing your free will and creativity. It is possible to experience life and all its wondrous offerings in joy, safety, and harmony, and that is a very beneficent belief.

You must learn to seek the harmony and purpose that is behind the impeccable and majestic order of existence.

There are always a multitude of favorable probabilities from which to choose. Please be aware of this potential and do not busy yourself with worries. Worry is a supreme waste of energy in any situation. It creates a disturbing vibration in your field and drains you of energy. And how do you avoid worry? You must deal with your beliefs concerning what you choose to worry about. Release your need to be in charge or in control of everything. Replace your worry with a statement that affirms your choice of safety, comfort, and peace of mind. Learn more about yourself by paying attention to how you manage energy. Be aware of what no longer works by recognizing how your inner ruminations become the movie of life that you meet in the outside world.

As your perceptions naturally blossom, you must take care to observe and learn from what is being shown. Select your words and thoughts with great consideration, for clarity of purpose will assist you in understanding how you create your reality. Your relationship to nature is of primary importance in the process of transformation. Spend more time in nature; go for a walk or take a stroll, and allow your attention to drift, like milkweeds in the wind, into the surrounding environment. The trees and flowers sense what you are thinking, and in fulfilling their purpose they will instantly harmonize their energies with yours, orchestrating a special series of vibrations, scents, shapes, colors, and sounds—the most appropriate energies in the moment for you to maintain your harmony and balance. When you are in relationship to nature, together you are constantly exchanging inner and outer energies. Plants exhale oxygen, and you exhale carbon dioxide—you are supported by a perfect relationship of giving through living.

You must learn to seek out the harmony and purpose that is behind the impeccable and majestic order of existence. If you are in an uncomfortable situation, lacking harmony or purpose, then intend clarity, own up to your feelings, and follow them back to the reason, the source concept or belief you hold that creates these results. Feelings change, just like the weather. Ask yourself what the outer world is attempting to reveal. And consider as well, what you are showing yourself by creating the reality in which you are engaged. Lay personality conflicts to rest and seek the bigger picture; look for the pattern and the larger message. Discover the teaching. Trust there is a teaching and purpose. Trust that you can create whatever you want, in and outside of time. Even though knowing the self can at times be the most intense journey you can make, you must learn to cultivate a deep desire to know yourself as never before. Living on Earth in these intense times is both extraordinarily challenging and a most noble undertaking for everyone involved. It appears that people are doing their best to transform their lives. Understanding the process in which you are immersed opens you up to the support of existence, which, by the way, if you happen to notice, is completely, totally, and gracefully sustaining you. We trust that you will pay greater attention to the untold realities that can be constructed as alternative possibilities for an eminently meaningful life.

You are a pioneer, and pioneers generally venture where no one has been before, so you must make the decision to trust yourself and believe in a safe existence. Energize the field around you with clear intent. Stay conscious and slow down. And when you are whining and tired, take a rest; cease with your criticism and complaints. Guilt arises out of manipulative behavior. Anger with blame implies victimhood and often reflects a lack of responsibility for one's decisions, as well as a lack of understanding of the many layers of purpose and meaning that underlie each event, whether personal or global in scope. Anger is often triggered when you feel backed up against a wall and limit yourself with only one interpretation of what is occurring. Remember, sometimes opportunity is disguised as loss. No matter what you think you have to do, there is always an option available for a harmonious resolution. Stop piling so much on your plate and let go of what you need to leave behind. Walk away if you must. When you blame circumstances outside yourself, you miss the wave of awareness, for you are really attracting the situation. Whenever you make excuses, you are not in the game. The nature of existence is friendly and significant, and as a designer of reality, ask yourself why you design what you do. Seize the moment and pay close attention to how you use your thoughts and words to create your outer environment. Do you really mean what you say? Do you know what you are saying? This level of awareness is most essential to grasp, for opportunities to naturally expand into new territories of intelligence will offer a bountiful harvest for sane and meaningful living. To heal and change your world, you must be willing to know some hard truths. This is your fortune, and it will set you free to know yourself and your place in existence. You are free to know and to change, and we watch and patiently wait, cheering you on, all the while wondering what you will do to succeed. For now, see if you can reach out with your mind to the field of frequencies we play on. It matters more than you think.

Your inner world and the intricate workings of your mind are rich with answers and solutions.

Within the larger framework of reality, everything you create through your thoughts and emotions is part of an intimate dance toward your spiritual growth, and your interpretation and response to a situation determine the outcome you experience. Taking the time to unwind and relax in a peaceful setting and focusing on your breath can do wonders for expanding your perspective. The simple act of asking why can also unlock your fixation and liberate your thinking, opening you to new vistas of possibility, as if you were taking a hot-air balloon ride over a glorious countryside and seeing the world in a new light. You must learn the art of detachment: to silently observe and pay attention to what your mind is saying. Allow yourself a few moments of illumination and look for the humor in the lesson being offered. Your inner world and the intricate workings of your mind are rich with answers and solutions; you must take the time to look within and pay attention to what your senses say.

People often want to know what will happen in the years ahead and the answer is, It depends on what you believe. A belief in an empowered existence, where all people are valued, will serve your world well. You must first accept that it is your responsibility to initiate the necessary changes required to achieve the desired results. What feelings do you have about change? Do you consider change a hard and difficult process, a struggle that sets you up for failure and loneliness, or does the notion of change call to mind the glorious and effortless unfolding of the seasons? As an exercise for exploring your beliefs about change, find thirteen photographs of yourself from various ages, ranging from early childhood to sometime near the present. Choose photos depicting only yourself in the scene, shots that are interesting rather than exclusively glamorous or unflattering. Then on the next new moon, full moon, eclipse, or whenever you feel like playing this game, set your intentions to open the timelines into various versions of yourself, and proceed to play with these thirteen pictures for three weeks—or longer, if you like. Find a convenient location in your home, a place you pass by often but where your project will remain undisturbed, and proceed to lay out your photos. Use your imagination and arrange them in various formations using geometric shapes, the zodiac, spirals—whatever comes to mind. Look at the pictures as often as you like. Talk to them. What do they say to you? Pay attention to any beliefs about change that the pictures bring up. Throughout the three weeks, rearrange the layout by changing the order and relationship of one photo to another. Be spontaneous and playful and allow the photos to teach you about yourself. Each photo holds a version of you, who in that moment had no idea of what the next moment held, yet each picture implies that change occurred again and again.

Your beliefs can become as flexible as you choose, like supple trees bending with the weight of winter snow patiently awaiting the warm security of spring's soothing sun. The current state of global uncertainty reflects the inner energy projected from the mass psyche. On one hand, the most exciting, life-liberating opportunities are coming to build sustainable probabilities: astounding new healing techniques through communication with other realms, an almost instantaneous changeover of energy resources, and amazing discoveries for providing clean water and air are just a few of the many discoveries hovering on the horizon. Other probabilities hold the course open for those who are angry and afraid to be in charge of their lives—and this path is not much fun. As you expand your consciousness and find other pastures to graze in, other mountains and mesas to climb from which to view reality, the most difficult aspect of the expansion will be watching those who choose not to change. You are here to witness, and a witness is one of the most difficult positions to occupy. A witness does not close his or her eyes; a witness sees and then reports about what transpires. It is tremendously challenging and often very difficult to experience the full range of emotional possibility—from the heights of exquisite joy and ultimate sexual orgasm to the depths of fear, hatred, and hopeless despair. As your heart opens, you will soar with those who fly and find it challenging to watch and feel with others who choose the depths of disempowerment. Watching and feeling the courage of others, while they experience those momentous melodies of emotion, takes you to your greatness. And for some, it can lead into insanity. It is a fine line that your world walks in these days of human transformation.

When you choose the path of empowerment, there are times when you must deal with life on a very profound level.

The very nature of a pioneer is to walk alone into new territory, to go where no one else has traveled. As a pioneer, you must learn to be alone with your discoveries. During times of instability, all of your fears can come up. Your emotions can take you deeper and deeper into the realm of feeling, where courage and love are required to encounter the wounds you carry. When you choose the path of empowerment, there are times when you must deal with life on a very profound level, and moments of despair can arise when you wish you simply did not know the bigger picture. Even the idea that ignorance is bliss can often appear appealing. This is a natural response because of the depth of emotional connections you are experiencing. Yet emotional states do not go on forever; the best and the most difficult are ephemeral and eventually slip away. Emotions can play you, and emotional depth is a unique and captivating aspect of your human experience. When you choose the stance of a victim, someone or something else is always to blame for what happens to you. To really claim your mind and free your spirit, you must consider your personal attitude as well as the criteria you use to interpret your experience. Do you see life and all you encounter with the glass half-full or half-empty? Are you in charge of your mind, body, and spirit, or does someone else always have more authority? Can you detect the feelings that define and confine your experiences? A change of attitude stems from a change in how you see and interpret your role in life and in all of your experiences. New interpretations create new feelings, which in turn fertilize the field of energy for new experiences.

As strange as it seems, accepting more responsibility for being the creator of your experience frees you to explore the shadow side of life; without shadows, you would see very little of life. Art is a dance between shades of color and tones of sound and light. When you examine your beliefs about the darker side of existence with another lens, it can free you to reexamine your life's creations from a different perspective. Perspective is every-thing. The essence of human experience is to participate in the full range of emotional expression; to learn how to navigate these unpredictable realms and to survive with your conscious-ness in alignment are some of the profound spiritual tests of the times. A deep inner knowing based on innocent trust is required to proceed on the path of empowerment. To swim and to dive deep into the immense pools of emotions, you must make the link between thoughts, feelings, and beliefs; otherwise, emotional energy can be a journey into madness where nothing makes any sense. When you consciously intend to investigate your feelings by being responsible for creating all of your experiences for a significant purpose, the resulting release of pent-up emotional energy can feel fantastic.

Emotional accessibility is the true gift of a seeking soul, for through deep feelings you learn what to do as well as what not to do. In the ideal, you will develop your emotional intelligence by learning to trust your feelings. Emotional energies can be difficult to deal with, yet feelings are always about something, otherwise they would not surface. When you begin to focus your attention on wanting to know the absolute cause and the ultimate purpose of your feelings, a bigger picture will unfold, showing you how your emotions are connected to more than you think. With compassionate acceptance of your body's innate wisdom and a steady focus on the power of your breath, your emotions can be used to successfully lead you to the awareness of your inner programs, which are created from beliefs in childhood, or may even be a limiting loop of genetic imprinting that an ancestor passed on when they perceived their own reality in a stunning and emotionally filled manner. Innumerable layers of perceptions are deeply encoded in the DNA, and you are called upon to become more consciously aware of the multitude of programs that you have inherited from your genetic line.

Once again, one of your challenges on the path of empowerment is to heal the pain and separation stored within your bloodline, and to utilize the wounds as well as the gifts in the transformation of your consciousness. You are on the forefront of personal growth, and as the times become more and more interesting, so, too, will your abilities. Kindness and caring are especially cherished values, for they open your heart and pave the way for paths of peace. The choice is always yours along the path of empowerment. Your true triumph is courage over fear and truth over deceit. Opportunities always abound. Remember that your beliefs decree your availability, and your attitude reveals your beliefs. Offering thanks and gratitude demonstrates a strong sense of responsibility and a willingness to see unexpected change as an opportunity for spiritual growth. You must remember to be very clear about what you want. Proceed with confidence, common sense, and courage, utilizing your own unique style and grace. Trust yourself to create harmonious resolutions, and remain calm with all that unfolds, affirming that everything will work out just fine. After all, life is a grand lesson in living.

Chapter Five

HEALING ON THE LINES OF TIME

*L*earning how to manage energy is an ever-unfolding process in all venues of existence. In your corner of the cosmos, humanity is deeply immersed in a worldwide spiritual transformation designed to clear away a vast accumulation of fearful beliefs from the human gene pool that carry energetic patterns of pain and separation. The ultimate purpose of this transformation is to open the way for new, pronounced frequencies of higher awareness to be available throughout the multiuniverse. All of humanity is here, along with a host of other-dimensional beings, including us, to make a unique contribution to a healing on the lines of time.

From the human standpoint, you must be fully present in your body to participate most effectively in this transformation. Your DNA is being beneficially enhanced during these times through cosmic ray exposure that is clearing vast amounts of lower-vibrational energies with roots deep in the human psyche. As the higher vibration of the nanosecond continues to accelerate, the gathering momentum of the transformation is fortifying through the process of entrainment—where the strongest, most vital life-enhancing frequencies build great electromagnetic power, selectively attracting other frequencies of consciousness to them.

Your perceptions of reality expand when you purposely look for new levels of significance, as well as the hidden meanings of life. When you enhance your awareness, you contribute your own unique frequencies to the ever-growing collective realization that as a human being you must accept ultimate responsibility for exercising the power you naturally embody. The healing requires remembering that you are an energetic being whose thoughts, feelings, and emotions create the world that you encounter. We are all engaged in this multidimensional drama because of an agreement between many realities to heal the mind, body, and spirit of humanity and all those connected to you. It is also an agreement to provide inspiration for a new vision of life throughout the multiverse.

As the great transformation of consciousness is played out on the lines of time, your physical body becomes the arena for your healing at all levels.

Change is occurring everywhere. People are seeing through the conditioned illusion that steers them away from greater self-reliance and personal empowerment. The forces that appear to restrict you actually provide a stimulus to motivate you toward greater personal achievement through the development of life-enhancing attitudes and abilities. Recognizing poor energy management in the worlds of business and government helps focus your attention on what is really important in your life. The corporate model for success is faltering. People are realizing that business based solely upon investment returns—where the accumulation of wealth supercedes any and all concerns for the health and well-being of the Earth and her creatures—provides no loving care or sustaining life force for anyone involved.

Consumerism has become a major preoccupation for millions of people; it can only last as long as people accept the hyper-marketing of credit that draws them farther into the wasteland of living through the endless loop of financial enslavement. As inner codes of consciousness awaken people to their inner truths, the new common sense knows that empowering one's life with an awakened mind makes an immense contribution to the welfare of humanity. Self-responsibility for nurturing an awakened mind is the real investment that will change the world by offering newfound freedoms and creative expressions as the best returns for your focus of energy.

Great change is occurring within the substrata of your cells as well. On a subatomic level, your body is being deeply affected by the energies emanating from a vast array of celestial influences that are providing information in the form of light-encoded frequencies. These energy codes are meant to trigger new levels of awareness to surface with stupendous momentum. As a result of this activity, you release pent-up psychic and emotional energies from your DNA code, which in turn attract into your life the very issues that are in need of resolution. The issues will manifest for you in physical reality because, as the great transformation of consciousness is played out on the lines of time, your physical body becomes the arena for your healing at all levels.

The human body functions in a fashion that is still unrecognized by the conventional medical sciences. From the larger perspective, you have been convinced that you are less than what you are. Each version of the human form is a unique code-reading device; you occupy a physical body in third-dimensional reality because this is the method, one of the foundational protocols used to experience and to explore the nuances of physicality. The so-called material world is based on a specific vibration of energy, and the specific tuning of your perceptions holds the mass agreement together. As you are learning, or may well already know, you are much more than just your physical body. The pressure from the energy acceleration is affecting your consciousness physically, mentally, emotionally, psychically, spiritually, and cosmically—each area of self is like a finger on your hand, individually capable of movement, yet so much more effective when working in cooperation with the rest of the body.

Among these various levels of experience, your emotions have by far the greatest impact upon the state of your personal well-being. Your emotions are what make you unique; and there is a direct link between emotions, brain activity, and how your body functions. Within an awakened human, vibrant health will be recognized as a sign of personal power, and happiness and peace of mind are the most important ingredients on an emotional level for achieving and maintaining excellent physical and mental well-being. Emotional comfort signals your brain by way of frequency to send positive messages to the rest of your body, calling forth the release of precise chemical combinations from your internal pharmacopoeia to strengthen and safeguard your immune system. When you are in emotional balance, your physical vehicle is more finely tuned to make sense of the interwoven connections from other levels of experience.

Your biological computer is more sophisticated than any manufactured technology, because it is directly influenced by the symphonic complexity of your emotional responses to life. Remember, your body is dutifully loyal in giving you feedback on the effects of your thoughts and feelings. Essentially, health is a state of mind. The decision to see your life as filled with inherent meaning, and the realization that everything occurs for a very good reason, are a prosperous use of your personal power.

Health is wealth, and a well-fortified immune system is the key to good health, and the simple key to a strong immune system is happiness. The transformation of human consciousness calls for you to accept personal responsibility for your health and healing, for you are the one who is ultimately in charge of your body and your life.

The ability to both give and receive love, in all its many shades of splendor, holds the true key to healing.

As we mentioned, genuine feelings of love and appreciation for your body convey a positive message containing essential life-sustaining signals that result in excellent health. In contrast, engaging in feelings of doom and despair, loneliness, helplessness, denial, anger, resentment, jealousy, greed, and fear conveys a negative message that promotes discord within the physical functions of the body. Negative attitudes bring about negative effects. Anger and hatred are the most damaging emotions because they close off the flow of life-force energy to the body. The ability to both give and receive love, in all its many shades of splendor, holds the true key to healing because it is the most life-sustaining and affirming form of emotional expression.

The decision to accept ultimate responsibility for creating your life experience will empower you toward attaining a state of mental clarity and physical vitality. For a few moments, quiet your mind, and after breathing deeply and rhythmically for a while, consider this important question: Is the world a dangerous, fear-ridden place or is it a great adventure filled with bountiful opportunities to awaken spiritual power and transcend established limitations? Your basic outlook on life is rooted in your foundational beliefs, and these beliefs outline the conditions of your experience by electromagnetically imprinting the field of existence with your expectations. All of your beliefs have a powerful impact on your health, because how you feel about yourself and the world at large directly affects the functions and operating systems of your physical form. Remember, your feelings are always connected to your beliefs—how you feel is a result of what you believe. No matter what you believe, your body will essentially follow your innermost commands— whether you send thought patterns of doom and despair or those that embrace vibrant health. You are in charge of your physical form, and the state of your health is a direct reflection of your inner world of thoughts, feelings, and emotions. And it is in these arenas of perception that the great spiritual healing will have a profound impact.

It is important to understand where limiting concepts about the nature of the body are sourced. Most ideas are learned at a very young age. In the womb babies are in great psychic rapport with both genetic parents, regardless of the proximity of the father. Untold generations of family behavioral patterns are stored in the blood; the beliefs and attitudes of each parent are well known by the child before birth. Young children develop their minds through testing, modeling, and mimicking the input from their surrounding physical, mental, and spiritual environments. When learned behavior stems from teachings that maintain a sense of helplessness to control your body's health, these ideas plant early seeds of doom that take root and grow into beliefs of doubt and despair, eventually disconnecting you from your abilities to create vibrant health from within.

The power of suggestion is well understood among the medical sciences, yet its negative applications can be readily seen with the relentless dire warnings about protecting yourself from harmful exposure to the sun and nature, or the need for vaccinations that are actually toxic chemical cocktails. And grave and foreboding announcements always anoint the arrival of the yearly flu season. Illness is now big business. You have to start thinking in terms of not catching everything that is going around, like going against the rules and not lifting your mitt to catch that fly ball. Millions of people frighten themselves into various stages of sickness and death and contribute to the business of fear because they have been taught to deny the connection between the mind and body.

A numbing, unquestioned acceptance of a given medical prognosis can stem from a variety of foundational beliefs; yet it will all boil down to a strong underlying belief in personal powerlessness that can be expressed as follows: "Who am I to question a medical authority? What do I know? Modern medicine has all the answers. I have to have medical insurance—what if something happens to me? I have no control over my body." The largely ineffective, costly health-care system is sustained by such beliefs. From a larger perspective, this sense of powerlessness over how to create physical well-being has resulted in poor energy management of physical and mental resources, which has manifested in the current epidemic of serious maladies. Illness is an internal battle, and people get sick in part because they stop their mental and emotional growth, which closes off accessibility to cosmic and spiritual connections and energies. Desiring to have someone else in charge of fixing and taking care of the body has created a cumbersome bureaucracy to deal with cradle-to-grave health concerns that are, for the most part, founded on conditioned fears contrived in the mind.

In order to live well and thrive during these times of transformational change, it is to your advantage to embrace a belief in vital health, and to accept responsibility for the ability to create it. As many are discovering, cure is not the overall intent of modern medicine, because treatment—involving the use of expensive poisons and medications—is far more lucrative than discovering the cause and purpose of the physical and/or mental imbalances. This pernicious approach to health only serves to put greater stress on the body. Masking the symptoms of an illness with medications only glosses over the destructive thinking processes and deep inner feelings of helplessness and powerlessness, which are at the root of the problem. Unresolved emotional traumas are the real core issues of disease. Weak thinking and leading a false life weaken the body, and the massive epidemic of serious illness is a direct result of most people over the past century accepting restrictive beliefs about how the body operates. In all fairness to yourself, you must ask: "Who really benefits from managing my self-concepts?"

Every illness actually serves as a positive message from one part of the self to another concerning your emotional responses to life.

You may have learned to fear your body because you were taught that it can break down for no apparent reason; that it is unpredictable, unreliable, and untrustworthy. These ideas are examples of limiting beliefs that restrict the flow of life-force energy within the body. Every illness is unique to its host, and it actually serves as a positive message from one part of the self to another concerning your emotional responses to life. A viewpoint of deep respect for your body's innate intelligence is required in order to understand the body's inner messages; the true validity and meaning of any experience of ill health are lost when you deny the power of your thoughts and emotions to heal yourself. Progressive health-care professionals, who affirm your power to be alive and vital in the moment, will consider it an honor and a pleasure to assist you in discovering the message your body is conveying.

A conscious commitment to live a better life must be made by you in order to induce the necessary changes required to create the ideal conditions of health and well-being over the apparent reality. You are here to awaken to a new understanding of how you create your reality for the purpose of overriding the internal programming that keeps you in a familiar, uncomfortable rut. Recognize your own worry and intentionally release it from your energy field. Restrictive beliefs and attitudes reduce the quality of life. Feelings of fear of the unknown can be replaced with the affirmation "I am always safe!" With a confident attitude, write down what you want to create, the same way you would make up a grocery list. Life is a vast learning experience. You must be willing to take command of your willpower and release old habits and patterns of thinking by ceasing the depleting mental and physical activities that wear you down. When you catch yourself in the act of self-sabotage, chuckle to yourself over your new revelation and remind yourself that learning how to manage energy in the material world is one of the main reasons you are here.

Developing strong foundational beliefs for vital health is of utmost importance, yet first and foremost you must accept that it is your personal responsibility to initiate the necessary changes required to achieve the desired results. The belief that an official authority can label and cure your body's so-called malfunctions with a magic pill will only set you up for a major disappointment. A super-pill is not the answer for a long, healthy life—emotional intelligence and nutritional awareness will grant you a self-reliance that will give far greater results. You must elevate your thinking concerning how the body operates;

all possible solutions exist as a frequency jump away from your current thinking. If you are really looking for the magic pill to heal your body and your life, it is in your mind. Illness can be understood as a physical manifestation of blocked emotional energy focused by your thinking—in other words, when emotions and feelings go unexpressed, the blocked energy leads to inappropriate activity that will eventually manifest as poor health.

Great significance underlies every illness, large or small, because your body is a biofeedback system for your attitudes. Managing energy involves managing your relationship with your emotional self. Examining your emotions is the bottom line for understanding the purpose of a particular health-related situation. Poor health does not just land in your lap. You are ultimately responsible for setting the stage of your body's inner terrain based on the choices you make, and you actually restrict your body's natural healing processes when you readily accept only conventional medical labels and categories for your condition. You deny the purpose and power of your body's intelligence when you believe that you "just caught something out of the blue," rather than realizing and accepting that your body is merely responding to your inner feelings and commands.

You are the ultimate authority when it comes to really knowing your body because you are the one managing the show. Either by clear intent or by way of beliefs, you will eventually manifest whatever it is that you command. Many of your commands are selected quite consciously regardless of their benefits. Other commands are hidden away, stored in the subconscious and unconscious minds, the onion field and potato patch of old family beliefs readily accepted and dutifully upheld without question. Passing on family limitations through the adoption of negative attitudes results in similar family illnesses over the generations. "My mother had a particular ailment, therefore I probably will as well." This is an example of taking on the challenges and limitations of others as your own. Your DNA carries many potential patterns, and you must choose your mental inheritance wisely. Discernment comes from observation, and you must learn to transcend a legacy of family confusion and create a more expansive experience by understanding the purpose of the limiting beliefs. Once you can see into the heart of the matter, you can release the patterns of pain and separation from your energetic field.

Your body is a magnificent self-healing, self-repairing system and an organic wonder that you have yet to truly appreciate.

You must take care of your body; it is a storehouse of power, yet so often your beliefs stop the power from flowing. Your beliefs are literal programs that affect cellular function. Your body is a magnificent self-healing, self-repairing system and an organic wonder that you have yet to truly appreciate. Clearly, your cells and organs, your blood and bones operate with a spontaneous intelligence based on a comfortable and familiar cooperation. Collectively and individually your cells know how to keep your body functioning, and if there is a problem, your body lets you know. There is always a point and purpose to every illness as well as to the pain that may accompany it. Remember, your body is loyally mirroring your beliefs to you. Feelings of self-pity, doubt, and worry send messages to your cells filled with announcements of helplessness and powerlessness, and in due order, your cells will align with the signals and follow these commands. On the other hand, when you choose to trust yourself, the conscious choice of this decision actually selects the operational codes of consciousness at a sub-atomic level, codes that maintain the probable patterns for branching off new versions of yourself. The choice to inherently trust yourself activates a thriving version of life based on a belief in self-empowerment. You are in charge of your life; feelings of tolerance, love, respect, sharing, caring, kindness, honesty, gratitude, and forgiveness not only build sound moral character, they bring peace of mind. When you affirm your desire for a safe and healthy existence, your senses open to subtle new attunements that stem from a reorganization of cellular codes of consciousness. These codes activate programs for new and extraordinary perceptions—literally creating a new avenue of life for you to travel.

The courage to claim your self-trust offers a new form of personal freedom. The choice to create a safe, honest, respectful, and pleasant experience in all realities is entirely up to you. When life-enhancing beliefs are embraced, a distinct vitality exudes from your physical form, and you are wired, so to speak, to the max. An exuberant state of mind makes you much more receptive to the vibrant effects of the cosmic radiated energy. When this energy enters into your chakras, your senses are open to new realizations; you can gain profound spiritual understanding of how events that have occurred in this lifetime are interwoven with events in other lines of time. Reality is fluid; time and space are flexible to change, conforming to the perceptions of the beholder. Your perceptual shifts in the here and now actually ripple throughout the lines of time, broadcasting your selection of new codes of consciousness. And this is how a healing along the lines of time occurs.

Events and experiences can always be reinterpreted because they are comprised of layers and layers of significant agreements;

when seen from other perspectives, the hills and vales of life take on a whole new purpose and meaning. The healing of the human gene pool is about releasing trapped pain and fear by transforming old thought patterns that contain restrictive attitudes, and bringing a state of higher awareness into the body. Asking "why" you create something changes your brain wave frequencies to open communication with the cosmic mind. Seeking greater meaning reestablishes the equilibrium of the body's natural power to cure itself; and from the bigger picture, on the playing field of existence, all healing is reinterpreting what you believe has happened to you.

Opportunities abound when you choose to heal your relationship with your physical form. The more you pay attention to and acknowledge your body's messages, especially the "gut feelings" that come from the brain in your belly, the more you will learn. Intuitive intelligence is a natural expression of your connection to the non-local cosmic mind, which transcends space and time. Trust yourself and follow your finest instincts. Your body does not work against you; however, if you work against your body by belittling, criticizing, and devaluing yourself, your body will obey your strongest commands. When strong emotions accompany specific beliefs, the relayed commands always convey a sense of urgency, which quickens the manifestation into being. The belief that "there is not enough time" will lead to a stress-packed life, and heart failure can occur if the command about time is the predominant or strongest message sent to the body. Holding on to the feeling of a "broken heart" can be equally damaging. The heart is the body's timekeeper; every beat marks a rhythm that is entrained with the cosmos, in tune with the Womb of the Mother, the Galactic Center.

All healing is reinterpreting what you believe has happened to you.

The widespread breakdown of the physical body, which has become a worldwide health crisis, makes a profound statement about the lack of pleasure and quality of life that is experienced by the dwellers of the so-called civilized world. The surfacing of deep emotional and physical pain among the people of Earth is a collective expression of a constriction of consciousness, which is based on foundational beliefs about what is and what is not possible. Humanity has developed a collective unconscious fear of having to take care of itself, and this belief creates a direct blockage of power in the body. Physically, the blockage, or obstruction, of energy can manifest in a wide variety of patterns that create chaos within the body's internal systems. The belief in a supreme being who will save you, or eventually judge and punish you for your transgressions, only serves to further discount and deny the magnitude of your power to heal your life from within.

Beliefs that focus on pain are plentiful in your world, and they appear to be justifiable because of experiences that appear to be real; however, the intense focus on the expectation of pain and suffering is what actually brings them about. Beliefs in pain have been woven into your biology; they hold court in your subconscious mind, often making you wary of life. Unresolved issues such as bitterness, anger, or wounds and death traumas are carried over from other lifetimes, often appearing as mysterious pains and chronic aches in the body. The patterns in your genes hold memories of your various reincarnations as well as the story of your genetic bloodline. Expectations of pain create patterns of avoidance in the body; as a result, certain events are automatically and unconsciously censored, sorted, and filtered through an invisible self-protecting process that strives, sometimes at all possible costs, to avoid painful encounters. Pain becomes the enemy, and taken to the extreme, any event becomes suspect. Eventually with this type of avoidance, the body begins to shut down. The repeated mentally and emotionally fueled command to avoid pain at all costs ends up overriding the body's natural intelligence, creating a stubborn obstruction within the field of cellular communication. This blockage may sooner or later be experienced as a diseased or displeasured body part, which is literally indicating where the painful beliefs and emotional issues are being played out.

The cells of your body continuously replace themselves, and in general you do not even think about this process, yet the vital new cells dutifully focus their attention on fulfilling your beliefs and commands. Even though the cells are new, they will keep replicating the same old you, if you keep giving them the same old commands. Your cells, molecules, atoms, and subatomic particles are all intelligent; they communicate with one another because their collective job is to respond to your input. You choose the codes of consciousness that best express your life aims based on the degree of awareness that you have developed. As chief belief-maker, please consider our inquiry: Do you send commands to wage war with your own biology based on concealed conflicts?

Your body is a repository of everything that you and your ancestral bloodline family have experienced—the joys, pains, and traumas from this lifetime and beyond. Everything is stored in your genes, and you must learn the art of stillness and silence to venture deep within and access this knowledge. You carry varying degrees of unresolved pain about what you believe was done to you—traumas that were never processed and integrated because they were never understood. Acts of violence and sexually invasive experiences mar the spirit, and like a groove in a record that replays the same old line, you repeat experiences again and again until you develop the greater vision to choose another outcome. Using words such as *always, never,* and *forever* to describe yourself or your behavior can be linguistic carryovers from other lives. Traumatic events create "unfinished business" that must be understood from a larger context to be released from the body. Deliberations and agreements to heal are constantly being renegotiated. Healing is dealing, and dealing is feeling, and feeling is healing. From a spiritual vista, you make agreements, such as: "I will take this issue on with you so that we can heal this unresolved issue with harmonious resolution." You have the free will to do what you want; our advice is to create no harm because no matter what you do, it will come back to you. When you bring harm to yourself and/or others, you lock yourself into a cycle of cause and effect: you play out similar scenarios for the purpose of exercising your free will or changing the outcome by changing your choices. No one is going to reserve a seat for you in hell if you are a sinner. The only way to really learn about your free will is to have what you create return to you. Existence is kind, interactive, compassionate, and just for this very reason.

Healing is dealing, and dealing is feeling, and feeling is healing.

For a moment, examine any thoughts and attitudes that deny your responsibility for being the creator of your life. Where, when, and how are you a victim? In what areas of life do you feel justified blaming others for your condition? Who has done what to you? Who has caused you harm? Who has violated you—in this lifetime and others? Beliefs that life is unkind, unfair, hard, and cruel; or that there are no solutions, or there is nothing you can do, or there is never enough, or it's someone else's fault, are most often accompanied by an underlying, seething resentment that ends up causing illness. These are only a few examples of limiting beliefs and attitudes that close off the flow of cosmic life-force energy that connects you to the mysteries of the multiverse. From a more self-empowered point of view, ask yourself: "What unresolved issues am I dealing with? Why are these people in my life? What is my contribution to this process? What is the overall spiritual lesson and purpose of these experiences? How can I change my actions and create harmonious resolution for these disempowering states of blame?"

You must act in favor of your own well-being by claiming your power and saying yes to new ways of experiencing your life. Otherwise, when you do not respond to the messages that signal you to change your life, the lessons can land in your body and create difficulties. You may feel shut down and in pain, and, out of necessity, forced to take the time to deal with a situation you have been dreading and avoiding. Balance your day by allotting time to quiet your mind. This is the only way you will successfully integrate the accelerated energies and keep your nervous system in balance. You must do the emotional clearing; feelings are meant to be felt. The accelerated energy will take you into deep places of memory that may be painful to recall; trauma is stored in your cells, and you must pass through the pain to remember the emotionally charged events blocking your health. Wounds from sexual violations that occurred at a very young age may be very difficult to remember, yet the pain can be released when you integrate the experience and clear your memories. Your life is significant and purposeful, and you have created all you have encountered to discover your personal power, and to make choices that liberate your spirit from endless loops of despair.

The nanosecond of accelerated energy is a massive multidimensional venture in healing to transmute the vast accumulation of fear that is stored in the human gene pool. When you transmute the patterns of fear stored in your genes, you create a frequency of personal empowerment that ripples through the present, into the past, and to the future, affecting other versions of yourself and all those connected to you. The great power for healing comes down to a choice between fear and love; by choosing love, you are fortified with the courage to meet your fears and to resolve them. People everywhere are learning to recognize the dramas of life as opportunities to initiate change, to create a quality life by transcending past limitations and choosing to activate their best possibilities. You will achieve your greatest victories when you suspend judgment and abandon victimhood by seeking the greater meaning of life. Forgiveness is the ultimate act of letting go, freeing yourself from the endless cycle of guilt and blame.

The underlying message behind any symptom can be clearly understood when associated with the function of the afflicted area.

Healing involves unblocking old pain. When your body is in discomfort or pain, note the specific area of distress, for the location will be a key to where your emotional issues have established obstructions. The underlying message behind any symptom of poor health can be clearly understood when associated with the practical and purposeful function of the afflicted area. What feelings are registered there? Communicate with your pain, get in touch with it, and describe it. In order to heal and be well, look to the part of the body in question and ask: "What is the message?" What actual function does that area of the body perform? For there you have a great clue as to the nature of your dissatisfaction. You can breathe into the area of your body that is sending signals—this focus will open up the area so you can have greater perceptual awareness as to what is happening.

If your genitals are calling for your attention, the second chakra is the place in your body where the energy is blocked. Examine your feelings about issues of male and female power, or the lack of it, in your life. Do you feel powerless to create what you want? After all, the sexual organs are used to create pleasure as well as to create life. Problems in the legs and feet involve issues of perseverance through forward movement, and difficulties in the arms and hands signify a lack of willingness to passionately embrace life and to actively create your desires. The neck and throat involve issues of flexibility and self-expression. The brain is the focal point for beliefs about intelligence, the eyes about sight, and the ears about hearing; the stomach is for assimilation, the intestines for accepting nourishment from life, and the bowels for releasing waste materials. Colds and flus are associated with indecision, weight imbalance with unfulfilled desires, while cancer is triggered by hate, often self-hatred, and anger and rage from believing you are less than who you are.

The liver is a detoxifying organ and if yours is not functioning properly, what contribution of toxic emotion is seething beneath the surface? Apply the meaning of the function to your life—if you understand the working function of the afflicted area, then you can understand the issues you are resisting, blocking, and stopping from finding healthy expression in your life. Fear of letting go and releasing the past is an underlying cause of illness. Your emotional responses to what you believe has happened to you are at the core of your beliefs. Scattered thoughts result from choosing fearful interpretations, which is a misuse and misunderstanding of energy, and is at the root of all illness. To achieve a higher level of understanding, a new mindset must be consciously developed to override the messages of despair that signal the body to malfunction. You must become focused to concentrate on replacing unproductive attitudes and changing your interpretations of your sensory impressions.

When the body exhibits a so-called symptom, there is always an underlying emotional component, and you must seek to eliminate the cause, not just eradicate the symptom. Connecting the dots between how you feel—about yourself, family, friends, and the world at large—and your body's physical functions provides an important key for understanding how you use your energy. Whether you are attracting colds and flus, or are challenged with more severe systemic blockages such as cancer and diabetes, or heart or organ failure, your emotions or how you feel are always involved. The message, or core purpose, of your body's condition is based on a friendly, cooperative relationship between your mind, your feelings, and your cells. Illness is a built-in service, a feeling-based feedback system activated by harmful input stemming from a personal misuse of energy. Certainly you have wondered why some people get sick and others remain healthy, many unaffected by exposure to the same alleged contagion.

In order to understand your body's input, it is important to remember that the seven body chakras transduce energy into your physical form. Look for the chakra closest to the area of your body giving you feedback, for that is the energy center that is directly affecting whatever malfunction you are experiencing. Look for the lesson in the issue, seek the positive purpose, and be honest with yourself. Offer thanks to your body for the input, for working with you and giving you feedback in response to the signals you are sending. Make the intention to become aware of any strong feelings you have in relationship to the specific area of your body calling for attention. What unexpressed emotions are stored there? A major part of self-healing involves visualization, practicing mind influencing matter, and seeing the desired outcome. Thoughts must be focused and directed to produce creative endeavors and bring forth results.

Developing emotional intelligence is one of the keys for learning how to manage energy in 3-D reality.

Developing emotional intelligence is one of the keys for learning how to manage energy in 3-D reality. You must be willing to open your heart with the intention of healing whatever it is that has hurt you. If you really want to know and understand what is activated in the deep recesses of your subconscious and unconscious minds, you can access this information by creating a special healing journal and using it to safely record your inner feelings. Writing things out can be very revealing, which in turn can be very healing. Before you start journaling, affirm your intentions, focus your attention, and then relax your tongue and jaw, and breathe rhythmically for a few minutes. Picture golden spirals of energy circulating throughout your body as you breathe. Then, on the first page, dedicate a letter of introduction from you to your cosmic mind. Clearly set forth your intentions for a healing energy to come through your writings; ask for assistance from your higher mind, and give thanks for all you will discover.

Intentions are processed in the cells at a subatomic level,

where probable realities are selected and maintained. Writing occasionally with your non-dominant hand can be a very effective method for tapping in to information below the beta-wave level of the conscious mind. Draw pictures if you like, or clip and paste items of importance into your journal. Be creative and enjoy this exercise. Trust yourself to access information from deep within your psyche, refrain from judgment, and do not be ashamed of what may come up. This is your private healing journal; your discoveries will be filled with flashes of memory that are important benchmarks on your path of healing. Stay with your feelings as you weave your way through your revelations. Remind yourself that you are moving through internal walls to create vibrant health by understanding and accepting yourself as the creator of your experience.

Illness and physical distress are also connected to stifled expression. Disease begins on an emotional level through unexpressed feelings that build in power, creating internal storms, volcanoes, quakes, and floods that will eventually disrupt your life. Remember, your feelings stem from your beliefs; examine your beliefs to identify the source material used for speaking your life into being. Look for feedback from your beliefs in day-to-day life. Reflect on how you feel about your body as well as your family, friends, relationships, work, food, money, sex, and religion. To discover how you block out life-force energy, you must be willing to acknowledge how you feel about any situation. Are you resisting or repressing, or not expressing and therefore suppressing, stuffing, and hiding deep feelings of victimization, resentment, hatred, envy, jealousy, shame, anger, guilt, or worry? If you can name your so-called poison, give thanks. We are being a bit facetious here; however, by naming your poison, you can catch yourself in the act of self-sabotage and change the program.

Remember, consciousness is awareness, and awareness is the ability to notice. You deny your consciousness when you ignore sensory input or when you do not extend and value your senses. Truly everything that you seek, you already have at your disposal; however, you must initiate your own spiritual archeological dig by honestly identifying and naming your feelings. "I am angry, I am frightened, I am very jealous" express feelings common to everyone at some point in life. Once you identify the feeling, you can trace the emotion to the belief that generated it. "I am angry because my parents locked me in a closet when I was little. I am angry because they told me what to do. I am angry because I was violated. I am angry because I did not receive love." The withdrawal or absence of love is at the root of all pain. When the feedback cycle of give and take, cause and effect is played out, you may well discover that you have to learn how to give love in order to receive it.

Wellness involves expressing your feelings in a mature and responsible manner. Your emotions are the most difficult aspect of mastering your biological being for playing the game of life within this system of consciousness. Emotions are like musical renditions being played on a two-mile-long piano—you must learn how to play all of the keys, not merely bang away on a few, or timidly touch the keys, or not venture to play any of them at all. You must affirm that you love yourself; that you have a right to live a pleasant, safe, healthy, and productive life; and that your present circumstances are the result of your own volition. As we keep emphasizing, love of self and self-acceptance are very essential attitudes for creating a positive, rewarding experience with respect to the human body. And, the more you are able to love yourself, the more you will have to question your choices. Why, if you love yourself, would you subject yourself to unpleasant, unfulfilling situations? Awareness is the ability to observe and notice what is occurring and then to make practical use of your assessments, all of which lead to an expansion of consciousness, self-reliance, and personal empowerment.

Your body is designed as a self-healing system.

Your body is designed as a self-healing system; it has intelligence, and with proper rest and nourishment it can produce whatever is required to bring about a state of health, once changes in both attitude and activity are engaged. A lack of love and appreciation for your body will be expressed through poor eating habits as well as a general disregard for the very activities that nurture and support optimum health. Once again, your body does not naturally work against you; it is designed to respond to your thoughts and beliefs. Your body thrives on the energy of love that you feel for yourself. You must affirm and act as if you are worthy of your own love, worthy of life, and that life is worth living. This belief, like any other, takes a commitment, and you must want it: you must want what you desire to create more than anything else.

There must be risk involved for growth because choice is essential to the development of free will. Learn to think without pain and set more expansive goals such as: "I am healthy. I am open to change. I am healing myself; I am healing the patterns of misplaced intent in my bloodline. I am transforming my energy. I am releasing all of my patterns of confusion and despair. I am feeling tremendous gratitude—for all that I know, for the joy of remembering, and the courage to heal. When I heal myself, I heal all my relations, on the lines of time." Guided imagery is also a very effective tool that can be used for reexperiencing emotional conflicts and substituting desired new outcomes. Your body is your connection to the multiverse, diligently assisting you when you direct a course of action. Answers appear when you begin to search for them, both from inside and from the outside world. Synchronicities occur to draw your attention to something. When, against all odds, a series of personally meaningful events unfold in a timely, yet unusual, manner to shed light and profound insight on a situation, you are getting a glance into the splendor of the multilayered world of significance. In the field of existence, time has no bounds; events are connected and enriched with the purposeful weavings of all forms of consciousness learning how to play the field.

To build the reality you want, create a clear, detailed mental image of your desired outcome; if you are ill, you must set your mind to full recovery with a healing phase that is short, easy, and sweet. Embrace the idea that everything works out just fine in a remarkable series of beneficial events. Imagination, visualization, activation of your willpower, expectation, and positive reinforcement are the keys to learning new behavioral patterns. You must expect results, otherwise there will be none; creative use of the imagination followed by action brings about results. When your body is not functioning properly, you have the power to change your attitude and heal yourself—this can be as simple as recognizing self-pity and changing it to self-acceptance; changing fear to desire, and anger and pain to forgiveness.

It is true that the denial of concepts as possibilities delays their emergence, whereas a safe expansion of knowledge can open to advantageous stages of living. In this lifetime you are here to actualize all of your abilities, and by choosing to produce the vibration of love, you become entrained with the immense cooperation and intelligence that permeate existence. Our intent is to inspire and remind you to allow the process of healing its due course. You must be willing to do the work of getting in touch with how you feel about the experiences you have stored inside. The work you do on yourself is tied to more than the healing of your bloodline—your family and friends, and the world at large, will all be affected by your taking a stance of responsibility for healing your life.

As you are learning to get well and stay that way, a belief in vital health is essential. Affirming what you want and then knowing that it will come about are the keys to manifestation. Knowing is based on trust—a state of mind where intuition reigns supreme. You must accept that it is entirely possible to create vital, life-enhancing health; accepting this belief puts you on the path to creating vibrant health. However, this may feel quite contrary to your present experience, and that is fine. But in order to change your experience, you must change your beliefs and stop the activities that are restricting you. As a demonstration of your intent to create health, based on your own realizations, write down the limiting beliefs you are discovering about yourself on small pieces of paper, one limiting belief per page. Examine each belief very carefully to see how you have designed your life around restrictive ideas; the words are symbols for how you have focused your energy. Once you have completed your initial housecleaning of beliefs, take the papers outdoors and find a secure spot where you can bury each belief beneath a rock and let it go.

When you complete this exercise, affirm the reality you want and consider the following: "I am a vital, healthy being now. I accept the responsibility and commitment that changing my life will involve. I am ready to embrace a new way of looking at life. I am excited about learning the many methods and techniques that will empower me to operate my physical body duty are to love and take care of my physical form.

Contemplate those words for a few moments, dear friend, for they are very empowering commands. Again, they may not reflect your current experience; however, words set forth the direction for energy to follow.

Establishing healthy boundaries and respecting the boundaries of others are important aspects of learning how to manage energy. You must be able to be yourself and still mix and mingle with others and not be adversely affected by their misuse of energy. Intend to respect the lessons of others, rather than becoming dragged into a negative probability. Using both your imagination and your breath, you can easily enliven and strengthen your energy field by picturing a stream of cosmic light entering your body through your crown chakra, at the top of your head. Relax and breathe the life-enhancing light deep into your body, journeying down to the very spacious subatomic level. With each in breath send the message you wish to convey: inner strength, safety, clarity of mind, protection, fortitude, healing, patience, love, understanding, compassion, and right action. Now imagine a great swirl of light in the center of your body, and then send it out through your third chakra, like a fountain of light exuding from your solar plexus. Use your imagination to play with creating this thought-form; it will establish a protective hoop of energy, a buffer zone equipped with heightened radar, because the boundaries of your sensibilities will be moved a few feet beyond your body.

Healthy boundaries also require the recognition of destructive behavioral patterns in yourself and others as being inappropriate for your personal well-being. Now and again you may find yourself engaged in a family quarrel; no one knows you better, or can push your buttons harder than your partner and the members of your family, but there is no one like your partner or bloodline to accept your dark side and be willing to forgive you. Emotional eruptions do happen periodically in order to clear the air; this is part of the process of learning how to manage energy. The trick is never to carry a grudge or resentment, for these feelings will drag you down, deteriorating the quality of your relationships as well as the vitality of your immune system. You have the power to change only yourself; you must graciously allow others the course they choose. Be patient. When you change your response, you remove your Velcro, so to speak: there is no stickiness from your side for anything to catch on to. As you grow in consciousness, eventually you will be an inspiration to those who appear to be currently resistant to change.

If you want to be really healthy, wealthy, and wise, you must be fully present in your body to use it most effectively.

Loving yourself is one of the best investments you can make, and it is also your best course of action; this means taking care of yourself in thought, word, and deed. The deeds of loving yourself include taking good care of your body, both inside and out. If you want to be really healthy, wealthy, and wise, you must be fully present in your body to use it most effectively. Good health and proper body management are true signs of inner wealth and right thinking, and creating better health often equates to changing old habits. Most importantly, you must be willing to learn about how the body's inner terrain functions. The body is highly adaptable; the genome is always actively engaged in responding to your requirements by changing and learning to perform new tasks in order to maintain the body's operability.

Life-force energy sustains you, and the electromagnetic codes, the patterns for healing your body, are in your genes. Even though your thoughts and feelings have immense power to set energy into motion, on a physical level the cells of your body require tender loving care to maintain support of the physical system. Your cells, blood supply, and organs are all affected by the food you eat, the water you drink, the quality of the air you breathe, and the amount of your sunlight exposure. The more wholesome your diet and the more oxygen you bring into your system, the more vital your cells. Even though the body is highly adaptable and capable of successfully transmuting many toxic energies, your biological system will still thrive best in specific supportive conditions. Nature provides you with the very best life-sustaining energies; take more time to nurture your senses in nature—along with the incomparable gift of beauty, nature provides the abundance of plants and trees that produce food and oxygen filled with cosmic energy.

In physicality, your breath is the most direct method for exchanging energy with the cosmos, and it is also the link between cosmic forces and the intricate operations of your body's neurological system. The quality of your breath is connected to the amount of breathing you do in natural sunlight. During the hours of daylight, you actually breathe in important information that is infused in the atmosphere. Good breathing habits are essential for clarity of mind, and when regularly applied, the results will always enhance your personal well-being. Remember to focus your attention on breathing consciously; this means paying attention to the process by directing your breath into the bottom of your lungs and moving the diaphragm out on the inhale, and in on the exhale. Find your rhythm and breathe. Over time the habit of shallow breathing, which is breathing into the upper lungs and chest only, slowly deprives the body of life-sustaining oxygen. Deep oxygenation restores your body's vitality, and with specific practices it can also be used to clear away the emotional debris stored in the body.

On Earth, the tradition of honoring the practice of breath-awareness is timeless. Making a conscious connection with your breath focuses your attention into the present moment, where you can enjoy the experience of having a body. Bringing oxygen into every level of the body is one of the greatest pathways to vital health. However, activities to enhance your health must also be accompanied by beliefs in your own self-value; the purest oxygen and the best organic food alone will not heal a diseased body under siege by beliefs of unworthiness.

It is common knowledge that your body thrives on water, yet people often needlessly suffer mysterious pain and physical distress—constipation, sexual dysfunction, and migraine headaches—related to severe dehydration of the body. To function at optimum capacity, you must hydrate your system by drinking *at least* two quarts of good, clean, non-fluorinated water every day to refuel your cells and flush out any toxic materials. Water is also a conductor of electricity, and a well-hydrated body will more easily accommodate the increase of cosmic electromagnetic frequencies that must be integrated. You will sleep better and have much more energy when you drink plenty of water. No matter what beliefs you profess, a steady diet of fast foods, greasy fried foods, processed foods with chemical additives, sugar substitutes, and soda pop provides none of the nourishment required for optimum performance of your cells. Do not delude yourself into thinking that you can just "think good thoughts" and your body will be healthy, while you continue to eat nutritionally impoverished food. You must be practical with respect to the laws of physical reality. Can you think yourself clean without taking a shower? Your body must utilize and process the quality and quantity of what you eat, and eventually if you pour enough sludge into your system, it will clog up and stop working.

You can learn to eat for health and let your food be your medicine.

It is essential that you eat wisely to enhance the strength of your immune system. The vital nutrients present in live foods feed your cells—grains, nuts, and raw fruits and vegetables balance the pH levels in your body toward alkaline. Juicing raw fruits or vegetables will also alkalize the body, as well as provide energy very quickly. Alcohol, meat, coffee, chocolate, wine—all the delectable goodies—make the body more acidic, and when the body is too acidic, disease is more likely to occur. States of emotional distress such as anxiety, worry, doubt, chronic uncertainty, anger, resentment, jealousy, and vengefulness also affect the body's chemical balance toward an acid pH. Maintaining alkalinity in the body's digestive and intestinal systems is a most practical approach for optimum health; an alkaline pH helps balance body weight, and it also balances the inner terrain by creating a natural immunization against sickness. Dietary enzyme supplements are pH balancing and aid in digestion. Foods such as coconut, honey, dried dates and prunes, as well as raw fruits and vegetables, not only establish an alkaline state in the body, they are antioxidants, which provide plant-based nutrients that balance the internal chemistry and eliminate constipation. The ideal balance is 80 percent alkaline foods to 20 percent acidic foods.

Eat wisely with respect for all that Earth provides. Add more raw live foods to your daily diet, and your body will respond quite positively to the life-force energies. Plants thrive on sunlight, which conveys the latest news from the sun to every part of the plant. Vary your diet, eat with the seasons, make certain you feel good about the food you eat, and drink plenty of good, pure water. You can energize your food by using the palms of your hands, which are naturally very highly charged with energy. Gently press them together and then open your hands, palms downward, over your food. Aloud or silently, with your eyes open or closed, offer sincere thanks for the foods you eat; state your intention for honoring your food and all of those involved in the process of bringing it to your table. Ask that what you eat harmonizes with your body for health, vitality, and clarity of mind. You can learn to eat for health and let your food be your medicine. Loving yourself means taking practical action—you must be the one to introduce hygienic and nutritional improvements. Start the day with a warm glass of water with a squeeze of lemon to alkaline the body. Add a green drink that is full of essential plant nutrients to your morning routine. When you are having a meal, chew each bite of your food many times, and eat slowly. Savor the taste and place your attention on the joy of eating.

In many areas the ground soil is completely depleted of minerals because of overuse and poor management; therefore, food is often nutritionally deficient, lacking the essential minerals required to keep your body's inner terrain in strong working order. As every good veterinarian knows, mineral deficiency has long been recognized as a main reason for poor health in farm animals. In addition, there is a real lack of love for the land in the modern world; humanity has forgotten the importance of communicating with nature through conscious attention. When the consciousness of the Earth is recognized as a viable presence among farmers, the quality of your food will be greatly improved. Even though a tremendous amount of energy is provided by the sun to vitalize your food, it is essential that, for the greater welfare of humanity, all food sources be dealt with in a much more conscious manner. The land responds to the intentions, attitudes, and moods of those tending it. Food that is grown with loving care and with conscious regard for harmonizing with the forces of nature will be super-energized with vital cosmic forces.

Direct communication with the land will open new levels of energy seeding that can be coded into the foods you eat.

Greater awareness is coming for the entire planet, and seeking to understand and apply consciousness to farming and gardening will bring about a revolution in your relationship with nature. Foods that are "goddess grown," for example, using menses blood to fertilize the soil, will carry a higher vibrational frequency. You must become much more aware of food, especially your attitude toward what you eat. Who prepares your food, and what temperament do they have? Food is filled with the vibration of the preparer. Vibrant food must be understood as more than just organic; food is an energy source that is affected by the consciousness of those who work with it and prepare it. Direct communication with the land will open you to many new levels of energy seeding that can be coded into the foods you eat. Gratitude and respect for the intelligent forces of nature will go a long way toward welcoming back the vitality of the land. Ceremonial practices that honor the land will become part of the process of healing the human spirit. People will learn to build gardens with frequencies of thought-focused energy, and the old tradition of "knowing the land" will once again have the respect and admiration of all humanity.

People have lived for a long, long time on your planet in great harmony with the sun. In contrast, modern-day science has manipulated the minds of the public into believing that the sun and nature are threatening. Research shows that many who are sick and depressed often have very little exposure to the sun. Numerous studies have also revealed that when sunscreens were first introduced to the public in the 1960s, the rates of all cancers began to rise. In these times of heightened awareness, the intensity and the frequency of the sun's energy will increase. And by design, your body thrives on sunlight. The rays of the sun are actually very good for you—the body makes vitamin D in response to sunlight, which also awakens your cells to enhance your body.

Intestinal health is of utmost importance for keeping your body functioning with ease. As the saying goes, "Staying regular is staying healthy." You must be able to effectively eliminate waste materials from your system; otherwise, a toxic residue of impacted fecal waste, which can be years in the making, builds a hard surface along the walls of the intestines. When unwanted waste material accumulates in the intestines, all sorts of physical problems occur. The intestines must be able to absorb the nutrients in the food that is broken down for digestion in the stomach. The next time you bathe, look down at your belly and notice if it is distended. Cleaning your colon twice a year, preferably both in the spring and the autumn, will do wonders to restore your health and vitality.

Food can become easily impacted in the colon due to a poor diet of overcooked, and processed foods, as well as a lack of water, and a sedentary lifestyle. Poor food combinations cause food to ferment and putrefy in the intestines, making a toxic site within the body. Red meats are difficult to digest; they stay in the system longer because the body works harder to process such heavy foods. Therefore, when you eat heavy foods, you will have less energy and feel much more tired. Your emotions are also a big contributor in how well even the best food is assimilated. Eating when you are angry is unhealthy, because the food will not be broken down in the body. Anger is a controlling, holding energy that prevents digestion and integration; so when you are feeling angry or controlling and holding, it is best to drink lots of water and herbal teas, and wait until you are more emotionally balanced before eating again.

A potent yet safe colon cleanse drink can be made by mixing six ounces of organic non-citrus fruit juice with an equal amount of good, pure, non-fluorinated water to make twelve ounces total. Add the liquid to a jar along with one tablespoon of each of the following: liquid chlorophyll, concentrated aloe vera juice, hydrated bentonite, and psyllium hulls. Cover the jar, shake the mixture well, and then drink the concoction within a few minutes. If the solution is not ingested within ten minutes, it will begin to thicken in the glass, turning to a pudding-like consistency, which is exactly what it is designed to do inside your intestinal tract. The colon cleanse drink is best taken on an empty stomach at least a half hour before breakfast. Stay away from coffee as it is very hard on your system and drink *at least* ten eight-ounce glasses of water each day to help flush out the colon. A mild vegetable laxative can be taken before bedtime to move things along. If you take the colon cleanse drink for at least twelve days and upward to four weeks, you will be amazed at what you will evacuate. Once you begin to clean the colon, however, you will also eliminate the good bacteria, so each evening before bed you must replenish the intestinal flora by supplementing your diet with a probiotic or the good bacteria found in certain yogurt cultures or in acidophilus. Eating an abundance of raw foods rich with enzymes will enhance the process of internal cleansing, as well as build, strengthen, and repair tissue. If you cannot do a twelve-day colon cleanse, have a "light day" once a week, or at least once a month, where you eat only organic watermelon or apples, both of which are wonderful internal cleansers.

Parasites are especially draining on your energy and can also be the source of many health problems.

Parasitic infestations are a much greater problem than most people realize, and a parasite cleanse is also highly recommended once the colon has been cleansed. Many alternative doctors are aware of a huge epidemic of parasitic infestations largely ignored and unrecognized within conventional medicine. Although not long ago, people regularly dewormed their bodies by drinking a potion of castor oil every month. The combination of a sedentary lifestyle and a poor diet contributes to stagnant bowels, establishing an environment where parasites thrive. Parasites are especially draining on your energy and can also be the source of many health problems—skin eruptions, chronic itching and scratching, digestive disorders, joint problems, bad breath; and they nest in tumors. Parasites get the nourishing food first, leaving your bloodstream polluted with their waste materials. These pesky critters thrive in an acidic environment and tend to be active in the body at both new and full moon cycles. Pay closer attention to your body's condition at the various lunar cycles.

Formulas using a combination of herbal remedies such as cloves, wormwood, black walnut hulls, and fennel are available commercially and can be taken to eliminate parasites; castor oil, figs, pumpkin seeds, fresh garlic, and cayenne pepper are foods commonly used for purging parasites from the body. The hull of the green walnut is known to kill parasites and worms in the body. For thousands of years, the walnut has been recognized as a special food because it is similar in shape to both the brain and intestines. Adding these foods to your diet on a regular basis can keep your body strong—parasites will not live in an alkaline environment. Some electronic frequency devices have also proven effective in killing parasites. On an emotional level, having parasites is a boundary issue: who is using you, draining you of energy, and what issues are you avoiding? Spiritually, parasites are linked to a denial of the body. With feelings of distrust or dislike of your body, you can actually vacate the body, which in turn makes room for various non-physical beings to enter and occupy what you do not want.

With the vast array of changes taking place, you must be careful not to overstimulate your body with disturbing vibrations. Nature is a mood elevator, so spend more time outdoors breathing fresh air. Walking and exercise reduce anxiety and depression. Bouncing on a trampoline moves the fluids in your body around and stimulates your brain to release your own natural "feel good" mood stabilizers. When you balance the energy in your body, you will have a clear and peaceful mind.

Time-tested natural herbal treatments are nature's contribution to the healing along the lines of time. Herbal knowledge in the form of wild-crafting—knowledge of the various properties of the plant kingdom—is essential for establishing a new health-care plan that is free of threatening suspicions of the body. Dried red clover in the form of a tea strengthens the nervous system. And gotu kola is a premier nervine and an herb that will thrive very well in the garden, even under neglectful conditions. Chamomile and lavender both have a soothing effect on your body; they can be brewed for tea or used for aromatherapy. Self-reliant health care gives you the ultimate sense of freedom—you are capable of drawing to yourself desirable life experiences and conditions when you understand that nature responds to and works in harmony with your conscious awareness.

If your emotional well-being is unstable, then living in a high geopathic stress zone, like an earthquake fault, can also be a factor in disrupting the flow of energy around your body. You may be aware that your own physical, mental, and emotional stress throws you off course; however, you must consider that your personal stress factor also delivers strong jarring frequencies into the land around you. The radiation from high-voltage transmission systems or power lines, as well as the energy of underground streams, can create great disturbance within the body. Ancient people could see the energy patterns in the land, sky, and water, and they learned how to harmonize these forces. They were treating nature in a friendly manner, and nature spoke to them in kind.

When you sleep you dream, and when you dream, you are practicing the creation of reality.

You also need plenty of restful sleep and quiet time to effectively navigate the many changes these times encompass. Prioritize your time by becoming really clear about what is essential to your well-being and what is not. Be kind to your body, a good night's sleep consists of *at least* seven hours of uninterrupted rest in a peaceful environment that is clean and pleasant. Your bedroom sets the stage for sexual intimacy, rest, and dreaming, and a room that is nurturing will go a long way toward enhancing your sense of security and well-being. Use candlelight to create a peaceful mood. Make your bedroom into a personal sanctuary, a special nest without computers, TV, and other electrical gadgets—technology is inappropriate for the bedroom. A battery-operated clock is preferable; digital clocks have a frequency that is disruptive to the delta-wave sleep state. Electricity leaks out of wall sockets and outlet protectors help somewhat to keep the electricity within the walls; electrical stimulation can bombard you with more than you can handle. Keep your bedroom on the low end of the electrical stimulation grid; in this case, less is best for managing accelerated energy.

The quality of your restful hours will become the bottom line in your stability, because how you sleep is of utmost importance to how you live. When you sleep you dream, and when you dream, you are practicing the creation of reality, whether you remember your dreams or not. In the dream state, you are testing and experimenting with reality, rolling out the dough of life, because every potential scenario, every probable decision, can be first safely explored while dreaming. In ancient times people would sleep to find the answers to life's many decisions—you can heal many situations in the realms of deep-sleep dreaming. Before sleep, make an intention to work out the solutions to life's challenges, or you can dream to heal the problems that are at the core of your physical malfunctions.

Remember that visualization, suggestion, and positive reinforcement are the major tools for learning new skills and imprinting new patterns of behavior. You can learn to set an intention for the time you choose to awaken, and trust that your body's internal clock will comply with your command. An alarm clock is very disruptive because it jolts you back into physical reality, whereas it is best to arrive back in physical reality by creating a bridge of memory between sleeping and waking. You venture out of your body when you are deep asleep in delta-wave states. Just before you awaken you begin to reintegrate your consciousness by changing brain wave states, coming back from delta, through theta and over alpha, and finally closer to beta, on into the conscious mind. Sometimes you can feel yourself jump back into your body; however, it is best to return with a long, smooth, graceful approach, like an eagle coming back to the nest after a very significant journey.

You can develop the presence of mind to remember your dreams and bring the memories back with you as you direct your awareness to land safely from your sleeping adventure. As a new lifelong habit, you can learn to balance your energy as you awaken. Before you open your eyes, use your imagination to activate and integrate both hemispheres of your brain. Visualize energy crossing over from right to left, and left to right, forming charming little paths, complex trails, and even super-highways that connect both sides. Be as creative as you like while visualizing each side merging and blending with the other. Create playful new ways to talk to your body by using your imagination. When you use your imagination, you are programming the subconscious mind to send out the command for the version of reality you want.

We advise you to become much more aware of how you use your physical form. First and foremost, it is essential that you embrace the knowledge that you are an unlimited being, wondrous and unique in your own experiences and capabilities. Slow down to enjoy life, and take more time for quiet, contemplative, and relaxing moments where you can be immersed in nature's healing vibrations. There is strength in calmness; inner peace is the source of wisdom. Yoga, qi gong, or any of the many methods of learning about energy and body management are essential for building both inner and outer stamina.

Good posture is essential to your development as a consciously aware being. A strong, flexible, stretched, and energized spine is the foundation of good health. The spine is a conduit for life-force energy; it is an antenna as well as the main switchboard for all incoming and outgoing signals. Moving the spinal fluid creates greater conductivity; you can cultivate the good habit of getting down on the floor a few times a day to rock your spine. Lie on a blanket or rug with your back on the floor. Relax for a few moments, then bring your knees to your chest and wrap your arms together behind your knees, and rock from head to toe for a few minutes. This exercise is a very effective method for moving the craniosacral fluid up and down the spine, as well as for maintaining wonderful flexibility. Develop the habit of stretching your spine and moving your body around so that you are not habitually in the same position. Adjustments to your spine are essential for integrating accelerated energy.

Bodywork therapies also move a lot of energy. Massage, shiatsu, Rolfing, deep-tissue work, chiropractic adjustments, acupuncture, acupressure, homeopathy, hypnotherapy, breath therapies, essential oils, and vibrational attunements with subtle energies, magnetic therapies, and pulsed electromagnetic fields can all be very beneficial in helping you to reduce old patterns of stress and trauma in the body. Herbal baths and saunas are relaxing and cleansing. The tradition of the sweat lodge is a very special practice for purifying the body physically, mentally, emotionally, and spiritually. Beyond all else, enjoy your body; be honest, trustworthy, creative, and aware that everything you do sends a frequency into the ether that affects the mass consciousness in many lines of time.

Ultimately, you must decide what your life is worth.

Remember to give yourself a wink when you look in the mirror and say, "I love you." If you are new at this practice and do not know how to love yourself, then you had best park your body in front of the mirror for a few days and make friends with yourself. You must focus on the development of your physical being; loving your self and taking care of your body are essential for maintaining vibrant health. Explore life with enthusiastic wonder and learn to feel good about learning something new. Call your creativity forward and use it to enhance your life; laughter keeps you young, so have fun. Love and a good sense of humor strengthen the entire body; remember your cells respond to your input. You activate deeper truths when you genuinely produce the feeling of love, and, of course, in order to produce the feeling of love you must first have a belief that you are worthy of love. Ultimately, you must decide what your life is worth.

Reality is a program—you enter it, and you leave it; at times you have conscious awareness of what you are doing. Sometimes it may appear that you are stuck on the wheel of cause and effect, yet what really happens is reality comes back to you to show you how you are using your energy. The twenty-five years of accelerated energy stem from a mass agreement among many forms of consciousness to create an opportunity for all of humanity to understand this aspect of cosmic law; this time is your creation, a gift from each of you to the multiverse that will share your discoveries of personal empowerment by way of frequency enhancement. To expand your spiritual and cosmic connections, you must take ultimate responsibility for your mental, spiritual, emotional, and physical well-being.

There is always good reason for the challenges in your life, because through your daily excursions of consciousness into physical reality, you are building your own version of the world. You are creating all of the time. Whatever you have drawn to yourself, do your best to accept responsibility for it and learn from it; if you muck things up, admit your errors and begin again. In the bigger picture of reality, there is really no such thing as failure; however, you do have to master challenges until you get them right. And what is getting them right? What is the game about? It is about how to manage energy in every aspect of the cosmos. And for you here, now, one of the most important aspects of managing energy is figuring out how your body actually operates in conjunction with cosmic law. Remember, you are at the forefront of a surge of energy that has been building for many thousands of years—numerous beings connected to you from other lines of time and other realities are invested in you figuring out the reality game from your vantage point. You have the best opportunity, out of all of the timeliners, to master it. And one of the biggest challenges is for you to learn how to manage your body, because from your vantage point your body is the vehicle for navigating the multiverse.

You are quietly pioneering a new frontier of thought, and you have not yet realized how real it is. Rest assured that you are not alone in building a purposefully significant probability. Your magical mind is really playing with beliefs, and as you learn to see beliefs more clearly, you will learn to transcend your concept of reality. The ability to explore the multiverse from other points of view is one of your most unused talents—to access many realities at once, understand them all, and create in each one is an exquisitely joyful and well-earned connection. When you learn to really balance your beliefs, you will see the power you have to heal yourself in any line of time. Think about that statement for a few moments. The belief in a vital, healthy existence is one of the wisest beliefs to embrace. And, as is true with all beliefs, the bottom line is that you must believe it! A key to vital health is the ability to sustain love for yourself and excitement for life. So, dear friend, there is no need to embrace any fearful labels of disease. Remember that forgiveness is a self-healing act that releases you from the lower vibrations of anger and judgment; forgiveness permits you to move forward in the game, so you can get on with the venture of living a joyful life. You are capable of accomplishing greatness when you believe in yourself. Remind yourself that you are a co-creator of the multiverse, that life is about change, and that everything can be healed, if you are willing to do the work.

We ask you to feel and think about the kind of life that is important for you to live. When you look back on these times from another vantage point, what will your life be noted for? How will you see yourself, "your character in this time," from two thousand years in the future? What is your contribution to the healing on the lines of time? You are the star of your own creation—like the sun rising on the horizon to awaken the world; be vigilant and aware, kind, compassionate, and just. Your task is to nurture yourself and develop a positive, life-enhancing attitude, especially in regard to your body. You must take charge of your life and realize that every moment offers a potential probability for connecting you to a future where you flourish and thrive.

Chapter Six

THE POWER OF HUMAN SEXUALITY

*E*verything is composed of energy that is in constant motion; from the inner space of your cells and atoms to the far reaches of the multiverse, the field of existence is an ever-evolving creative expression engaged in a magnificent dance of intelligent cosmic energy. During these times of acceleration, your main challenge is to learn how to manage subtle energy in order to evolve to the next phase of conscious awareness. Energy assumes numerous shapes and forms, and you must learn to direct it wisely, for on every level of reality creative expression is only optimum when in harmony with cosmic law.

The field of existence is composed of a collective of consciousness that is both united as a whole and separate in its parts. Each part learns about itself through curiosity and separation; by journeying into new territory for the purpose of initiating creative experiences, it then returns instilled with unique perceptions and different expressions of energy to contribute to the motions of the dance. On all levels, consciousness is learning about itself. As your solar system traverses new areas of the cosmos, it encounters patterns of consciousness that dance in those areas of the great celestial sea. Cosmic particles are living intelligences carrying patterns and codes of consciousness that stimulate tremendous activity throughout the heavens.

On a personal level, coming into contact with these codes will arouse a deep yearning within your subconscious mind to heal itself and become whole, aligned with the inner knowledge that life is a self-selected sacred journey into the depths of the dance of creation.

As the years unfold many astounding changes will transpire on Earth to enhance the development of human consciousness. In the present you are learning about aspects of reality that will in some way enhance your own personal plans for the future expression of your creativity. Your approach to life is always based on choice. When you intentionally select the path of empowerment, your decision notifies the field of existence that you are calling for opportunities to learn how to refine your use of energy so that you can be in charge of your life. Remember, your beliefs establish the conditions for your participation in this reality; they are the foundation of ideas that you build your life upon. These beliefs are interwoven with layers of multidimensional decisions and agreements made by you for the purpose of exploring specific aspects of third dimensional existence that will augment your spiritual self with unique creative insight.

Sexual energy, in regard to what it is and how you use it, can contribute to a restoration of all that is sacred and missing in your life.

Part of the multidimensional learning curve is dealing with your emotional capabilities. When the fine dance of emotional energy is unraveled, it will invariably reveal your beliefs. Emotions are individually unique personal expressions of perceptual interpretations of reality. Emotional intelligence, which can be one of the most difficult aspects of physical reality to master, is learned and developed through responsibility and accountability. The chief challenge to emotional balance is sexual energy, perhaps both the most difficult and most dangerous of energies to understand because the power of sex can make life as well as destroy it. As a contribution to the healing along the lines of time, an open and honest exploration of sexual energy, in regard to what it is and how you use it, can contribute to a restoration of all that is sacred and missing in your life. We ask you to consider, what have you learned about yourself and life through your sexual experiences, and even more, what new realizations hover on the horizon of your awakening mind? When you learn how to manage your body with confidence and grace, especially in regard to your sexuality, you will find greater pleasure, creative fulfillment, and enjoyment in the purpose and meaning of life.

Sex is a dance of energy; it is your contact point with the vital force of creation as well as a declaration of your identity in physical reality. Sexuality is an essential aspect of your creativity; when founded upon worthy values, your sexual experiences will offer romance, excitement, trust, sharing, intimacy, passion, pleasure, fun, exuberance, caring, love, and self-worth. Sexual territory is like a huge forest filled with unknown mysteries. Sex is life; you are always sexual and you cannot avoid your genitals, yet your beliefs about your sexuality can be the source of many inner conflicts resulting in an avoidance of true sexual understanding. Hidden beliefs about love and your body can serve as the root causes of a basic denial of pleasure. Your sexual expression is conditioned by who you believe you are, as well as by what you believe you are worth.

Sexual relationships are not random events; at times sexual encounters can span the lines of time, involving simultaneous love affairs or other situations that are ongoing or in need of resolution from another dimension. Have you ever felt—in the midst of lovemaking—that you "know" your partner from another time and place, yet in different physical form? Sexual energy is also a karmic opening to your personal timeline, and especially during this time of acceleration—where it is like living hundreds of lifetimes all rolled into one—you may attract people from your so-called past lives to re-create specific experiences for the purpose of healing unresolved issues. By achieving a higher level of awareness, you can reinterpret events with greater insight and release the blocks of the victim/victimizer energy that keep you and other versions of yourself in a relentless holding pattern, circling around the same issues while never landing for nurturing forgiveness. Embrace your power to heal your sexual identity. Insight is ripe for the picking during the nanosecond. Reality is open-ended and so too are your sexual experiences.

In today's society, even though the media uses sex extensively as a commodity to program your attention by implying that you will be sexier if you buy or do whatever is suggested, sex is nevertheless still a selectively private and very personal affair. Before you learn about and experience sex, it is one of the biggest mysteries of life; yet once you encounter the mystery, you can become seemingly lost in the confusing psychic energy that sexuality inevitably involves. Sexual territory can range from a fragmented, isolated, and pain-filled part of your identity to that of an ecstatic ever-evolving integration of mental, physical, emotional, and spiritual awareness. In essence, sexual energy is a personal expression of the raw primal energy stored in your body; it is the most vital energy available to you because it is the ultimate creative expression for making and enlivening life. During these times of transformation, an extremely devalued version of sex is being marketed to the masses in a not-so-subtle attempt to steer you away from the wholesome, vibrant, loving, and nourishing aspects of a healthy sexual union. Many people have become terrified of the genitals and/or obsessed by them, and have dissociated from one of the greatest spiritual experiences of a biological being. This deprives both yourself and the planet of a true abundance of health, wealth, happiness, and world peace.

On some level of reality, you structure the parameters of your availability—what you are and are not available for in this life. Yet in physical reality, as you well know, most often you have no idea what plans you set in motion before you came here. In accordance with the mass agreements of third dimensional reality, all life-forms within the system of nature are programmed to procreate. Creating life through sexual expression imprints the DNA code with the perceptual experiences of each generation, essentially building and adding to the records in Earth's living library. You are composed of layers of energy connected to a spiritual self that journeys into and out of many different realities. When you come to Earth, you adapt to a set of mass agreements, specifically accepting a body with a gender-genital identity as a vehicle for experiencing physical reality. Your spiritual self naturally conforms to any particular time frame through the celestial imprint your body receives at birth, as well as to the mass belief system of your particular culture and the genetic belief system of your family and local community. Accepting sexual expression is a mass agreement that is essential for the continuity of this third dimensional experiment of energy. When you make children, you create life and contribute to the living library, assuring the continuity of this version of the game of consciousness. Even though sex is essential to the perpetuity of your species, you always have a choice whether or not to express your sexual energy for the purpose of making life, and if having or not having a child is part of your plan, you may set up specific agreements to help you stick with these intentions.

Sex is about attracting a partner willing to work with you on the specific issues that are pivotal for your personal growth and transformation.

The power and use of sexual energy are much more complex than physical attractions founded on good looks and social status. Sexual energy is like money; how you manage your sexual energy and the value you place upon your experiences are the basis of your personal wealth and self-worth. When a sexual attraction occurs between two people, they are responding to a telepathic exchange of energy and recognition of each other's intentions of availability. Sexual identity has its own distinct frequency, and your sexual values are broadcast into the field of existence, usually without either you or the other party being consciously aware of the process. You will meet a potential mate or partner when you follow your interests and impulses. Because thoughts and desires seed the field of existence with your intentions, you will notice and be drawn to someone you have something in common with. Sex is about attracting partnerships; relationships enrich personal growth and development; therefore, you will attract a partner who is willing on some level to work with you on the specific issues that are pivotal for your personal growth and transformation. Even though relationships can be full of challenges, you must value yourself enough to draw someone who values you and what you have to offer in return. The quality of the love you receive mirrors the value you place on yourself.

Through the intimacy of a sexual union, you get to "know one another," and with open honesty and good intentions unresolved issues can be jointly explored through the exchange of energy that occurs. The risk involved with partnership is allowing yourself to be vulnerable and less focused on performing, more receiving rather than controlling; by doing so you will find a deeper spiritual connection through sexual surrender. Sex stimulates your chakras to open and spin in alignment with the new currents of energy your partner embodies. Together you share and merge your energy fields through the intimate act of sharing your genitals, and with each shared orgasm, you probe much deeper into your partner's psychic forest.

Your beliefs about your body, whether conscious or unconscious, determine the nature of your sexual experiences. Feelings of fear and shame about your body are an indication of unresolved pain-filled memories and beliefs that energize your field of intent and qualify the conditions of your availability. Sexual energy magnifies your frequency into the field of existence. If you are involved in a relationship that is draining you of energy and/or fighting is the normal state of affairs, then it is best to jointly identify and resolve the root problems, recognizing them as signs and symbols of blocked energy. Remember, the emotion of fear is the root cause of blocked energy, and your power ends where your fear begins. Sometimes it is well worth the time and dedication to work things out, and sometimes it is time to let go and graciously move on. You must be willing to recognize what does and does not work for you. Your issues are rich with many layers of meaning, yet they all boil down to how you manage energy.

When you trust your sexual nature, you are open to explore the rich territory of sensual pleasure and will attract a like-minded partner, and together you will produce a distinct frequency that reflects your combined energies. When a good sex life is considered by you and your partner to be inherent to a successful relationship, then the exploration of sexual energy will provide all of the lessons and tests required to teach that sex can open the doors to the world of spiritual awareness, where the qualities of love, trust, respect, self-realization, and mutual admiration are vastly enhanced. Laughing together is a sign that a relationship is doing well. From an empowering perspective, sex is sacred and wonderful divine fun; it is an invigorating, stimulating, natural activity that offers mental, physical, and emotional pleasure as well as a spiritual connection to the cosmic mind. Sexual expression is essential for vibrant health and well-being, and when seasoned with truthfulness, trust, and love, it is your personal connection to the cosmos, where doorways open to the sacred mysteries of the multiverse.

Your genitals are your body's version of a sacred site.

Sexual energy is best approached with conscious awareness and as a consensual agreement between two people to create pleasure within the bounds of personal integrity—with respect for your own, as well as society's, moral values. Do your expressions of sex involve honesty, integrity, and a respect for your privacy and that of others? Do your experiences involve more than just the transience of desire? Sexual energy is psychic energy, and when you have sex with someone you literally take on your partner's energetic field. When two people stay together, after a period of time they can become very telepathic with one another, sometimes taking for granted the ability to read each other's minds. In the trust and familiarity of a long-term partnership, sexual intimacy builds powerful psychic structures, like clearing paths that lead deeper and deeper into a magical forest. Your genitals are your body's version of a sacred site, and when you explore your sexuality, you open the gates to the forest to traverse the paths of power within your personal sacred terrain. Earth has a treasure trove of areas that are considered sacred because of the confluence of energies that naturally occur there. Throughout time the land was loved and honored by those who could see and feel the power of these energies, and who taught one another to live in harmony with respect for the forces of creation. Sexual energy is just as sacred because it embodies the power of creation, and within your body, it is the most powerful source of energy you have to master. When you establish strong boundaries and qualify your sexuality with clear, conscious intentions based on very distinct values, your sacred site experience will be greatly enhanced.

Sex can also be a double-edged sword. As you venture farther into the state of sexual love, it can stimulate exhilarating feelings that will stir you with new wonder for your body's remarkable capabilities to produce mind-altering chemical responses. Happy hormones conduct an ancient ceremonial rite to keep you in the hold of a blissful love vibration. The love and ecstasy you experience with another person create a profound sexual chemistry, and without this rapturous hormonal seduction, it would be far easier to turn your back on partnerships, with all of their accompanying complexities.

In astrology, marriage and partnerships are ruled by the balance and beauty of Libra, while sexual energy is affiliated with the deeply transformative aspects of Scorpio and Pluto, and for a good reason—sexual energy digs into the psyche to excavate old, unresolved issues. Sexual activity roots out secrets and issues of power, and there may be times when the discoveries appear to be dark and menacing. Sex can bring up all of your fears, and yet if you can see it as an opportunity to work through them, which involves both listening and speaking with honesty and trust, you can have a much more ecstatic experience with your partner. The more you share with one another, the greater the strength and beauty of your energetic bond. Opening your sacred site to sexual activity is an act of surrender to your vulnerability because it roots out emotional pain, limiting beliefs, blockages of energy—essentially anything that clutters and pollutes the elegant beauty of your site and keeps you from functioning as an integrated human being.

Emotional expression is essential to the development of your intelligence; therefore, emotional issues will naturally surface before, during, and after sex. Emotions put the juice behind the thoughts you are sending out, and while engaged in sexual activity, your thoughts are quite amplified. Telepathy is very strong in the bedroom, whether the exchange of information is acknowledged or not. Remember, you can fool yourself, but you cannot fool others with your frequency, and as energy accelerates, the "knowing" shared between two people will be especially highly accentuated. Even if your sex life is "hot under the covers," you still have to deal with the emotional issues that sex stirs up, because you cannot have sex without emotional and psychic involvement. Feelings need to be felt, and accepting responsibility for how you feel will not only put you in touch with your beliefs, you will also be acting from a stance of empowerment.

There may have been times when you were really enjoying yourself on the physical level, and then suddenly, a tidal wave of emotion appeared as fast as a volatile summer thunderstorm on a hot, sultry afternoon. Emotional issues must be clearly addressed; otherwise, you will back away from your partner, or project your issues outward and blame your partner for your feelings, creating an endless cycle of entrapment of the disempowering victim/victimizer dance. Sexual activity is the real reason that things get stirred up. Sexual energy will always bring up suppressed emotions because activating the second chakra will certainly create activity in the third chakra. Remember, you attract someone for good reason, and if you can work through your difficulties with the intention of becoming a better person, and if you have enough common ground to build upon, sex will create a far-reaching bond with your partner that can restore and revitalize your whole identity, healing your body, mind, and spirit.

Your sexual expressions are part of learning about how to operate your biological computer: how fast to drive it, what to feed it.

You will gain greater insight into your life when you are kinder in your analysis of your sexual experiences. If you are too critical of your sexual activities, you will miss learning that some actions lead to pleasant, uplifting experiences and other actions lead to states of confusion and denial usually stemming from acts of deceit, disrespect, manipulation, violation, and destruction. You must value your sexual experiences; even though some of them may be very difficult to accept, these experiences help you identify who you really are. Your sexual expressions are part of learning about how to operate your biological computer: how fast to drive it, what to feed it, what makes it feel good, and what leaves it feeling lousy. When you are activating sexual energy, what are you thinking about? Are you aware of what is happening in your body on a cellular level? What is your heart feeling, and what about the sensations in your genitals? What else is occurring besides the obvious outwardly physical aspects of the sexual experience? How do you feel in the days following your sexual activities? Are your moods stable or do they fluctuate? Are you higher than a kite or feeling like you have been set adrift on a garbage barge? What is on your mind, are you drawn into a specific groove of thought? What is your energy like a day or two before your sexual encounter?

With sexual energy you loosen the hold of your senses on 3-D reality, time can appear to be suspended, and your psychic senses are activated to help you become more fully aware of your precognitive skills. Being clairvoyant, clairsentient, and clairaudient, you may tune in to concurrent vistas of reality, or even vignettes of simultaneous lives. You may see and sense people that you know now, and gain insight as to what they are doing. When you have a sexual experience, the vortex of energy created can open doors to multidimensional vistas of reality, catapulting you into earlier memories from this lifetime or those of another line of time. You must learn to pay attention to how sex alters your frequency and how it affects your personal field of energy. And most importantly, ask yourself, what is the point and positive purpose of the information you are tuning in to?

Sexual attraction creates tremendous energy between two people; yet to really build a solid union, trust between sexual partners is the bedrock for greater appreciation of intimacy. Even subtle touching and deep eye contact create a highly charged field of electrical and psychic energy, stimulating levels of excitement that will culminate in much better sex. The rituals of intimacy—touching, exploring, kissing, rubbing, tickling, licking, stroking, holding, and caring for another—stimulate excitement on a cellular level of awareness that switches the genes on and off. In the state of sexual arousal, as your relaxation increases, you switch your mind and body to off, releasing your conscious hold on physical reality and allowing your cells to access codes of consciousness that express more of who you are. In a sexual experience, you are nestled, immersed, occupied, and enthralled. Next time, see if you can observe what else is happening energetically. Together you and your partner can learn to extend your feelings of pleasure and ride them to make your orgasms last longer; and while in the midst of this exhilaration, you can learn to focus your awareness on your heightened sensibilities.

There is always so much more happening between two people on a non-physical level than what appears in 3-D reality, yet translating and understanding these ephemeral sensations can be difficult to accomplish because both your physical body and emotional responses most often take precedence over other-dimensional sensibilities. Using the same focus of attention you would use for remembering dreams, focus your attention on noticing and then capturing the essence of your multilayered sexual experience. After a sexual encounter you are more psychically tuned in to your partner as well as your environment, and this will increase as you and your partner have more sex. Sexual-psychic energy allows you to experience reality from an expanded vista; at times you may feel as if you have, for the moment, left your body and turned into someone else. The familiar comfort of your bedroom can dissolve and fold in on itself; suddenly you may find yourself lying on the ground, gazing at the dome of heaven from a hilltop covered in short, silky-soft grass. You may be sprawled beneath the velvet richness of a dark night sky spangled with dazzling bursts of light—cosmic particles can relay codes of consciousness that excite your cells—and you feel at one with the dance of intelligent cosmic energy.

When a strong impression comes to mind, be willing to share your realizations with your partner; pillow talk, spontaneous laughter, and gentle teasing open doors to psychic intuition. When you truly value the energy produced through sex, you can make great progress in understanding more of who you are, and how sexual energy opens your senses to function beyond the confines of linear time. Remember, the understanding and awareness you achieve here, based on accepting responsibility for your life, can ripple into many realities as a frequency of self-empowerment to contribute to a healing along the lines of time.

You can also develop a greater understanding of the subtle nuances of energy by paying attention to the cycles of the moon. The waxing phase, from new to full moon, is highly energetic—magnifying, lengthening, swelling, extending, spreading, accelerating, and expanding; the waning phase, from full to new moon, involves a decrease of energy, being tired and worn, and retreating into invisibility. The moon completes a turn through the twelve signs of the zodiac approximately every twenty-nine and a half days, changing signs every two and a half days. The moon, with its rapid orbital cycle around the zodiac, triggers specific patterns of energy on a monthly basis that have a significant bearing on your moods and behavior. On some level of consciousness, you are always responding to the effects of lunar and planetary cycles; how you interpret these influences can have a profound impact on your sexual experiences. The moon has a strong bearing on your emotions; for example, when the moon is in Cancer, you may want to be a homebody, nestling and snuggling and feeling secure; in Leo, it is time for romance and play, accompanied by feelings of excitement. Virgo is about making order and being fully present; feelings of crankiness may surface or feelings about perfection. When the moon is in Libra, you will feel in balance. A few days later, when the moon enters Scorpio, your emotions may feel more intense as the energy delves into secret aspects of your identity; and by the time it reaches Sagittarius, feelings of understanding the bigger picture unfold, so that the feeling of responsibility is embraced with the moon in Capricorn. Sex can bring up all kinds of energy, triggering a range of emotional responses by accessing and playing all of the black-and-white keys on your two-mile-long emotional piano. The colors black and white are also symbols for woman and man, and like the keys on the piano, the colors are keys to understanding the spark of life that the polarity of sexual energy provides.

The orgasmic experience connects you with your spirit, reorganizing and revitalizing your cells.

Sex is one of the most powerful expressions of your biology, and the most personally empowering aspect of sex is the orgasmic experience. The orgasmic state excites your body on all levels. The cells in the body respond as they would to the effects of a powerful gong being sounded to realign the body and fill the space with vibrant energy. Sometimes called "the little death," an orgasm releases your conscious mind of its rigid hold on the body, and for a short while you are floating, suspended in a space between waking and dreaming; here, your cells and subatomic particles free fall with layers of your consciousness into a state of exuberant healing. Through sex you remind your cells of your own vitality. Sexual energy is designed to keep you tuned up; it is part of what heals your body. The orgasmic experience connects you with your spirit, reorganizing and revitalizing your cells. The hormones released during sex alter your brain wave patterns toward balance and integration, activating the awakened cosmic mind. An orgasm can be a genital experience, a full-body experience, or a multibodied, full-chakra opening taking you on a journey into the multiverse.

Orgasms provide healing for the physical body; with an orgasm you are refreshed and enlivened on a cellular level, and you are reconnected with the essence of your spiritual self. You are suspended between probabilities with the various layers of your body—mental, physical, emotional, and spiritual—lifted up and aligned. At the peak of orgasm, your body is pulsating with vitality, which bursts forth into the atmosphere, distributing what you want and who you think you are into the field of existence. You can learn to focus your attention on riding the energy of your orgasm through breath synchronization with your partner and by directing the energy with your imagination. Like a surfer riding an enormous wave curling across the ocean, use your imagination to move up with the rising swell of energy passing through your body's seven chakra centers, and then swirling out the crown and spiraling farther upward, dancing in and out of the cosmic chakra openings. While remaining fully present, grounded, and connected with one another through the seven body chakras, you can ride the eighth, ninth, tenth, eleventh, twelfth, and thirteenth chakras into the mysteries of the multiverse. People have long used sex for building psychic energy to transcend the bounds of physical reality; with the right partner and in harmony with cosmic law, sexual energy can be used to venture just about anywhere you choose to travel.

The essential ingredients for a healthy, well-balanced sexual relationship are trust, comfort, and compatibility, aligned with honesty and integrity. When you allow yourself to love and accept your body and the pleasure potential stored within it, you will have much better health. Orgasms create a healing on a cellular level, and the healthiest people have an orgasmic experience on a regular basis. The sex act initiates deep heavy breathing that oxygenates your body and expands its vital energy. An increase in oxygen into the blood brings about a heightened sense of awareness and mental clarity. Making love provides a boost to your immune system; endorphins are released during orgasm, providing relief from pain, stress, and tension. Love and a happy sex life go hand in hand with vibrant health and a longer life. Remember, your state of mind during an orgasm, along with your accompanying beliefs, will qualify your venture into the forest of sexual mysteries. When orgasm is shared in a loving, trusting relationship, it can create the ulti-mate of healing in the physical body; healthy sexual expression and great sex with the right person can reorganize the body at all levels. Trust creates a comfort zone where you can really con-nect with one another. Sex is healing because when you are relaxed and in your comfort zone and open to pleasure, you can really feel the love vibration between you and your partner. When heart chakra love is present, the nurturing, sustaining, and regenerating energy stimulates your cells to respond with a big Yes! This is creation! This is the primal nature of existence; this is it! This feeling between two people is healing sex.

Remember, the orgasmic state creates a suspension on the cellular level; you are a bit above gravity, floating into deep relaxation. People who do not have orgasms cannot really relax, and if you cannot relax, then you are missing out on the many multisensory pleasures of life. No one owes you an orgasm if you have been unable to discover for yourself your body's own orgasmic pleasure. You owe yourself the experience of under standing what an orgasm is by learning how to pleasure yourself. Society has created taboos about the body, yet it is one thing to have someone else tie your shoes, and quite another to tie them yourself. You must learn about your body; it is yours. The idea that sex is sinful or that there is something wrong with your body is an example of ingrained cultural programs and self-selected limiting beliefs. Nevertheless, you will always feel best when you use your body with integrity.

Sex is like a rocket booster, and coupled with conscious intent, it can propel you into aspects of reality that can enrich your life.

The highest of empowerment that sexuality offers is to take you into the stars for the ultimate remote-viewing experience. Long ago, men and women knew how to entwine their spiritual selves with their physical forms to explore Earth, the moon, and the planets; they observed weather patterns, and watched celestial activities or scouted locations suitable for new living quarters. They wanted to know the others who were occupying this plane of reality along with them. Distant family and friends, both living and deceased, could be contacted because the sacred dance of life was connected and understood. Animals easily shifted between dimensions, and they were watched and at times consulted for their wisdom from this position between the layers of reality.

Sex is like a rocket booster, and coupled with conscious intent, it can propel you into aspects of reality that can enrich your life. Sex with a loving partner is like riding a magic carpet and traveling anywhere you want. When you are having sex, you are stirring the life-force kundalini energy nestled at the bottom of the spine, and inviting this serpent-like energy to come out of its cave to teach you how to dance with life. It is your responsibility to know and understand your body and the many ways it can be played, touched, and positioned to bring greater pleasure, and to allow this energy to run up your spine and spiral out through all reality. Activating kundalini energy by means of sexual pleasure can create direct openings into simultaneous dimensional experiences that have a complete interface with the life you are presently living.

An orgasm with sensations of ecstatic pleasure localized in the genitals may entice the kundalini up to the second chakra. Lifting the energy farther up the body is accomplished through extending your time of pleasure, deep breathing, relaxing, surrendering to the joy of the process, and using your imagination to raise and ride the wave of energy. Thoughts of performance anxiety will shorten the process. When you slow down and truly allow your sexual sensations the time to unfold, you will build more energy. With your partner, be creative and condition this energy by dedicating the explorations of your body and your sexual ecstasy toward your goals and intentions in life. You can also send out the energy of love to awaken family members and friends, and to all of humanity for world peace. The second-chakra experience can offer a great genital orgasm, but not a full-body, full-chakra, multiverse orgasm. When energy rises to the third chakra, you will both be engaged with the feeling zones of the belly, clearly picking up each others' emotional states of mind. In healthy long-term relationships, the energy will move beyond the belly into the fourth or heart chakra, where there will be love, trust, and mutual admiration between partners. With heart chakras open, two people may stay together for a lifetime; many couples will build families and truly love each other, having established comfort and honesty in important day-to-day things. Even so, they may never speak their deepest truths, or hear another's, if the energy does not reach the throat chakra.

When there is energy in the fifth center, or when kundalini has risen this far, two people will really communicate what is on their minds, safely expressing their fears, joys, memories, and opinions. With this truly essential accomplishment, kundalini energy can move beyond the throat chakra to activate the sixth and seventh energy centers of the higher mind. As this energy circles the brain, an orgasm will reverberate through the body, building successive waves of intense, pleasurable sensations. Full-body and full-chakra orgasms cannot be experienced in non-consensual sex. Rape, incest, and cult rituals involving sex with children and animals produce a very low-frequency form of sexual energy. Participants in such activities are in most cases possessed by entities directing the human hosts to carry out the sex acts that the possessions actually desire. Some people may derive great pleasure from these activities, even if they are violating someone else. Pleasure combined with sex is relative to your values; however, the pursuit of pleasure does not give you permission to do anything you want. The purpose of the acceleration involves learning how to manage energy, and in the countdown to 2012, what is set in motion returns faster and faster as the field of existence offers direct, quick-service feedback on what you are creating. Negative acts create negative consequences.

Part of humanity's healing at this time involves recognizing and releasing dysfunctional patterns passed on from generation to generation.

You are a product of genetic propensities, and part of humanity's healing at this time involves recognizing and releasing the dysfunctional patterns of behavior passed on from generation to generation. You are called upon to use your awareness to understand the meaning of these patterns, and then to override them with new beliefs that serve your positive intentions. If you come from a line of people who repress their sexuality, you have those codes stored within, yet that does not mean you will follow the pattern. You are not stuck with your genes and their propensities; however, the programming is there for how reality can be explored, especially sexually. Sexual energy is deeply encoded into the body; it is raw primal energy. Women in particular have inherited patterns of perception that have restricted their ability and desire to have an orgasm; actually there are many women who have never had an orgasm. Some women have learned to fake an orgasm and get away with it because their partners are too self-absorbed with their own gratification to pay attention. A woman knows that something is supposed to happen, and sometimes she will ride the moans and groans of her partner, imitating the sounds, but never really feeling her own luxurious surges of arousal and passion. A woman will pretend to be aroused because she does not know and accept her body, nor does she understand what she is missing. Men have an external demonstration of their excitement, sparking their sacred energy outward through an ejaculation that generally accompanies an orgasm. A woman's contact with the sacred sexual part of her being is an internal path, into dark, mysterious depths. For these basic reasons, the two differing sexual identities have been used as a basis for understanding the power of energy stored in the body. To utilize the body for optimum fulfillment in every endeavor, and especially in sex, you must be in your body, fully occupying every particle of your being.

Even though you have a prominent gender, you have both male and female vibrations within you: the left side of your body is feminine and ruled by the right brain, and the right side is masculine, ruled by the left brain. According to your biology, your genitals decree the identity you are learning how to become, although the degree of male or female energy will vary. There are no mistakes in biology, and no mistakes in who you are and the identity you have chosen. You did not get stuck at the bottom of the list and have no choice in the matter. Each and every life you live is significantly interwoven with layers of purpose and plans that are connected in a much larger vista of reality. You have been both man and woman on your multidimensional journey through the human form, and even though you may not consciously recall your various identities, your personal timeline records are stored in various layers of the subconscious and unconscious minds. Sometimes bleed-through talents and abilities will create more masculine-like qualities in a woman, and feminine characteristics in a man. Self-acceptance is not only an important key to understanding your identity; it is the sign of an awakening mind. You are a self-selected expression of a larger form of consciousness learning about itself through the intricate wonders of the game of existence. On some level, you are predisposed to outline your life as a man or woman, yet how you manage energy throughout your various dips and dives into physical reality and beyond definitely determines and qualifies what you are available for.

Sexuality and psychic sensitivities naturally intertwine with one another, and with the acceleration of energy activating a spiritual awakening within humanity, both men and women the world over are breaking their bonds with the limiting beliefs and thought patterns that have trapped and stifled the creative mind. Women in general currently have the greater tendency to switch their attention from one reality to another and most women do so, often without realizing it. This ability is inherent in the human form. Women also tend to establish a deeper connection with their biological structure and are more naturally psychic because of their monthly menstrual cycle, which generally begins around the age of twelve or thirteen and ceases during the forties, fifties, or even sixties. At the onset of womanhood, the appearance of the first blood creates a psychic-spiritual vortex of energy, a personal power portal entrained to the lunar cycles. Pregnancy and childbirth can further intensify a woman's bond with her body. Unfortunately many women have denied themselves the pleasures of the body, because both men and woman have been taught over long periods of time to regard the menstruation process with extreme disfavor—while ironically accepting the violated, pain-ridden blood of war. When women condemn the body for its natural functions, they only call forth physical problems because their cells follow their commands. The dislike and ignorance for this life-giving process have resulted in all sorts of modern-day female ailments. The bleeding cycle is the very characteristic of the female body that embodies the fertile, nurturing mother-goddess energy, and during the special time of month when the blood appears, the doors to transcending 3-D reality have been flung wide open.

A woman's blood knowledge was once cherished and respected, far back in time.

During the past two thousand years, the power of the female body and the menstrual cycle have been ridiculed and diminished, yet a woman's blood knowledge was once cherished and respected, far back in time. In the rhythm of a woman's life, the appearance of her blood is when and how she makes contact with nature's mysteries. This is the depth of her magic—to be able to lead the way for humanity with grace and compassion into the system of nature, to provide the gift of bringing forth life. The presence of the menses, or moon blood, produces varying degrees of psychic sensitivity depending upon the individual; the ether is always full of activity, and when women get psychically opened each month, havoc can be created if they do not understand what is happening. Sometimes women want to retreat, withdraw, and hide for a few days to buffer themselves from the barrage of frequencies they can sense but so often do not understand. The male vibration is the grounding force for this natural psychic opening, so men need to honor and respect their own part in balancing the power of the menstruation cycle.

Throughout history, men have certainly demonstrated their own immense psychic abilities and feats of renown. However, just as with women over the past two thousand years, the mental, physical, emotional, and spiritual suffering—through war and the persecution of magical psychic practices—has imprinted the gene pool with tremendous records of fear and pain, particularly in the male vibration. Men are learning to accept that their sensitivities and vulnerabilities are indeed their true inner strengths, and that honesty is the key to a clear conscience and peace of mind. Men are challenged as well to accept responsibility for their sexual power, which has a completely different energetic charge than what women experience. Men need to understand that their personal power resides in activating and embracing their feelings, a side of themselves they have not duly considered. When a man's feelings are actively engaged with his sexual energy, he will experience new levels of intimacy. Although it is very important to have a well-structured body, real strength is about trusting one's self, family, and partner, and other men and women. The task for men is to trust others with their truth, to recognize the arrogant ignorance and folly of war, and to honor and respect and nurture all life.

Your biology is driven to procreate so you can learn first-hand how to manage the energy of creation. Pregnancy is a symbol of growth, a promise of renewal and responsibility. When a man and woman have good, earthy sex—fully occupying their bodies and enjoying the pleasure their bodies provide, while laughing and loving their way into a cosmic experience—they vastly enrich their connection to each other and the cosmos. A child conceived in such an environment, will be a stalwart member of the human race, especially when the sensuous energy of nature is added to support the endeavor—making love outdoors in a private setting under the light of the silvery moon, or the heat of the sun's life-enhancing rays. Sex for the purpose of creating life is best when filled with joyful pleasure, for it conditions the relationship between man, woman, and child. During the actual process of inception, egg and sperm tweetle and chirp at each other as the sperm rush in to bring their song to the goddess. The egg actually makes an inaudible sound, like a mating call. The sperm that genetically best suits the requirements of the non-physical being desiring birth through this union will then resonate with the song and match the egg's vibration. This sperm will be pulled forward by the resonation, appearing to beat out the other sperm. If only the so-called hardiest sperm won, then you would have physically perfect but not spiritually aligned babies. Remember, you qualify for your genealogy and time of birth, so pregnancy and the birth process involve many layers of agreements. If you want children, then it is best to first make contact with them through the dream state; before going to sleep, focus on your intentions on finding and communicating with the spiritual energies that will become your future children—call them and welcome them into your life.

Sex keeps you young and strong, and through sexual intimacy with another person, you make contact with your spirit.

Although you can go for years and years without having sex, sexual activity is actually a necessity for overall physical well-being. Sex keeps you young and strong, and through sexual intimacy with another person, you make contact with your spirit. As people get older, even if they are still in a marriage or some arranged partnership, they often stop having sex for one reason or another. In this case, they can self-pleasure themselves. Health professionals are realizing that masturbation and other forms of self-pleasuring are essential for personal development and overall well-being. People who go without sex for long periods of time often experience a variety of physical problems. Stimulating the physical body is essential, and is far more fun and productive with a partner. As you age and become more discriminating, you are better able to tune in to your partner because you are both more psychic and have the wisdom that experience affords. Your sacred site has been visited more than a few times, and you have also cycled the sun many times to claim knowledge from the cosmos. Sex naturally becomes more than just a genital or physical experience and only gets better with age; you have wisdom, you have built paths into the forest, and you have ideally reached a point of accepting your body, having overcome the awkward self-conscious body fixations of youth. You are now making love to a person, not just using a body for self-stimulation, so love handles, a softer tummy, and a less firm derriere do not make so much of a difference.

In any long-term relationship, you will ride a roller coaster in regard to your sex life. If you were always climbing Everest, it would become rather exhausting; traversing sexual peaks and valleys is part of a mature relationship. However, as you get to know one another better, you will notice that there is lots of great energy around after great sex. Sex is a super-exchange of energy. Sexual expression is your contact with the creator, and sex is really about how you use sacred power. If you have a secret sex life or have to manipulate energy—yours or another's—to have sex, then this is a direct misuse of your integrity and responsibility as a human being; such activities vibrate at the lower end of the spectrum of conscious awareness. You and only you are responsible for raising your standards, and by doing so, you will discover the gourmet version of sexual energy.

The dark and dangerous side to the powers of sexual energy involves possession by non-physical entities. In regard to managing energy, you must ask yourself, "Am I fully occupying my body and am I having sex of my own volition? Are my sexual experiences consensual, joyful expressions of lovemaking based on intimacy, trust, and truthfulness with my partner?" If you have strong sexual urges, but intimacy, trust, and truthfulness are lacking, boredom with sex can take a hold that will lead to edgier and edgier explorations—sometimes involving pain and humiliation to bring about genital arousal. The desire for this extreme type of stimulation leads you farther and farther away from the bounds of self-respectability and deeper into the dark caverns of entity possession. Remember, when you open sexual vortexes, you are playing with the raw primal power of creation, and entities from other dimensions are very attracted to the sexual energy and life force generated. With the presence of intimacy and love, dynamic higher-vibrational energies make subtle contact with you during sex for the purpose of reconnecting your physical body with the higher dimensions of your spiritual identity, which make you invulnerable to possession.

When intimacy is feared and real value and respect for the

sharing of sacred creative energies are lacking, sex becomes a mere gratification of transient desires. Such an approach is ripe for attracting lower-vibrational entities that seek a way into physical reality without having to take on the responsibility for fully occupying, owning, and caring for a body. Entity possession is like an invisible plague, and many people cannot break their cycles of dysfunctional sex because they have devalued the sex act and now have entities attached to their energy fields. Sex has been degraded and perverted in today's world because millions of people have allowed their second chakras to be taken over by beings that use humanity to fulfill their twisted sexual desires. The real impulse behind an addiction to perversion is possession. In most cases, when a person is engaged in non-consensual and/or indiscriminate sex, such as rape and having sex with children or animals, he or she will be in the throes of sexual deceit, which is a signature that non-physical entities are involved. People have the right, in this program of reality, to explore the hills and vales of life according to their own choices; we are not here to judge these explorations. However, for those seeking a higher level of consciousness, their moral values and the degree of their conscious awareness in all activities will determine the type of experiences that they draw to themselves.

If you have unresolved painful sexual issues from previous ventures into sexual reality, your beliefs around these experiences will surface when you have sex. The darker side of sex is painful, frightening, forceful, controlling, abusive, degrading, destructive, and humiliating. Remember, sex naturally opens the doors of psychic knowledge, whether you want them open or not. Intense sexual experiences, particularly those in childhood, are often carryover issues or agreements from other lines of time. Sexual abuse can create severe trauma in an individual, resulting in fragmentation, disorientation, dissociation of the personality, and, most often, amnesia concerning the very events that caused the trauma. You do not lose your mind without reason. At the extreme, the shocking experience of sexual abuse can cause people to go insane, or to develop identity disorders, where they apparently lose or relinquish contact with their core center because it is too painful to encounter. In any case, trauma of any kind can induce a dramatic heightening of physical and psychic sensitivities, activating the body's natural response to upgrade itself in preparation for states of enhanced vigilance.

If sex were considered a sacred act, the world would not be in the turmoil it is today.

If sex were considered a sacred act, the world would not be in the turmoil it is today. The sex slave market is a multibillion-dollar operation, with tentacles reaching into every continent, where men, women, and children are bought and sold as sexual objects. A variety of nefarious groups engage in organized sexual abuse, using sexual energy to exhibit control over others, and in rituals as a life-force offering for calling up dark, demonic entities and enticing them into physical reality. Sexual energy is the most vital of forces that exists within you, and for this reason those engaged in mind control activities use sexual energy to control and direct their slaves. Sex produces a tremendous amount of energy, and like atomic energy, it blows holes open into other realities. This is why people who have non-consensual and/or indiscriminate sex attract lower-vibrational entities that will match and meet the fantasy thought-forms the person is entertaining. Thoughts and desires are charged-up with the power of sexual energy. The entities will then occupy and take over the body and run the person's sexuality. It is very easy to have a non-physical entity take over your genitals when you have no value for your sexuality. If you are attracted to pornography and are delving into dark versions of sex, you are more than likely being used by these forces to debase the value of sex. It is also possible to become possessed when you have no emotional, mental, physical, or spiritual boundaries. If you operate in a sea of confusion and can barely commit to a decision in life, or operate without love for yourself and your body, then you are basically hanging out a vacancy sign advertising free room and board.

Sometimes wounds in this reality are simultaneously occurring in another vista of experience, with another version of you, in a different line of time. Be more aware of the bridging of events from linear time to multidimensional time-beyond-time by blending your emotional intelligence with your intuition, and acknowledging with mental clarity the synchronic nature of life's events. A higher version of yourself is always working with you to assist with your spiritual integration. Remember, the opportunities for spiritual connections are so immense in this time that the healings you realize now create a ripple of vibrations and frequencies into the web of existence—your creative contributions to the motion of the dance. It is important to know that your consciousness is always working to integrate and heal, to gain full insight and knowledge into the whys and wherefores of your experiences. Sexual abuse can be seen as a personally empowering experience, if you ask yourself the true purpose of your wounding, and seek to understand the multilayered significance concerned with its healing. What did you learn about yourself and those who played with your sexual energy? Your realizations will give you the opportunity to come face-to-face with your self, through this intimate contact with another human being, who may mirror hidden aspects of yourself, as well as have karmic connections.

Lifestyles and sex styles that have been popularized in the media, such as multiple-partner relationships, do not represent a healthy, nurturing life; energetically the process of multiple partners becomes very, very confusing and draining to all involved. When there are too many people involved in a relationship, the levels of honesty and depth and integrity are compromised. Your cells know when they are not being valued. If you are going to be in a relationship, whether it is a same-sex relationship or opposite-sex relationship, be committed to it. Explore the subtle nuances of romance and allow the mysteries of sensuality to blossom. Be certain that if you are having sex with someone, you have feelings of love, appreciation, and trust for that person. If you are having sex with someone who you do not trust—run! Healthy, wholesome sex has honesty and truthfulness at the foundation. When you can build a relationship of intimacy based on reliability, trust, integrity, and good fun, you can begin to activate all kinds of awareness codes in the DNA, enhancing your life through the knowledge you gain.

A neighborhood with strong family bonds based on love and good sex is going to make a better community.

Sexuality that is expressed and qualified and cherished will attract vibrational entities that will imbue the coupling with a cosmic knowledge experience. This was known long ago on your planet as the ultimate gift of love for balancing a community. A good, bonded, loving experience between two people, creating a good, honest, loving orgasm, will ripple into the neighborhood. Energy is not confined by walls. A neighborhood with strong family bonds based on love and good sex is going to make a better community, providing peace and prosperity throughout the land. Imagine whole towns of people treasuring their sexual explorations, couples loving, laughing, and valuing each other in the privacy of their own discoveries. When sexual expression is honored as a doorway to the creative energy of existence, the whole world will vibrate with a much greater awareness of the spiritual purpose of life. Sex is vibrant creative energy, and used wisely, it can change the world. When you are suspended in orgasm, you are experiencing the healing energy of creation, and these energetic frequencies contribute their vibrations to the community and to the Earth itself. Good sex is good business for all. You contribute to the great dance of energy when you accept yourself as a sexual being and ideally reexamine your sexual experiences in a new light, seeing them as great teachings for managing energy.

The Pleiades star cluster has long been affiliated with spiritual growth through sexual development, producing an energetic frequency to provide wealth and beauty in the material world. Our home, in the sign Taurus the bull, is noted for vigorous, fertile, and high-spirited energy. Various planetary, lunar, and solar alignments with the Pleiades provide new codes for sexual dignity, the effects of which will heighten your value and understanding of sexual pleasure. Strong bonds of love and trust in a partnership are essential for the deep exploration of multidimensional realities through sexual energy. A relationship grounds you in this reality, so that in your journeys to the stars you remember who you are and where you are from. There are many ways to use your body that you have not yet believed into being, and as you change your beliefs about sex and your body, you will be the recipient of untold rewarding realizations.

The nanosecond provides the opportunity to understand

the energy of empowerment through developing different perspectives of reality. It is important to know that challenging
situations arise to initiate change; the resolution of old issues—
and there are none more potent than sexual issues—frees you to
have a more meaningful, emotionally fulfilling connection to
life. Use your body as an honored and respected sexual vehicle
to explore your identity and to receive the teachings of knowledge as mature sexual codes. Sexuality has long been practiced
as a form of receiving and transmitting energy, so when you are
in the midst of the lovemaking process, by all means enjoy
where you are. However, you can learn to enhance the immedi-
acy of your physical pleasure by being present in the moment
and aware of other "nows." Remember, sexual energy is powerful stuff; it creates the boost needed to open windows and doors
to other dimensions, and it is healing and rejuvenating, and
ignites your creativity. Great passion has an even greater purpose, so please be aware of the power you are playing with.
Remember as well, the quality and clarity of your intent will set
the frequency for what you experience, and this holds true for
any endeavor. Once again, complete trust and honesty in a relationship will ground the sexual energies in your body, allowing
for a much more exciting ride.

The new frontier of multidimensional living and healing
attracts stalwart pioneers. Many of you made agreements to
learn lessons and to heal, to make connections and bridge realities in ways that are foreign to society's current system of
beliefs. In the journey of consciousness, how you earn a living is
much less important than how you manage energy. Now, the
opportunity you are immersed in is both immense and subtle at
the same time. Everything is happening quickly, and quite simply you are in it and challenged to integrate many teachings,
including Pleiadian and galactic-centered transmissions. Be

open to the virtues and fortitude of the human body, think of it as venerable and value sexual activity as an admirable and celebrated art form of creation. Remember to pay closer attention to what your body is saying. How has sex enhanced your spiritual growth and what have you learned about yourself through your sexual experiences? Sexual contact can stimulate the cells to become a sensual library of knowledge—a tribute to beauty, and pleasure, and love. Allow yourself to feel the power and vitality that are naturally yours, and live to express it. Dear friend, it is your personal responsibility to seek sexual pleasure with awareness of the sacred way—as an honorable being, with respect for your body and your partner, and with reverence for the knowing that you too can enhance the cosmic dance.

Chapter Seven

THE GAME OF EXISTENCE

A tidal wave of light-encoded energy, emanating from
the center of the Milky Way Galaxy, permeates the
new territories of space that your solar system is currently passing through on its journey through the cosmos. This energy is
being deliberately introduced to your world to quickly enhance
and upgrade human awareness in multiple levels of reality. The
cosmos is rich with life, and consciously advanced civilizations
distribute their knowledge and achievements throughout the
field of existence using light frequencies as carrier waves for
information. Massive influxes of ever-increasing cosmic radiation carry patterns and codes for peaceful and sustainable
solutions to your global challenges, revealing to humanity a
grander understanding of the design of existence. Once selected,
these codes can elevate human consciousness and inspire it to
resolve the raging conflict over ideas that currently separate
humanity through the acts of war, greed, and tyranny. The proliferation of chaos and confusion in world society is actually
stimulating humanity to awaken to a higher order of values. You
are stronger than you think, and with this in mind, you must
allow the multiverse to gift you with something even greater
than you can imagine.

Rotating on its tilted axis, Earth is like a rare, priceless gem radiating its luster into the depths of space and time. From your vantage point on Earth, the sun and moon appear to be of the same size; yet in actuality, if the sun were a beach ball, the moon would be a grain of sand. The precise positioning of the Earth, moon, and sun allows for the periodicity of the lunar and solar eclipse cycles to occur, which have a penetrating and powerful impact on the entire system of nature. Eclipses follow distinct cycles that methodically disrupt the normal rhythm of the well-established relationship patterns between daylight and darkness. Eclipses initiate change by stimulating new levels of intense interrelatedness; essentially, they stir the pot of awareness. The tilting of the axis in relationship to the solar orbital plane creates the changing seasons; as you move farther away from the equatorial zones, variations in temperature and ratios of light and dark increase dramatically.

Your body thrives on sunlight; the entire system of nature functions on pulsed light vibration.

The vernal and autumn equinoxes are recognized for providing an ancient code of balance for Earth and all of her creatures. Twice each year, the sun appears directly overhead in the equatorial zones, creating an equal distribution of daylight and darkness in both Northern and Southern Hemispheres. This apparent balance between the hours of daylight and darkness is like a cosmic reset button that realigns and updates both the system of nature and that of humanity. Your body thrives on sunlight; actually, the entire system of nature functions on pulsed light vibration. Information is distributed on light frequencies, so as the daylight hours diminish or increase, your consciousness is deeply affected. With less light in autumn and winter, you naturally journey farther inward to reflect upon and reassess your place in the game of existence—which is about managing energy in every aspect of the cosmos. When the light increases, you are naturally more attracted to your external environment as the place to play, create, and initiate action.

Each year, springtime brings the fulfillment of nature's promise of renewal. As the land awakens from winter's slumber, you awaken as well. The cells of your body sense the quickening of light and respond by nudging your consciousness to stretch and reach outward into reality, to take action on the ideas you have been reflecting upon during the quieter winter moons. Your cells know that an increase in light is an opportunity for growth and expanded awareness. Each spring your body is stimulated to become entrained with the new light frequencies, to meet and match the strongest ones and to integrate them into your personal cellular storehouse of knowledge. Your consciousness expands along with the light because the light frequencies, which penetrate your body to a subatomic level, are encoded with symbols conveying new information.

The multiverse maintains contact with all dimensions and versions of reality through an elegant web of interconnected electromagnetic frequencies. As the hours of daylight lengthen, your senses grow anew, and just like plants, you learn to adjust to the atmospheric changes that include new levels of sensitivity to the high-spectrum radiation carried by the light. Radiation is energy that is emitted in either particles or waves moving away from their source. In the cosmos, energy emitted by one body is transmitted in wavelengths along the electromagnetic spectrum through the medium of space, to be absorbed by another body. From an earthly perspective, frequencies are measured in hertz, signifying how many cycles per second energy moves along a wavelength. The higher the frequency, the shorter the wavelength; waveforms with higher frequencies bring about entrainment, causing weaker frequencies to basically join in and resonate along with them—somewhat like vines joining together to climb a tree in order to reach more light.

You are a cosmic force producing your own form of radiation through your thoughts and feelings.

People everywhere are becoming much more sensitive to the effects of the increase in energy from the cosmic radiation. At this time, living on Earth involves learning how to manage energy from the perspective of the physical body. Accepting the ever-growing mass realization that thought creates reality is the bedrock foundation for the transformation of consciousness and the spiritual awakening of humanity. Even though other forms of Cosmic Intelligence are offering their higher wisdom to assist you in navigating these times, it is incumbent on you to rise above the ever-pervasive tyranny of fear by applying the power of your conscious mind to create your reality.

You are a cosmic force producing your own form of radiation through your thoughts and feelings. Just as others offer assistance to your world, whatever you learn and accomplish here in physical reality ripples as a frequency of inspiration into the field of existence; and some realities eagerly await your contributions. Your personal and collective achievements make significant contributions to all realities; your victories are gifts that provide frequencies of humanity's version of spiritual transformation. The steady influx of intense cosmic energy will activate new degrees of emotional awareness and expression that will further the development of your psychic sensitivities; these energies stimulate you to reach for a new understanding of yourself with respect to your power to create whatever you direct your energy and attention toward. It is also important to remember that to anchor the codes for expanded awareness into physical reality, not only must you maintain balance in all aspects of life, you must also be aware of how you conduct yourself.

The sun is the governor of your solar system; life as you know it requires an orb of light to flourish. Unusual and unprecedented solar activity will continue to deliver intense high-radiation frequencies to your sector of existence through-out the nanosecond. These transmissions alter the fabric of physical reality. Cosmic radiation has a powerful effect on your body because greater activity in the heavens creates greater stimulation and communication on a cellular level. Cosmic energy interacts with you and your version of the field of existence by digging through layers of patterns in the DNA that have been encoded with a thorough accumulation of generations of ancestral perceptions. The energy can rearrange your perceptions, putting them in a new perspective where you can more easily untangle any self-destructive emotional behavioral patterns—such as victimhood or fear, hatred or vengeance, and violence—by seeing and understanding the purpose of these feelings, as well as the affiliated events from a larger, interconnected picture of cause and effect. To leave the endless, boring loop of repetition on the road of disempowerment, you must make a choice, and then creatively imagine your own exit.

The internal space and structure of your atoms are comparable to the vast expanse of the heavens. Just as outer space is filled with twinkling stars, on a subatomic level your inner depths are filled with blinking patterns of light. Cosmic radiation travels along the electromagnetic spectrum carrying encoded patterns of energy that are like maps and blueprints for locating and building probable realities. As these powerful frequencies entrain with your cells, your nervous system converts the cosmic signals to electrical energy, delivering the messages both to your brain and throughout the body. Cell receptors accept these frequencies, which then pass through cell membranes to roam the depths of subatomic inner space. They streak in and out of this inner reality like a meteor shower gracing a velvety-dark night sky. Just as words are symbols for ideas, these blinking lights are symbols that carry the codes and patterns for an abundance of probable choices and options for enhancing physical reality; however, it is up to you to choose the codes that embody the path of empowerment.

The codes and patterns offer instructions that the cells can use to maintain your body at a higher level of awareness, so that you can adapt to the great social and environmental changes that characterize these times. Cells read the environment; everything is identified by the cell as a vibrational frequency. Life-force energy is actually in the environment and passes through the cells offering an unlimited array of potential selections. Your genes are programmed to respond to stimuli, and with the new codes streaming through the body, the DNA can be played like an electronic circuit board, with the various signals decoded and translated on a subatomic level. The sun, along with a supporting cast of other cosmic forces, plays the lead role during this time of transformation by delivering frequencies that your body, your cells, and your conscious mind can use to enhance your life. As your entire solar system traverses new areas of space, the sun translates the incoming codes of consciousness and then eloquently disperses them throughout the entire system.

Your body is highly receptive to light frequencies that carry encoded instructions for navigating the fabric of multidimensional reality.

Remember, in order to experience the unique qualities of physical reality, your spiritual self takes up occupancy in a physical body, which is actually an elaborate code-reading device for analyzing the environment. Your body is highly adaptable and very receptive to the light frequencies that carry encoded instructions for navigating and managing the fabric of multidimensional reality. Unlike the conscious mind, the cells, molecules, atoms, and subatomic particles operate with an intelligence that is not confined to linear time. Your DNA is inscribed with an accumulation of ancestral perceptions and other-lifetime memories that serve as a foundation for your physical identity to build upon. An inner communication system sustains your organs, your continuity of memory, and your ability to move and function. And it simultaneously assesses and maintains a myriad of communications between so-called past and future situations that affect your present reality.

Any vista of time can be reinterpreted when seen from another perspective. A new vision of past, present, and future events creates an alternative route for consciousness to move, explore, expand, and heal. Even though you participate in life believing that you are fully aware of what is happening, quite simultaneously other aspects of yourself co-exist with your consciousness. These other aspects are more aware of your multidimensionality than your conscious mind, and are able to operate out of your body, using the same cells, the same molecules, and the same organs simply by adapting to a different frequency. They can perceive legitimate vistas of reality that you and other parts of your self may be completely unaware of.

Your body is always operating as a multileveled code-reading device. Codes of consciousness dance through the vacuum of inner and outer space for the purpose of seeding and shaping realities with energetic patterns. The patterns are symbols and signposts for consciousness to explore—like markers on a map; they point the way to various cosmic crossroads of energy where realities merge. The incoming codes stimulate you to consciously reevaluate your ideas about yourself and to elevate your thinking above and beyond your own self-imposed limitations, as well as those fostered by factions of society still steeped in denial. To be fully actualized, the codes must be selected and integrated by your conscious mind.

For a few moments, relax your tongue, gently separate your jaw, and focus your attention on your breath. As you read along, clear your throat, straighten your spine, and open the front of your chest by rotating your shoulders backward, in alignment with your spine. Now, use your imagination to visualize a vibrant influx of golden spirals of energy dancing their way into your body as you inhale oxygen and life-force energy deep into the bottom of your lungs. Consciously follow the feelings of expansion and contraction in your lungs, as well as the outward and inward movement of your diaphragm. Picture the swirling spirals of energy easily speeding through the walls of your lungs to enrich your bloodstream with the latest cosmic codes of consciousness. As you continue to breathe in a deep, rhythmic manner, direct your consciousness into your body's inner world to consider the versions of reality where your cells, molecules, atoms, and subatomic particles participate. Whom or what are they communicating with? Use the deep rhythms of your breath to entrain with your cells; allow your cells to show you what they know.

Enhanced awareness is based on the ability to read and discern symbols, to recognize the significance of patterns and cycles.

In both inner and outer worlds, enhanced awareness is based on the ability to read and discern symbols, to recognize the significance of patterns and cycles through observation. Symbols are the interface between the field of existence and consciousness. Symbols are a way of notching the field with significance. When you pay attention to the dance of subtle energies, reality is altered through the introduction of your consciousness. Your perceptions condition the fabric of reality to conform to your expectations; when you thrust your thinking toward experiencing new realities, you create a new waveform of awareness that carries your intentions into subatomic levels and seeks to entrain with the appropriate probabilities.

The nature of your reality is abundantly rich with meaning. Everything in your world is highly symbolic; symbols express and unlock larger ideas. You are a symbolic representation of your inner identity. Your body contains a highly structured map of interwoven energetic forces; the lines on the palms of your hands, the bottoms of your feet, your eyes, the structure of your face, the shape of your body, how you stand, speak, and move all convey a vast amount of information about who you are. Your particular style of handwriting and how you form the symbols of the alphabet, your astrological birth data and numerology all offer deeper insight into the layers of intentions you are playing with in the game of existence.

Within the current world culture, a challenging aspect of the game of consciousness in 3-D reality has been to forget that you are a part of the field of existence. You had to sever connections with other levels of reality, to be separated for a while from your greater identity, and to appear not to know the details of the larger plan on a conscious level. Although there are many ways of playing the field, it can definitely be a tough and challenging assignment to appear to be cut off from your higher-self awareness. Nevertheless, your higher self is still working with you to map out positive, purposeful probable realities from a place where time is suspended. The more adept you are at recognizing patterns within the symbols of 3-D reality, the faster you learn to reestablish contact with your higher self, thus opening and activating the codes for new levels of life-enhancing, sustainable probabilities.

Remember, conscious thought is a powerful force; it ripples into realities beyond your perceptual awareness, affecting both physical matter and other layers of life. While a portion of your identity is firmly focused in the present, consciousness on a subatomic level experiences existence as being non-local—meaning there are no walls or boundaries to separate space and time. Non-local implies being everywhere at once—omnipresent with existence—and this is why your cells are precognitive. Each moment is important because it contains untold probable choices; you must therefore take complete responsibility for every moment. You actually select probable versions of reality as easily as you choose food items from grocery shelves. Each and every potential decision you face creates a vortex of energy—a point of power where potential realities line up awaiting selection. Each time you make a decision, you select a personal vortex of energy to fortify your version of the world. When your mind is clear and your body is operating with optimum health, it is much easier to focus your attention on the version of reality that you consciously choose to occupy. The ability to consciously focus your attention and energetically choose what you want is the sign of an awakening mind.

When you select and direct your thoughts with clear intentions, you actually tune your attention to a specific show of reality, like adjusting the dial of a radio to a specific broadcast. Intentionality ripples beyond the present into the past and future because thought is not confined by space and time. In a larger sense, thoughts freely explore the non-local multiverse, making new realities in every moment of the past, present, and future. New events can happen in "anytime," and every "now" is engaged in making new versions of itself. You make the choice, and you always have a choice. The multiverse is in constant motion, seeking to find the ideal balance to support and sustain each and every part of itself. As you are now fully aware, part of your challenge is to awaken your perceptual awareness to a much higher purpose of life. You are not stuck in or destined to a doomsday version of reality—reality is refreshed and newly selected by everyone each and every moment—and this, dear friend, you would be wise to remember.

Your ancestors were capable of navigating reality with ways and means that are foreign to most people in the modern world.

Your ancestors in both the distant and recent past were capable of navigating reality with ways and means that are foreign to most people in the modern world. Nearly all of written history has been purged of the fascinating aspects of life involving experiences with paranormal versions of reality. Over the ages human beings have been led to believe that they are less than who they really are. In other times people were more capable of navigating and playing with reality simply for the fun of it. They knew the joys of exploring non-local existence and were able to activate DNA codes etched with the circuitry to bring them back to their home station. They knew their place in time, yet they were not confined to it. They did not need the technology that you require today to go to Mars, nor did they need weather forecasters to predict pending storms. People could travel the cosmos and explore their greater reality; the Mayans knew of the black hole at the center of the Milky Way Galaxy, yet from a modern astronomical perspective this is only a recent discovery.

Your ancestors knew that their senses were for interacting with nature, and when they wanted someone to watch their children, they were able to create an energy vortex around a favorite tree. They could then walk into the forests and fields and maintain communication with the tree, and the tree would use its own energy, in cooperation with the mother and father, to watch their children. People once knew that the system of nature was a necessity of life, and they used the knowledge to empower themselves to survive and thrive in cooperation with the natural world.

One of the most subversive battles for control of the human mind began thousands of years ago as organized religions sought to draw people away from their sacred connection with nature by convincing them to "worship the gods" in buildings designed to mimic nature's majesty. Much later, with the advent of the Industrial Revolution of the late 1700s, an even greater dislocation separated people from nature. The accelerated pace of economic change brought factories into the towns, which in turn created a drastic increase in people leaving the countryside to seek urban living. Insanity and poor health became more common as people lost their connection to nature and then, too, lost the ability to tell the difference between one stream of time and another.

An accumulation of rigid social and cultural beliefs, limiting the confines of time and space, have disconnected you from the experience of direct learning from nature. The resulting systemic confusion within your cellular circuit board has become detrimental to humanity's spiritual growth. At this time all of humanity is deeply immersed in fulfilling a crucial mass agreement to restore the physical body's code-reading capabilities. By claiming your inherent abilities to move your conscious awareness around the field of existence, you will experience direct knowledge and be able to tell the difference between truth and deceit. And you must reclaim these abilities to reach beyond the confines of physical reality to understand the power and intent of the forces that challenge you to awaken.

As mediated confusion intensifies the world over, political and sexual charades are used to purposely confound, demoralize, and separate humanity into opposing factions. The seemingly endless tidal wave of war propaganda, and a barrage of double-talk scripted to program human consciousness, will continue to offer a version of reality full of forebodings of fear, hopelessness, doom, and despair. Even though the political management of your planet appears to be racing out of control; from a higher perspective, the flamboyant scourge of lies and deceit stimulates your growing awareness to awaken to your true spiritual identity, while you occupy a human form during these times of tumultuous transformation. As spiritual common sense prevails, an agenda of fear-based entrainment has no hold on an awakened mind. Conscious awareness, dear friend, is the key to unraveling the mysteries of the multiverse. And like hobbits discovering their strengths on their journey through Middle Earth, you will also discover how strong you really are.

You are integrating cosmic energies for the purpose of restoring the function of the specific codes of consciousness within the human form.

Physical reality is founded upon the creative process. The concepts we share with you at this time are for the purpose of refreshing your memory and reminding you of your power to implement change into physical reality. It is time to activate your imagination, to clarify your intentions, focus your energy, take action, and expect results. You are integrating cosmic energies for the purpose of restoring the function of the specific codes of consciousness within the human form. You must respond by expanding your field of possibilities and trust in your power within the scheme of existence. A much larger framework of consciousness supports the positive versions of reality that you agree to participate in. A frequency away, forms of intelligence watch, interact and cooperate with, and sustain your version of reality. Our advice is to be very, very clear about what you are and are not available for; this way it will be much easier to receive the live updates from the appropriate cosmic energies, and avoid having your body's computer compromised by so-called nasty lower-vibrational bugs.

During these times of perceptual changes, you will be tested to strengthen your resolve and demonstrate your version of the power of the human spirit. While you are being adjusted by waveforms of energy that you cannot see, your body is being recircuited and fine-tuned to adapt to the accelerated energy. You select the codes best suited to your values and intentions.

All realities occur concurrently, each one fortified by the power of thoughts and emotions invested in it. So, the all-important question comes down to, which program do you want to be a part of?

Stretching your mind beyond the walls of mass agreements that structure 3-D reality is an empowering achievement, which adds greater awareness and meaningful new understanding of the whys and wherefores of life. You are here to learn how to manage energy—the intricacies of your own individual energy in concert with the magical, mystical field of existence. Collectively and individually, this undertaking is no small task. In every venue of reality, it is essential to understand how the governing influences of cosmic and spiritual laws operate in concert with the ancient mass agreements that guide your inter-play with the field of existence. As you are learning, not only do your thoughts create your reality, they operate on many levels of the mind, as well as in multiple layers of reality.

Spiritual or esoteric knowledge uses the language of metaphor and symbolism to convey the subtle meanings of exis-tence, meanings that transcend the physical and material world, yet have a profound effect upon it. From a larger picture of real-ity, you are swimming in a sea of symbols. The human mind readily responds to symbols; they are easily imprinted and stored in your DNA, as well as in the deep memory banks of the subconscious and unconscious minds. Without symbols, how would you express yourself? Language is based upon telepathic agreements where inherent meaning is assigned to sound sym-bols; yet when people speak, they take the act for granted, rarely wondering where their next words are coming from, or even aware that they are molding ideas into words and playing with the power of naming, qualifying, identifying, and creating exis-tence. Words convey information, but information is not in the words; they symbolize meanings based on mass agreements of consensual reality, and help form it.

Writing is a form of magic that was once readily accepted and developed as a method for affecting reality.

With the art of writing, specific two-dimensional lines and squiggles utilize a code—an alphabet—and the words they form can literally make something out of nothing, because the physical act of writing creates and directs energy. Writing is a form of magic that was once readily accepted and developed as a method for affecting reality. Over time the meaning of the symbols of every language has changed, adapting to the requirements, intelligence, and curiosity of the people of each culture. Yet sometimes certain words were purposely altered, or reinvented, or even banished from the vernacular, because they had special power and were forbidden to be used.

In times long past, the ability to identify and name life's unfolding mysteries and their forces within nature was recognized as an act of power for exercising influence over the magical properties of those forces. Nature was recognized as the staging ground for the manifestation of spiritual and cosmic laws and forces within a particular dimension, allowing consciousness to explore reality from this particular vantage point. An innate sense of curiosity is embedded in all forms of consciousness, and people of old sought to understand the interplay and relationship between all of these cosmic laws and forces. They sought knowledge that would assist them in utilizing the mystical properties of nature and the atmosphere—to influence and play in the vast field of existence.

The tradition of noting the sun's position in the heavens

was utilized by your ancestors for the purpose of locating their place in existence, and as a way of marking time. They knew that understanding the cycles of the heavens offered important keys to unraveling their greater identity. In modern culture, people have misplaced their sense of curiosity, and few of them now recognize the power and significance of noting the seasons as a way of counting time, or as a method for finding their place within the grand scheme of existence. People of the ancient world readily recognized and acknowledged the forces of nature. In the Northern Hemisphere, long before the rise of Christianity, December 25 was a special day for acknowledging the promise of the yearly return of light that would soon deliver the northern world from long, dark nights. Born anew on the horizon, the heavenly sun was finally beginning to move upward into the sky after reaching its peak of light in the southern latitudes on the December winter solstice.

As Earth completes a twenty-four-hour rotation on its tilted axis, it soars through space in complete synchronization with your solar system, revolving around the sun in an orbit of about 365 days. Due to the tilting of the polar axis, the sun appears to alter its position in the sky, seeming to seasonally migrate north and south while casting new shadows and reflections through a continuous transmission of light-encoded information. The sun is your most important source of energy; as the ruler of your solar system, it dependably provides light, which sustains life as you know it. The sign of the cross, or two intersecting straight lines, is an ancient multilayered symbol that was originally used in very ancient times as a locator point, and as a sign for representing the sun and stars. The cross was a symbol for other meanings as well: it signified "where spirit meets matter," or where the sky appeared to meet the Earth at the horizon to form a cosmic cross. In ancient times the atmosphere, or ether, was always symbolically positioned in the center of the cross; the ether was filled with cosmic life-force energy, and where the lines joined, the abundance of vitality opened portals to other dimensions of reality.

It was well known that activities carried out in the exact center point of the two crossed lines had great power to affect many versions of reality.

Long ago, when people utilized the sun as a way of locating their place in existence, they maneuvered stone markers into specific placements on the Earth's surface to discover the pattern that the movement of the sun's rays displayed. People observed the positions of all heavenly bodies—the moon, planets, comets, and stars—to understand the keys to the celestial symbols and patterns that defined and emblazoned the scenery of existence. As a marker and locator point, the cross also became the symbol for denoting the four directions: north, east, south, and west. And for those who understood and respected the power of the goddess energies, the crossroads were always considered among her sacred places. With its utter simplicity as a symbol, the cross came to signify a number of important themes: the significance of the sun and stars, where spirit meets matter, a notation for sacred places, the mark for the four directions, the four cross-quarter points, the four seasons, and the four elements—earth, air, fire, and water. And in those times, it was well known that activities carried out in the exact center point of the two crossed lines had great power to affect many versions of reality; for the two lines meet to form a point of power, where the ether—the vital force of existence—is always signified.

The checkerboard, or game board, pattern is a more complex version of the cross—an extension that naturally evolved from connecting a series of intersected crosses. The checkerboard is a grid pattern composed of sixty-four squares—eight squares per side alternating in a black-and-white design. This familiar set of symbols can be found the world over, as well as throughout many lines of time. Hiding in plain sight, this black-and-white pattern of squares is an ancient design that was created as a very simple, yet powerful, tool to remind humanity of the vast expanse of the field of existence, and most importantly, how to navigate it. This symbol was easily imprinted on the deeper layers of the human mind and passed on in the innate patterns of perception from one generation to another. The interlocking pattern was a multilayered teaching that conveyed the encoded complexities of the multiverse. Each cross point on the grid was a vortex and portal of energy where realities merged, and each square was a symbol for a specific quality of energy—black for negative and white for positive—just like the negative and positive charges of electricity.

The checkerboard is a symbol that has captured the ultimate complexity of the field of existence in a design that is layered with symbolic meaning.

Synthesizing this crucial information into a two-dimensional form in third-dimensional reality, the intent was to portray the importance of polarity within the natural order of the multiverse by way of symbolic metaphor. The checkerboard is a symbol that has captured the ultimate complexity of the field of existence in a design that is layered with symbolic meaning, yet presents itself with the ultimate of simplicity—an innocent presence in world culture appearing as nothing more than a board for playing games. People of old knew that, in the vast game of existence, they would live again and again, and they also knew that how they perceived and interpreted reality determined the quality of their life experience here and beyond. They further knew that the game board was created as a symbol to imprint their memory banks so as to remember and be able to call forth what was learned from lifetime to lifetime.

Like the cross, the checkerboard, or game board, contained layers and layers of meaningful information. Because symbols can be used to affect and direct consciousness in many subtle ways, the lines and alternating colors spoke to the deep layers of the subconscious and unconscious minds, areas that readily respond to and recognize symbols that the conscious mind may barely notice. People use their minds in different fashions; the ancients grasped that the mind was affected by the forces of nature and that everything is part of a cosmic dance of energy. The game board became their treasured symbol for consciously playing the game of existence. The sixty-four squares—six plus four equals ten, revealing one and zero—form an eight-sided design on a two-dimensional surface in third-dimensional reality, a metaphor for revealing the essence of cosmic law and the basic instructions for building energy in any reality. Black and white symbolized the female and male polarities, negative and positive forces, dark and light, night and day, blood and semen, zero and one, vagina and penis, chalice and blade; the oval, dome, and altar; and the obelisk, pillar, and steeple. Even the Eastern symbol of yin and yang, the black-and-white swirl traditionally representing the balance of energy, was inherent in the design.

The alternating pattern of black-and-white symbols triggered the mind to remember the higher cosmic and spiritual laws for working with energy. In Indonesia, on the island of Bali, the local culture has long used the checkerboard pattern as a reminder for dealing wisely with the necessary balance between the forces of dark and light. Around the world numerous ancient power sites contain calendars and computers made from stone and based on this same principle: a stone and a space, a pillar and a space, a one and zero, or white and black. And, right in line with a very clever and knowledgeable use of energy, modern-day computers are, interestingly enough, based on the exact same system of primary symbols: one and zero, pillar and space, or male and female energy.

Ancient temples and churches were always located at the points, or crossroads, where the powerful Earth energy lines intersected, for the intent was to tap in to the energy of the great planetary grid and use it for amassing energy and power. In the old world and new, buildings were constructed according to the very ancient art of using the forces of polarity at these sites, with consideration for geological anomalies, to create and direct energy. Remnants of the game board can be found all over the world: on the floors of old structures, such as those in the ruins of Pompeii; and on the ceilings and walls of churches and mosques that were decorated in black and white. In the modern era, the design has been consistently used for the foyers of state and federal buildings, Masonic temples, and the meeting places of the New World Order clan.

Manipulating and managing reality from behind the scenes is an age-old practice.

Fashion and advertising industries invariably use the pattern. In auto racing, the black-and-white checkered flag is raised as a signal to "start your engines," and then it is lowered to give notice that the game has begun. Secret societies have long used the board to affect their own consciousness, as well as that of the masses. Manipulating and managing reality from behind the scenes is an age-old practice. Even though many modern societies willingly participate in various displays of public rituals using ancient symbols, they have no real knowledge or awareness that these symbols are being used to open portals of energy, often for covert reasons. The power points and their uses have been a well-guarded secret. Symbols that represent layers and layers of hidden meanings are used profusely in the architecture of churches and public buildings; they are also on uniforms, military insignia, and regal attire; and they are found in religious ceremonies in both the ancient and modern worlds as well as in advertising on street corners today.

Within the board are layers and layers of codes signifying various divisions of time; numerically, the outer edge is composed of twenty-eight squares, corresponding to the approximate number of days within both lunar and menstrual cycles; the next layer in has twenty squares, noting the approximate number of years in an eclipse series, which is established by the moon's north and south nodal patterns—known as the head and tail of the celestial dragon—that complete a rotational cycle. The moon's nodes are a symbol for the energetic cross points of the orbital planes of the Earth and the moon, which are imaginary positions used to calculate distances and directions, both astronomically and astrologically. The next layer has twelve squares signifying the twelve signs of the zodiac and the twelve months of the calendar year; the innermost layer is made of four squares joining around the center point of a cross, symbolizing the four directions surrounding the ether power point. Each numerical symbol represents important information for the designing and building of reality, as well as for understanding the intricately significant patterns of the celestial cycles.

When diagonal lines are drawn across the board from corner to corner, as the lines cross the intersection of the north/south and east/west axes, they divide each quarter in half, creating eight sections with the new lines marking off the all-important four cross-quarter points: the four times a year—the first of February, May, August, and November—when the sun is halfway between the next solstice or equinox. Some cultures celebrated the four cross-quarter dates as times of important spiritual renewal, while the traditional four seasons of the year, marked by the solstices and the equinoxes, were celebrated as earthly festivals. Remember, time serves as a locator and organizer of realities, creating invisible boundaries as containers for creation. The eight directional points were used for marking and telling time; determining their relationship to the cosmic calendar was crucial for knowing exactly when the energies of spirit meeting matter would peak.

Today, what is the game really about? What are the components? How is it influencing you? Perhaps you are wondering how you can learn to play on the game board, working your way up to multidimensional chess. The game is about managing energy in every aspect of the cosmos. It is a game of awareness, and the board represents the field of existence, which is the neutral playing field of energy that supports and expands consciousness; its presence announces and reminds you, on very deep levels of consciousness, that "you are playing the field." As you are by now well aware, one of the primary reasons for your presence here on Earth is to learn how to manage energy during a time of rapidly unfolding awareness. Remember, the point of awareness is to take note of what you are observing; to assess, evaluate, and apply the present information as a piece to a much larger puzzle in the tapestry of reality. Every day of your life, you are being triggered by symbols you are completely unaware of; these activations take place in the part of the self that is holding ancient memories. To become more fully aware of the significance of symbols in your reality and to achieve the healings you came here to receive, areas of your mind and body that store memory must link up and operate from a higher state of consciousness. Once you place your attention on these possibilities, your curiosity will elevate your understanding of reality to a new level.

The game board conveys that the nature of existence is multidimensional and is composed of light and dark forces that require constant balance.

The symbol of the game board can serve as a tool for expanding your consciousness. Remember, the game board conveys the important message that the nature of existence is multidimensional and that it is composed of light and dark forces that require constant balance. When you see the game board, it is a reminder that you are in the game; and on a subconscious level, you agree to the rules. We have a suggestion for playing a game of awareness, and if you choose to participate, you will be amazed at how much you will learn. On your next venture to the store, purchase a disposable color-film camera with twenty-seven exposures. This is your game board camera. When you first buy the camera, write the date on it, because this is when your version of this game of awareness begins. Next, you must carry the camera around with you, fully prepared to snap a photograph of the celebrated checkerboard wherever you see it. Be certain to use your intention, creativity, and intuition to condition the field for what you want to encounter. The camera game involves developing various degrees of awareness; looking for the game board is a way of training your eyes to notice even more of the symbolic nature of 3-D reality, such as the subtle proliferation of ones and zeros throughout all world cultures.

Like a child, you learn best through play, and by playing this game, you will discover that everything is a game of energy. The camera is a symbol of your intent to notice and record specific symbols in 3-D reality; your participation will open multidimensional levels of the game, and your psychic abilities will be enhanced as you focus the path of your attention. Be certain to notice where, when, how, and by whom the black-and-white checkerboard is being displayed. Be creative and have fun, because this is also the purpose. There is no time constraint to this game; it may take you three weeks, months, or years, depending upon how you use your awareness and the clarity of your intent.

With your final photo, note the date; once the pictures are developed, study them because they will contain teachings from your subconscious mind. Look for synchronicities and subtle patterns beyond the apparent black-and-white design. What other symbols are present? Can you recall where all of the photographs were taken? How often were you following your intuition when you found a game board? What was your biggest surprise? How do you feel about your collection of photos? You may notice other things in the pictures besides the game board. The exposure numbers and dates taken will reveal the numerological story behind the meaning of symbols. When you purchase the camera, the game begins; and when you take the final shot, the game is over. Remember, whenever you see the game board, take note that, on some level of reality, your cells are very aware that you are being notified, "You are now on the board and you are playing the game." Please consider this exercise; our intention is to playfully stretch and expand your mind into new levels of perceptual acuity.

The game board is a tool, a synopsis, and a metaphor in 3-D reality of a two-dimensional model for the multiverse; it is a simple springboard and trampoline to trigger your consciousness into remembering the complexities of "all that is." We suggest that you use it to gain good measure in your life. Learn from it; notice how it affects your consciousness, and learn how you can use it to focus and direct energy toward what you want to create. As you take note of the extensive use of this symbol throughout world culture, other signs and symbols will appear to assist you in connecting the dots. When you see the game board, it is a notification, to various levels of your mind, that a game of symbols is being used to affect your mind—an invisible, yet very powerful, ancient game of energy. As you further consider the idea that everything is a symbol, what do you feel you and your life are a symbol for?

Now, take a few deep inhalations and exhalations to get your body ready for an internal exploration of the nuances of the game. Make yourself comfortable by adjusting both your spine and pelvis, and then by opening the front of your chest. Clear your throat, relax your tongue, and gently separate your jaw. Have your eyes follow the words on the page as you concurrently follow the sound of your breath. Be certain to breathe long and deep into your diaphragm, and as you make the sound of a gentle wind passing between two caves, notice the feeling of your breath as it moves over your larynx and into the very bottom of your lungs. Picture your breath filled with dancing golden spirals of energy swirling into your body; then see them graciously moving through the walls of your lungs and into your bloodstream to provide a rich, exuberant vitality of newly charged energy. You are breathing the field, the breath of life, the vital force, the ether and chi energy—all that is. Use your imagination to distribute this energy throughout your body as you journey with your conscious mind down to the cellular level; once you are there, picture a version of yourself simultaneously present in each and every cell. Then journey farther inside to enter the molecular structure of your body; and then again, down farther still into the atomic layers and beyond, where you will reach the vast expanse of your own inner space.

As you ride the golden spirals of your breath, imagine a miniature version of yourself seated on a game-board carpet, soaring through a sea of subatomic particles. Your mind is clear and in complete balance; you feel exhilarated and very secure on your game-board carpet as it responds to your every command. Inner space looks somewhat like the heavens, wide open and filled with blinking lights, yet inner space is buzzing with constant movement and activity. As you explore the depths of your inner terrain, you will notice patterns of light that join to form structures, somewhat like inner rivers and streams of consciousness; if you are attracted to a specific formation, tune in, study the symbols, and feel their presence. What do they represent? If the energy is something you want to connect with, meet the entrainment and join in by similarity. You can jump these rivers of light just as genes jump around the genome. Change is an inherent ability within the DNA. Clusters of consciousness open and close gates, and build bridges and ladders within the genome complex, which is ever changing and evolving. The light frequencies that penetrate your body down to a subatomic level are encoded with symbols conveying new information vital to the transformation of your consciousness.

As you travel around the subatomic world on your game-board carpet, think about the kind of outer world you would like to inhabit. If a peaceful, non-violent world is your choice, then you must imagine and energize it into being by visualizing every aspect that is important to you. As you see yourself establishing a consciousness presence in the depths of your inner space, you are free to energize and select the versions of reality you require to safely evolve as a spiritual being occupying a human form. Acknowledge your intent to always be in the right place at the right time, in balance and displaying a wise and appropriate use of your creative energies, all the while living with peace and joyful humor in a world filled with new and exciting ideas for optimum growth. You must see and select the qualities you desire.

When you take an inner journey, you exercise your mind and stimulate new degrees of psychic sensitivity that empower you with greater clarity to create your chosen version of reality. Such openings provide you with a firsthand encounter with the knowledge you seek to further understand the truth of humanity's legacy. And when you are back in the outer world of day-to-day living, remember to apply the same abilities that you use for navigating inner space to reach out and touch the stars. Metaphors, like symbols, are tools for describing the abstract, to help your mind grasp the ungraspable. Problems arise when you mistake the symbols for reality.

Cosmic law states that you have free will to do as you choose; however, what you do *will* come back to you. It may just be a game of consciousness; however, you *will* face the consequences of your activities in 3-D reality and beyond. The time lag may vary, and a million years can go down the pike before a swing back occurs; however, during a time of accelerated energy such as the current nanosecond, remember that everything is drastically sped up. In an ever-expanding multiverse, this law is a generous gift to all forms of consciousness, a compassionate teaching that decrees: Do as you will. The advice, dear friend, is to create no harm; this is, however, only advice, not the law. You have the free will to choose how you want to experience existence—to create seeds, to plant them in 3-D reality, and to reap the harvest of what you have sown. In this manner of generosity, you learn about the responsibilities of co-creating reality. As energy continues to increase in intensity, and solar flares and coronal mass ejections alter human consciousness, those operating from positions of corruption—lying, cheating, stealing, raping, torturing, and killing—will find themselves with very loose footing on a very slippery slope, tumbling head over heels on the fast track to self-destruction. Deception and violence only fuel a need for ever-greater violence and deception. As the light-encoded energies increase in frequency, "what you do" comes back to you with ever-quickening exactitude, and this is the generous gift of the multiverse.

Your awareness is of the essence; otherwise, you will become a pawn in someone else's version of the game.

During the time of acceleration from 1987 to 2012, the energy increases in magnitude each year and will continue to escalate in order to give everyone an opportunity to understand the game of awareness. There are multiple levels at which this game has been played over time to manipulate human consciousness. In our own version of reality, we are also learning how to manage energy—one could say this is a lesson common to all forms of consciousness within the field of existence. Within other levels of the game, there are forms of consciousness that we call game masters; these are players who design and unify systems of learning through the creative expression of cosmic laws, for the purpose of discovering the potentials of the multiverse. Game masters are unbounded and can take on any form they choose. A game master is widely dispersed within its own creations, similar to someone on Earth writing a software program and then embedding his or her consciousness within the program, thus being ever-present to experience the creation and always available to work out the bugs in the system. We offer this information to you as a reminder of your own capabilities for exploring the ever-expanding opportunity to manage energy, to be present in the moment, and to realize that every moment has the potential power to create the version of the world you most desire. In this regard, your awareness is of the essence; otherwise, you will become a pawn in someone else's version of the game of life.

Awareness is the ability to observe, take note of, integrate, and make use of the information presented for the purpose of expanding your perceptions of reality. New realizations offer renewed opportunities for personal growth and expansion of consciousness. As the energies of these fortuitous times continue to accelerate, it is important to remember that everyone on Earth is immersed in a steep learning curve, a fast-track course for understanding and respecting the very basic cosmic laws for living in balance. Once you can see through the script of beliefs and ideas that entrap your use of energy, you liberate your mind and free up your energy to be managed from a more consciously empowered position. When you take the time to notice and observe, to pay attention and to reinstate your curiosity, then your awareness will flourish—like a well-tended garden catching the latest news from the sun. A season of super-enhanced awareness is now upon you, and understanding that everything is a symbol for an expression of energy will reveal new and exciting levels of the game. And playing with the creativity of your naturally curious mind will serve you well as you process all that is churning deep inside, in preparation for another round of awakening.

We are connected to you by multidimensional agreements, and we earnestly share our energy and our perspectives for the purpose of fulfilling those agreements. Like you, we are here to play our part in the process of restoring and activating humanity's inner codes of consciousness for a healing along the lines of time. As the seasons pass and you continue to journey around the sun, many new discoveries will be revealed as knowledge buried deep within your biological being is stirred by the increased intensity of cosmic radiation. Cherish one another, enjoy life, and be willing to bring forth the best of your abilities to play the game of awareness within the game of existence. As you venture farther into the multiverse, remember the choice is always yours to create joy, safety, and harmony as essential qualities for paving the way for all of your explorations.

Chapter Eight

PROBABLE CHOICE

*H*uman consciousness is blossoming and maturing with great momentum these days, and the bustling commerce in the trade of information appears to be stimulating more and more people to wake up to the realization that a massive unraveling of reality is rippling across the globe. People are now able to grasp new ideas very quickly—ideas and concepts that at one time may have taken months, years, or even entire lifetimes to accept and integrate. Potent cosmic energies are responsible for the tremendous changes in every arena of life. And as traditional beliefs and expectations continue to crack and crumble like old, stale bread, the ability to quickly grasp new interpretations of life is crucial for navigating the swiftly churning currents of a world seemingly in a rapid race toward chaos.

As everything continues to accelerate, monumental changes will transpire, and your beliefs about reality can be altered in the twinkling of an eye.

The pressure to change is even greater than you can imagine. The nanosecond in the annals of time is hosting a massive

transformation of consciousness that catalyzes the spiritualiza-
tion of matter and restores awareness of your multidimensional
existence. The awakening of consciousness is being cast to the
forefront of your own life because you are here at this time to
learn how to manage your energy. Will you overcome the program of fear as a qualifier of your experience? Will you pursue
the quest of transformation by trusting yourself and your intuition? You are called upon to think for yourself, to believe in
yourself, and to consciously create a peaceful and sustainable
version of reality by accepting complete responsibility for your
life. The nanosecond is especially important because as everything continues to accelerate, monumental changes will
transpire, and your beliefs about reality—and the very nature of
reality itself—can be altered in the twinkling of an eye.

The collective mass consciousness of humanity is profoundly affected by the restless stirring of new levels of
awareness that are coming to life across the globe. Impetus is
building as people steadily emerge from various stages of deep
denial due to the accelerated energy that is changing, at super-
sonic speed, the consciousness of Earth and all her inhabitants.
Like a few billion Rip van Winkles suddenly coming back to
life, many people are waking up in a very different reality than
the one in which they dozed off. The ever-increasing influx of
cosmic energy shakes up everything at a subatomic level, nudging humanity to recognize and grow beyond the dysfunctional
patterns that separate world society into factions thriving on
discord and disagreement.

These twenty-five years of accelerated energy involve a
huge transformation of consciousness that will collectively clear
perceptual limitations and expand your perspective, essentially
freeing humanity from a state of bondage that is, as yet, largely
unrecognized. The quickening of energy you are receiving, from

new areas of space that your solar system encounters, is literally blowing your paradigm wide open, triggering a huge leap in your ability to select probabilities that support, sustain, and value life. This passage is generating new flurries of solar flares and coronal mass ejections that hurl through space—riding the solar wind with massive, unprecedented bursts of cosmic radiated energy—and quicken every subatomic particle of your body. These super-intense transmissions from the sun totally rearrange your consciousness on multiple levels of reality by tuning your perceptions and enhancing your senses, especially if you have been working to become more spiritually and psychically aware.

Enormous changes are occurring on Earth, as well as within and beyond your solar system. The sun is displaying increasingly high levels of solar storm and electrical activity, as well as a distinct increase in its brightness and a sizably stronger magnetic field. An increase in brightness can also be seen on the planets and their moons, some of which now appear to be glowing. Scientists and astronomers have noted magnetic pole shifts, huge changes in atmospheric pressures and temperatures, and unusual fluctuations in magnetic fields throughout the entire solar system. The steady increase of celestial activity by way of comets, meteors, and asteroids is also an obvious sign that something very big is occurring; yet most people are so wrapped up with day-to-day diversions and distractions, they barely acknowledge the significance of these all-important celestial changes.

The probabilities of the nanosecond involve a cosmic identity crisis that is steeped in enormous complexity. You are being challenged to completely reevaluate who you are in relationship to the ever-expanding map of cosmic existence. It is important to understand that numerous extraterrestrial races have been interacting with humanity and operating on Earth for more millennia than you can imagine. Throughout the centuries, a myriad of highly unusual objects have been observed in the atmosphere whose size, shape, and performance cannot be explained by the known laws of science. Due to the effects of the current acceleration, UFO activity has escalated to an all-time high, making it near impossible for government and military establishments to continue the charade of ignoring or hiding what is happening in the heavens.

A so-called official acknowledgment of the presence of intelligent life-forms that share time and space with you is just around the corner. Once this occurs the pace of change will speed up. As your life takes on an array of new complexities, you will be challenged to recognize the difference between genuine occurrences and stage-managed events designed to deceive you and distract your attention. A full acknowledgment of the extra-terrestrial presence will unravel society's traditional religious beliefs concerning your origins. Your heritage is from the stars, and understanding the multilayered complexities of this truth is of premier importance to the spiritual transformation of humanity. For those still chained to the old, crumbling paradigm, where the mainstream media and the words of public officials are never doubted, it will become exceedingly more difficult and confusing to sort out the truth.

The courage to fearlessly ask questions is at the core of your spiritual awakening.

Various mundane and cosmic forces are in a desperate battle for your attention, because your attention represents where and how you focus your energy for creating the reality you encounter. The courage to fearlessly ask questions is at the core of your spiritual awakening. People have been clinging to various stages of denial for a long time; as a result of this inattentiveness to life, a behind-the-scenes breeding ground for carrying out despicable deeds was easily fostered. Such behavior by your leaders is a symbol for society's denial to effectively deal with the truth, and by playing out exaggerated versions of lies and deceit, they test your abilities of discernment. By claiming your rightful ability to move your conscious awareness around the field of existence, you will experience direct knowledge and be able to tell the difference between truth and deceit. And you must claim this ability to reach beyond the confines of physical reality to understand the power of the forces that challenge you to awaken. Then you will not be so easily deceived.

The controlled mainstream media is used as a tool to pull your attention into a probable world that is devoid of vitality and creativity. By enticing your attention into a reality of violence and war, your thoughts and beliefs are conditioned to enslave you in victimhood and complete disempowerment. Will you choose pessimism or empowerment, be browbeaten or make use of the new energy and soar to new heights of achievement? The twenty-five years of acceleration offer an opportunity to live a life of empowerment by developing your attention and conscious awareness to the extent that you can recognize the larger truths of your spiritual heritage and actively participate in creating a world that embraces this understanding.

In direct opposition to the ever-increasing attempts to confound the public, the incoming cosmic energies balance the playing field by opening the floodgates of human awareness, deliberately stimulating you to pay closer attention to a new source of information stemming from deep inside—your own inner-knowledge genie. Once this all-powerful genie is finally out of the bottle, newly realized psychic and intuitive abilities will help you quickly achieve new levels of personal empowerment to assist you in dealing with the spiritual dynamics of the transformation. With humanity's inner abilities strengthened and unleashed, the truth, on all levels, will be increasingly difficult to hide. As the veil of denial is whisked away, tremendous disclosures of hidden information will come to light, and all that was formerly secret will become more and more transparent. Do not be alarmed by these revelations, for your ability to deal with change on a conscious level and to effectively change the world through conscious choice is a sign of your empowerment. With everything moving at an ever-increasing pace, those entrained with the awakening can achieve massive leaps in conscious awareness and learn how to manage humanity's newly unveiled mental, emotional, and intuitive capabilities. Eventually, it will be apparent that all forms of consciousness engaged with 3-D reality are learning extremely valuable, if sometimes volatile, lessons concerning the effects and ramifications of playing with the power of these subtle energies.

All forms of consciousness swim in a sea of subatomic particles that is in constant motion. These particles are differentiated by your conscious mind and selected for use at your discretion. Subatomic particles are actively engaged in building realities because they are in continuous contact with the entire field of existence. As the acceleration progresses and your solar system moves through the new areas of space, you must personally incorporate the new dance of energy these areas provide. Many types of celestial activities will be pivotal in catapulting the collective awareness to new levels of understanding by activating the codes of consciousness for restoring honor, dignity, purpose, and sanctity of life.

How *you use your awareness and your attention will determine the version of the world you create.*

Many conscious life-forms that co-exist with you in the same space, separated only by a barrier of time, are also involved in the transformation. The changes your world is experiencing are actually occurring subatomically, and one could say, with a bit of humor, that you are just along for the ride. As a human being, you experience the changes in 3-D reality, yet as you learn to integrate and incorporate more of this accelerated energy, you will invariably discover that what you are experiencing is also being played out in numerous layers of reality, involving a wide cast of characters. How you use your awareness and your attention will prove to be of utmost importance, for it will determine the version of the world you create. Part of your challenge during the transformation is to ride the wave of the multidimensional acceleration, while learning to manage and direct your own awakening consciousness with clear intent by remaining grounded and empowered in 3-D reality.

One of the most important aspects of the path of empowerment involves uncovering the true history of your planet, for you must understand who you are and where you have come from. While the cosmos is calling on you to participate as a citizen of a greater reality—to open your eyes to your stellar heritage—global controllers and their non-physical puppet masters, playing their part in the game, do their best to steer you away from seeing the truth. Before your incarnation here, you knew of the strange and unusual events that would transpire during the time of accelerated energy, and you came to participate in these life-changing events to make a difference. The old adage of the glass being half-empty or half-full exemplifies what you are facing—for how you interpret what you see unfolding each day, and the choices you make, will determine your experience and energize a probable reality.

A natural part of the awakening process involves dealing with and finding answers to the seemingly endless flood of questions that arise from deep within. Questioning the framework of your personal and collective reality is actually a wise and healthy endeavor, because it unlocks the conditioned mind-set used to exploit your understanding of life on Earth, as well as your place in the scheme of existence. A probing, questing mind always has a tremendous impact on the mass consciousness, and like seeds sown to the wind, there is no telling where your thoughts will land and take root once they are free from restraint. As the pace of life continues to quicken, a vista of reality is being revealed where the truth is indeed far stranger than any fiction ever contrived.

Even though the so-called official versions of reality are now being questioned, many people still harbor the illusion that the opening years of the twenty-first century are on the cutting edge of unprecedented technological achievement, a time and place in history where civilization has reached an apex of progress and sophistication far surpassing anything that has ever transpired. In actuality, history, as it has been taught and recorded, is a massive hoax. Humanity has been conditioned to believe that educational institutions, and especially the sciences, strive to elevate the standard of life through a noble pursuit of new ideas and inventions. Yet this is hardly the case. Most of the life-liberating, worthy discoveries have been selectively hidden from the masses—independent inventors are harassed and harnessed when they explore alternative energy sources; pioneers in the health field are often threatened or killed when they find inexpensive cures for disease; and geologists, journalists, and archeologists are particularly targeted when they present information that runs counter to the "official versions" of reality.

Earth is far more ancient than anyone dare officially proclaim, and for billions of years nature has remained the one constant factor. Modern humans are by no means the most sophisticated race your planet has ever seen, and humankind is not the first intelligent race in the solar system. Mystifying artifacts on Earth and in space tell of ancient civilizations with advanced knowledge far earlier in time than present-day science is willing to admit. There is abundant and intriguing evidence indicating that modern humanity is not at the top of the evolutionary ladder, yet for millennia only certain people have been privy to the secret that a wide variety of intelligent life-forms have always shared Earth along with you.

The controllers of your planet play the game well to make certain that you will not understand the mysteries of Earth.

The evidence of truly grand engineering feats of the past—on Earth, the moon, and Mars—has yet to be revealed to the masses; and for those who work at controlling the truth, the job of hiding the truth is growing exceedingly more stressful due to the acceleration of awareness. The controllers of your planet play the game well by doing their best to make certain that you will not understand the mysteries of Earth. For millennia they have succeeded in creating chaos in order to distract everyone from understanding and integrating the layers of lessons and the important achievements, the dramas of life and death, and the opportunities for spiritual growth that are the legacy of every civilization.

Earth also has a long and well-known history of tremendous geological upheavals in response to great stress on the natural environment. Even though there is no official recognition of prior intelligent life on Earth, many archaeological discoveries point to the existence of very ancient and advanced civilizations that were destroyed and wiped from the surface, leaving only bits and pieces of their once-thriving cultures. Myths and legends are a collective symbology used to convey much larger relevant truths. Stories from various world cultures refer to creator gods who were engaged in epic struggles between the forces of good and evil. In days long gone, civilizations of old misused the keys of higher knowledge in their development of advanced technologies. Due to their reckless disregard, extreme hubris, and exuberant foolishness, many of them experienced vast disruptions in the stability of Earth's ecosystem. At times, in the blink of an eye, entire civilizations disappeared as their reality buckled, lost shape, and collapsed.

Such mind-boggling events induced a state of global shock, creating severe trauma, amnesia, and dissociation among both the living and the discarnate. There were always some survivors who felt compelled to explore the haunting wisps of memory from past events. Over time, a few people would eventually integrate their memories of the disasters by daring to delve past the barriers that the mind naturally builds in response to severe trauma. Through great perseverance they breached the mind's walls to recall the painful traumas that were stored in their cells as unresolved memories. By undertaking this difficult task, they relived the wisdom and folly of their ancestral selves; as the teachings and lessons of very ancient times were remembered, they were filled with awe and their understanding of life was renewed.

The people of old and the survivors of the great cataclysms shared their knowledge of the Earth through oral teachings—

spoken word, poems, songs, and epic ballads were more than mere entertainment. Many people were fully aware that a multidimensional sharing of reality was an ongoing and compelling aspect of life on Earth, and their tales emphasized the importance of understanding and recognizing the deeds of the wide stratification of intelligent life with which they shared time and space. Millions, even billions, of years ago, intelligent life-forms were observing Earth from their palaces in the sky—their celestial homes appeared as small mobile moons slowly orbiting Earth and maintaining constant surveillance. At various times, intelligent life lived far, far, far beneath the surface of Earth, and sometimes entire civilizations chose to live underground, hiding from beings who roamed the heavens to hunt them down.

Nature is a symbol for a system that sustains your identity in cooperation with celestial activities that provide meaning to earthly existence.

Everything is a symbol for a certain expression of energy, and symbols are as prolific in the field of existence as insects are on Earth. Nature is a symbol for a system that supports and sustains your identity, and does so in cooperation with celestial activities that continuously provide structure and meaning to earthly existence. In order to wake up and accept your personal power, you must be willing to emerge from denial and activate psychic sensitivities to discern truth from deceit. The storm of chaos that is disturbing your world is a symbol of your own awakening consciousness. In the past, humans collectively chose to close down their psychic intuition, and now they are paying the full price of this self-imposed ignorance. On Earth, the divinity of nature presides at the core of all life, and a sense of its precise planning and impeccable order can be easily recognized by the mathematical eloquence embedded in nature's designs. Far earlier than the last massive global upheavals almost twelve thousand years ago, people lived with respect for nature's order and used it to further their understanding of her mystical technology. At various times throughout the ages, Earth was honored as an ancestor of creation, and when she was recognized as a living being, her conscious awareness of all that transpired within and beyond her domain was shared with her numerous inhabitants. The most important aspect of this shared knowledge was that the precision of nature connected the smallest part to the grandest of cosmic schemes.

There was a time when secret societies were established for the guardianship of important ancient knowledge. These organizations were originally well intentioned in their shared belief that preserving the knowledge of the past would be of tremendous value for the future. These societies felt that when people healed from the severe trauma of global catastrophe, they would be more fully capable of grasping the full and vast complexities of their legacy. The responsibility of caretaking secret information is a daunting task, and over time and through many tests of character, the guardians of ancient knowledge lost their way. Misusing their power, many of them became obsessed with hoarding, controlling, and withholding essential information from the masses. Repeating another cycle, and another version of the game of life on Earth, most people abdicated their higher abilities to remember and to heal, and chose instead to live in fear with their self-imposed ignorance. The keepers of ancient information eventually became the ruling elite, who used what they safeguarded for their own means. By exerting control from behind the scenes, they distorted the truth by destroying or removing evidence of past civilizations. In time, various secret societies united in a conspiracy of silence and branched out into every arena of world culture to exert their covert influence on the patterns of progress. As deceit became their norm, they attracted non-physical energies of a very manipulative nature who began to manipulate the secret societies.

In modern times the most valued tales of old—those that regaled the rise and fall of many a unique civilization—have been gathered into the dustbins of myth and legend. Throughout the past six thousand years, history was completely rewritten; events from the past were purposely changed, edited, homogenized, or even deleted from the records. Occasionally, important knowledge was encrypted within certain texts to preserve a truth that was known only to a select few. Most often, however, the chroniclers of history were instructed by authority figures to embroider the records with falsehoods, and only allude to the truth through allegory and metaphor. Today, with the pressure from the increasingly intense cosmic energies and the resulting rapid exchange of new ideas, these layers and layers of deception can no longer hold; they are flaking off and peeling away, like old coats of paint, revealing what has long been undercover.

Military organizations are an example of highly compartmentalized secret societies, and those at the very top of the chain of command have a long history of applying ancient esoteric information and magical practices as standard operating procedures. Military organizations know the secrets of the land, sea, and sky, because their forces are always called upon to secure areas where unusual phenomena occur. And modern military campaigns rely on satellite technology for providing the latest surveillance for activities beneath the Earth, on the Earth's surface, and in the heavens. Conducting a war has often been used as a cover for entering an area to plunder and destroy, or to steal records of the past, and to traumatize a people into forgetfulness. Wiping out history is standard military procedure.

Deep emotional experiences through the exploration of memory can open the doors to a unique state of awareness, expanding the mind to the presence of a greater innate intelligence. However, when both memories and emotional intelligence are suppressed, the ability to link up to the higher mind is shut down, and in the absence of emotional morality, countless petty reasons for war can be devised. The rationale for war has always been based on the belief that "right is might," and because so many people still carry ancient unclaimed memories of severe trauma in their genes, they cannot remember the past and are therefore easily swayed by propaganda.

War instigates unhealthy social chaos; it releases emotional repression based on feelings of victimhood and disempowerment.

War instigates unhealthy social chaos, because it releases long-term emotional repression based on feelings of victimhood and disempowerment. Violence and hostility create the very intense negative energies of fear, and when the frequency of fear runs rampant, the whole Earth feels the collective stress. War has been used to entice humans into the practice of ritual sacrifice—with the Earth herself serving as the holy altar. Time and again people have been called forth to leave their homes to fight and even die, shedding their blood for the official noble cause of a nation or a religion. Thousands of years of conditioning have instilled the belief that it is an honor to die for your country or your god. The furious turmoil of war is not constrained in time; it can explode into other dimensions with devastating force. The death and destruction of war have often been secretly used as an offering to the gods of old, as a blood sacrifice to beings of other dimensions who are drawn here by their attraction to the pain-ridden chaos that wars serve to create.

Throughout time, violence and bloodshed have attracted many beings who require the dark energies of pain and confusion to hold liege over those humans controlling the planet. In the game, the dark forces play their parts well and are too powerful to be destroyed; they must be met and transformed through compassionate understanding of their purpose. From a larger vista of understanding, it takes a highly evolved being to take on the role of evil so as not to become indefinitely entrapped in the character. The controllers are actually important players in the game of freedom; they rule by psychological and spiritual manipulation because humanity refuses to confront its collective fear of remembering the past. Even with their power over humanity, the controllers are lonely and lacking in truth and trust. And the risk of entrapment remains ever present.

Symbols are tools for describing the abstract—to help your mind grasp the ungraspable, to anchor meaning into your reality. As the inner world is a reflection of the outer, what does war symbolize? Even though acts of war are rewarded, the history and agenda of war on Earth are always a battle over thinking that "there is not enough" land, food, fuel, or gold. Earth has been used as a portal and testing ground for war; many beings are here on your planet to overcome their tendency to rape, torture, kill, and conquer to feel more powerful. This lesson is not localized to Earth, and the destruction of life is an issue that various forms of consciousness play out as part of the game of existence; and you have the free will to do the same or decline. And every once in a while, when the field of existence is off balance, the system accelerates a bit and "rights itself." Part of humanity's learning curve involves understanding the pain and destruction of war, and choosing to rise above it as a form of emotional expression. No one wins in war; it rips families apart and creates an endless loop of violence that is etched in the DNA. In a world with unlimited funds for war, women make babies and raise them for the battlefield. How can success or purpose in life be based on rape, killing, pillage, and destruction? War is poison to the spirit, and the game of awareness calls upon humanity to consciously recognize the futility of war and to lay to rest this particular form of emotional expression.

People of the Earth must wake up rather than support the fraudulent intentions of all acts of war.

Threats of war and the creation of enemies serve to keep the masses under control by falsely arousing fearful emotions. Humanity's challenge is to understand the effects of war through time and the gridlocking trauma that has ensued. You must learn to recognize the patterns and symbols that define your reality, and intuit a new understanding behind their apparent meaning. Remember, symbols are a sign, a manifestation, and an expression of energy; do not get so attached to the symbols that you miss their greater teaching. People of the Earth must wake up rather than support the fraudulent intentions of all acts of war. There are only a few who want to kill, a few who are obsessed with destroying others. There are many who want the Earth to live and thrive. Will the many or the few control the world? Will the many create the world they want, or will the few succeed with their desperate, despotic game plans to separate humanity and destroy life? At the end of the day, through their audacious acts and assaults on life, the few may well succeed in waking up the many to the value of freedom, the power of the mind, and the endurance of the spirit.

When an individual encounters shocking events, the mind instantly perceives the trauma, and a natural self-protecting process of dissociation occurs. The normal state of conscious awareness often moves off to the side, shocked, shattered, and incapable of integrating and making sense of the new reality. Simultaneously, an alternate personality is naturally created— one that will hold and contain the trauma. When the trauma is handled in a sustaining, loving way, based on understanding the event, a bridge is built in the mind between the separate personality compartments; eventually the trauma can be integrated into the conscious system of beliefs and experiences. If the trauma is repeated, either through personal experience or mediated exploitation, the state of dissociation grows; the greater the trauma, the greater the separation between the alternate and core personalities. It is also very important to understand that the body-mind complex is highly programmable in a dissociated, traumatized state. In the face of such trauma, a person's consciousness vacates his or her body and is very reluctant to return. When you are disconnected from your conscious will, you become an unwitting participant in behavior-modifying manipulations. A purposefully designed reality of fear and chaos distracts your attention away from the massive spiritual awakening that defines these times. The trauma state has its gifts, and it can be integrated through honest discussion, touch, love, good food, and conscious intent to understand the reason "why." Questioning is the difficult part, and as the "whys" grow, this is an excellent sign of personal empowerment.

When the lessons of the past are ignored, history repeats itself, playing out age-old dramas with maddening exactitude, only in different eras of time. Everyone involved in war is traumatized when savage brutality overtakes the lives of even the most stable humans. Dissociation, or the separation of consciousness, is the inevitable result of trauma, and traumatized people often take lifelong vacations from their conscious awareness because of a deep reluctance to integrate their shockingly painful memories. Dissociative people can experience missing pieces of time, having no idea what comes over them. Trauma comes in many shapes and sizes, and basically stems from encountering versions of reality that shock the senses. Trauma also ripples through the dimensions, and there are many restless, wandering spirits in need of being laid to rest. Extensive healing by both physical and non-physical beings continues to lift up the dissociated spirits of those who died in tragic events. Many are returned to a place where they can understand their participation in traumatic events from a larger vista of awareness. Traumatic events jolt the mass psyche into super-sensitive states of consciousness. Trauma can trigger supreme psychic abilities, where a connection with the higher realms becomes a self-empowering tool for dealing with and resolving feelings of being stuck in the limiting realms of fear.

Many people never fully realize the disinformation that steers them away from seeing the bigger picture of reality.

Deception is an old tool that is only effective because you choose denial rather than facing the implications of what is obvious. Awareness is an all-empowering tool for recognizing the failure to acknowledge ignorance. You must learn to trust your feelings, as well as your intuition, and then you will know when a truth or a falsehood is presented. Unfortunately, many people never fully realize the disinformation that steers them away from seeing the bigger picture of reality. How far must the lies and deceit proceed until humanity is willing to relinquish its denial? To understand Earth, you must journey into the depths of your inner being, where you can reclaim your sensibilities from patterns tucked away in the ancient code of your DNA. Never underestimate your own personal power to change the world, for as you emerge from denial, your probable choices dramatically increase. Remember to always ask yourself: Why did I create this? What are my lessons, the gifts of opportunity, and what can I learn from them?

Our intent is to convey layers of information that will trigger memories stored deep inside of you. Your cells are always exchanging information, with the cosmos and with the Earth, throughout layers of time. We ask you to open yourself to explore Earth's mysteries. A substantial portion of the civilized world appears to be rapidly racing toward doom by investing in beliefs of immense falsehoods. Earth is always alert and ever aware, and works in great cooperation with the thought-forms—the ideas and feelings—that she receives. It is most important to have respect for yourself and respect for Earth, and even if you do not understand her many mysteries, spend time with her and she will reveal them to you. No matter what you think is occurring, many more layers of purpose are always involved. Your greatest gift to the human legacy is the achievement of an open, questing mind, which is at home with the rapid reconsideration of reality steadily redefining the course of human experience.

The technique of producing mass trauma to control people has been used time and time again. The fraudulent creation of an enemy is an old ploy used to foster fear and to intentionally create instability in order to divide and conquer the natural brilliance that resides in each human being. Humankind is fast awakening to the challenging test of questioning the purpose of existence, and in many ways the traumas and dramas that fill your world open the fast track to higher consciousness. When faced with chaos, turmoil, and sudden, shocking, and surprising change, the core of an individual's spiritual essence advances. It is well known that humans are invested with an indomitable spirit; that under auspicious circumstances, it can be called forth to birth brilliant and remarkable accomplishments. Your spiritual brilliance is based upon a supreme cooperation with all of existence. You are birthed from spirit, seeking to explore this reality during a time when the dark veil of ignorance is being lifted—and this is no easy task. You are to be acknowledged as a creator. All actions and the resulting events stem from a cooperation that involves many levels of reality, and recognizing that you are multilayered and multidimensional is the core challenge to living your destiny.

World managers have long understood that the human spirit is powerful and complex, basically creative and peace loving. Wars and violence must therefore be instigated through human agents, who are often possessed by non-physical entities of a cunning and bloodthirsty nature. In other realms of existence, the invisible, emotional frequencies that you so readily provide are read, felt, and understood. These frequencies can also be used in many capacities. In your world, you look at books and the written word as objects of information; however, from other avenues of reality, frequencies play a primary role and are seen as a tool of consciousness with form and purpose. When extreme fear is created en masse, the vibration is like a multitude of atomic detonations traveling into the various levels and layers of alternate realities. Unfortunately, there are others who feed on the frequency of your fear and use its production to control you.

There has long been a plan by nefarious world controllers to herd the attention of all humanity into one probable line of time. Remember, when you abdicate your role of responsibility in creating your life, you create others who will control it for you. The deceitful mechanizations behind the events of 9/11 are an example of a classic ritual working of dark magic as an attempt to control and manage time—to distort it, to make a trap, and to lead as many people as possible through the portal of fear by means of planned media programming. Events can always be orchestrated; however, the outcome cannot be predetermined, for the uncertainty principle reigns, and in any moment the freedom to choose prevails.

All around the globe people are pressed to consciously create their reality and anchor the energy of self-responsibility onto the planet.

You are in a severe test to learn how to manage your energy. Will you buy fear? Will you believe what you are told in every newspaper? Or will you pursue the quest to question by trusting yourself and trusting your intuition? All around the globe people are pressed to think for themselves, to believe in themselves, to consciously create their reality and anchor the energy of self-responsibility and self-respectability onto the planet. The awakening is not about good against evil, or light against dark; it embodies a fine cooperation of good and evil and light and dark, playing with the energies of your world with infinite patience in order for you to learn. Each person on Earth had prior knowledge of this era and chose to be alive for this momentous, unprecedented, and profound spiritual awakening. The risks are high where consciousness moves from density to light, where matter is spiritualized, and where it is said that the human spirit arises to instigate a majestic ripple of inspiration and healing, which will ultimately transmit the frequency of heightened spiritual achievement throughout all of the corridors of time.

Many attempts will be made by various physical and non-physical beings to control and lock time in order to create fewer probable choices. The media plays out this control every day by producing the same fearful imagery and distorted ideas, intentionally programming your beliefs. You must learn to think for yourself. You are challenged to recognize the programming of fear that is designed to break down individual psychological and spiritual strength—to render you helpless and hopelessly confused. Look around. The choice is in front of you. The seasons change and so can you. Be receptive to the truth; you must have the faith to believe that you are the director of your experience, and if you really pay attention, you will see that your world is safe by your own creation. You must have the courage to see a bigger picture of reality and anchor in new solutions.

When you really believe in yourself, you will know that the frequency you broadcast is growing more powerful than any of the signals that antennas and satellites exude. Machinery cannot surpass the power of your innate biology, and you will learn to realize this great truth by exploring the deep nuances of who you really are. The great irony is that events of a traumatic and tragic nature often bring forth the best of the human spirit. Trauma is a many-faceted tool, and given that the game of awakening occurs in many realities, many intentions set the stage. You agree to be part of what you experience. Individual and collective dream states explore the various dramas and probabilities and offer the opportunity to work out reality before it happens. You always have a choice. If you seek to understand the many spiritual opportunities resulting from the events of the nanosecond, your consciousness will grow in awareness as will your spirit grow in confidence.

You must believe in the peaceful stability that you can provide for an awakening world through the intervention of compassionate benevolence in all lives and probabilities. Evil plays an important role, and you must learn to recognize it. Too often those in positions of the greatest trust point their fingers at evil, yet in actuality they are really pointing to themselves. Many of your heroes and leaders will fall from grace as part of a necessary collapse of power, for all that is rotten and decayed will crumble. Betrayal and desperation are all around you, and so are honesty and love. Turn your attention to the purpose of your heightened sensitivities and know the truth when you feel it. You must be willing to cherish and protect your children. Children will adjust according to their own personalities, based on the truth that you share with them and the realities that you model. They may either relate or rebel against what you are modeling. Our advice is to always be truthful with your children, to explain to them in simple terms what is transpiring, and allow them to make their own choices about how to interpret it. Instill them with confidence that you are there for them. Give your children truth, love, responsibility, and rules; they need boundaries and guidelines. A bit of telepathy now and again can work wonders to get your intentions across. And, let them know that you trust them and that they can trust you. Every parent is building a citizen for the world's future—which world are you preparing your children for?

We come through time to be here, to support you, respect you, and learn from you. Our intent is to explain the events of your world from another point of view, to bring you truth with grace. And even though some of these truths may be hard truths, they are worthy of consideration. We are multidimensional personalities; we exist in your world, and ours, and many others as well. We can communicate and operate with various degrees of success in these different arenas, and we model for you your own multidimensional destiny. You are becoming multidimensional in awareness and each day of these fleeting twenty-five years draws you closer to the truth of your identity. What you do in the here and now affects an ancient karmic drama, one that has been stuck on repeat mode, playing again and again through the great cycles of existence. The same old trauma drama involves managed fear and violence purposefully told and sold with layers of lies. And for those who are able to see, those whose job it is to explain and explore and question in order to uplift humankind, the truth is easy to recognize. We will hold out, dear friend, for the world where a peaceful and sustaining probability is created. Our question is, will you?

You must learn to value the dynamics of creation rather than fall prey to the mind-management projects that characterize these times.

There may be some hard realizations along the road ahead, as well as a few great miracles of intervention. Even some actors of evil may be retiring their roles in an epiphany, a new realization that their part in the secrets of hurting and hiding is no longer required. These times are astounding—riveting, pivotal, and outrageously filled with the opportunity of many lifetimes—and the greatest challenge you have is to eradicate fear from the planet. The fear-based vibrations from the human drama trauma have been sustaining non-physical entities for eons. You must learn to value the dynamics of creation rather than fall prey to the mind-management projects that characterize these times. With this in mind, focus your intent and connect your heart to the Pleiades, then to the Galactic Center, and then to the core of Earth, and transmit the frequency of love. Even though you are a vibrating being of energy spanning many realities, you are primarily focused in the here and now to learn and grow and make a difference. Our intention is to open the door to a new probability, yet we cannot create your reality—only you can create your world. We offer ideas just as your newscasters do, and it is up to you to choose what to believe: doom and gloom, or a safe, sustainable, and self-created world where the cooperation of the multiverse awaits your attention.

Your journey on Earth is part of your spiritual legacy, for death does not destroy consciousness—you continue to learn and grow and experience life in numerous cycles of time. Part of living involves knowing how to die; you can learn to intentionally walk through your fear of the unknown and to use your will and intent to ride your consciousness into another reality, graciously leaving behind your physical form. Death is part of life. It is not a random act; it is rather a timely agreement, and you have more power over your life and death than you realize. You must learn to interpret your reality from a multidimensional vista that is imbued with purpose and intention; otherwise you will be drawn into scenarios of disempowerment such as war, famine, illness, or any of the other magical ways you choose to limit yourself. The choice everyone faces comes down to the selection of the frequency of fear or the frequency of love; love is the fuel, and your greatest gift to the world is your version of the love frequency.

When you seek self-empowerment, you truly begin to live. It is wise to remember that you are here for reasons that will continue to be revealed, and just because you cannot see something does not mean it does not exist. Electricity, radio waves, microwaves, cosmic radiation, thought-forms, and beings from other realities oftentimes exert strong influence on your life without you being the slightest bit aware. It takes courage to live in these times. It takes confidence, stamina, stability, and most definitely the love of self and the understanding that you chose to be here for very good reasons. We ask you to make a difference, to contribute all that you can by consciously creating thoughts that will fortify and empower you to catch and ride the waves of new potential. Remember, choosing to take a risk is an essential aspect of living a life of freedom.

To sleep and dream is to live. The dream state is pliable and flexible; learn to use it in a more creative and empowering manner. Before you go to sleep, make clear intentions for what you want to create or resolve in the outer world of physical matter. Intend to dream about whatever it is that you really want to manifest. Even though you may not remember your dreams, you can certainly dream with the intent of creating harmonious resolution to all of your challenges. Sleep is necessary, and when sleep and dreams are disturbed for prolonged periods of time, you slide into a state of dullness, and with this loss of creativity, you are easily controlled. Sleep deprivation has long been used as a tool for mind control. You literally learn about physical reality from the dream state as you dream yourself into being. Use the tools at hand to empower your reality—you have great freedom in the dream state to test out events, and to check out various probable choices and outcomes for all events in the waking world.

Civilization is based on an agreement, and in this time you are called upon to offer your visions of harmony and cooperation to the world.

You are here to experience delight in what life has to offer, to contribute your unique ideas to the world and to bring forth personal excellence. Civilization is based on an agreement, and in this time of crossing the bridge from one world to another, you are called upon to offer your visions of harmony and cooperation to the world at large. Strive for noble values and live with honorable intentions. Power is always a test of character; so empower yourself with questions. Be responsible and accept responsibility for your life, for this is the greatest contribution you can make to your civilization. Your response to any event or situation determines the outcome. You must allow yourself the inherent luxury of loving yourself by opening your heart and feeling gratitude for all you have created. In a sense, you must count your gifts and read the signs that are revealing the transformation of your consciousness.

The very best way to deal with these times of accelerated energies is to get grounded and stable. Eliminate any distractions that are signs of escape and denial, and for stability of your attention, empty and clear your mind, then observe. You must be present and in your body in order to expand your capabilities, and you can begin by picturing all states of consciousness uniting in harmony as you create a frequency composed of your heart's desire to live in a safe, consciously inspired world. You must learn to live with the times, to adapt and to adjust your attitude by intending your path and proceeding with confidence and trust. You must identify destructive thinking and then change it. Fear destroys the imagination and numbs the body. You are here to restore peace and dignity to the human race, so you must value the homeland of your spirit by valuing both your inner and outer realities. True security stems from trust and confidence as well as from a strong and solid inner foundation of resolve, which is based on an emotional and spiritual understanding of life. Your inner security is your security in the outer world.

The frequency of heart chakra love creates the space for joyful and safe, uplifting changes to occur. A calm, confident, and relaxed outlook goes a very long way toward creating solutions. When worry and tension are absent from your electromagnetic vibration, you can pass through any crisis with ease. Holding on to tension is like building a fortress around your mind, and when you create blockages, you close off your range of motion on many levels of reality. The life-enhancing solar energies and the vital force of cosmic radiation will not connect with your inner communication centers if you close down or collapse your energy field through fear. You must choose to recognize and then dispel your fears and develop the frequencies that will boost your mind into a more vigorous and awakened state by creating balance in your life. Use the power and beauty of nature, for they are natural remedies for a restless or troubled mind. An overexposure to electronic images and the printed word has suppressed the full capabilities of human imagination, and returning to nature will rebalance and restore your innate sense of self.

Nature will not become obsolete by a scientific fanaticism bent on capturing the souls of people and transforming them into robotic, electronic beings.

The sight and scent of flowers and the busy sound of buzzing bees and chirping birds will adjust your brain wave frequencies and balance your right and left hemispheres so that you are in synchronization with the cosmic mind. Nature will not become obsolete or outdone by a scientific fanaticism bent upon capturing the souls and spirits of people and transforming them into robotic, electronic beings. A reality built on the misuse of energy cannot sustain itself. Civilizations evolve and grow from the ideas that are fed into them, and you are a highly creative being free to build any version of the world you want. The energies and events of your current era bring about changes and challenges that confront you with your innermost truths, truths that make you claim who you really are. You are a powerful being in the midst of changes that will bring out the best in the human spirit, and by changing the way you think of yourself, you will change the world.

It is of the utmost importance for humanity to realize the ramifications of war. This is an old issue that follows you through time awaiting your enlightenment. Not only is war an unnecessary act, it is an abomination to your spiritual evolution and perpetuates another tedious round of living and dying with a fear of the truth. Everything is built first in the mind. Peace is the solution, and peace now begins within. In order to have a world at peace, the people of the world must really desire peace and be willing to make the vibrations necessary to create it. A few can control the many; however, it takes more than just a few to fix the masses. Your thoughts and intentions are greatly amplified when joined with others. To have an impact on your country and community that establishes world peace now, join with a group of like-minded individuals each month at the new moon, the traditional time for planting and seeding reality. Customize your own respectful ceremonies and concentrate your energy and intentions for peace now. The forces of nature will feel your intentions as they ripple along the ley lines, the subtle energy paths that run across the surface of the Earth.

People once felt a kinship with nature and practiced their own natural magic, with telepathy and dreaming as their primary tools. You must learn a new level of respect for the power of your intentions to condition and objectify the space around you. You must wake up to the exquisite value of life. There are only a few who want to kill, a few who are obsessed with destroying the people of Earth. There are many who want Earth, her people, and her creatures to live and thrive. A world of war must invest time, intention, attention, and energy to manifest an environment ripe for destruction. A safe world is also an investment of energy and intent. Each person makes the choice. Knowing what you know and watching others make their choices will be one of the most difficult aspects of the transformation. You are here to participate, and you are also here to watch and witness all that transpires. How you process your emotions and the quality of the symphonies that you play on your two-mile-long piano will determine the codes you are eventually able to release when you entrain with incoming energies.

As energy continues to accelerate, and billions of people awaken from their slumber, the choice must be made by everyone to take a stand on the value of life. Recent readings of environmental indicators show that certain ecological factors that have been stable for the past half-million years have changed rapidly in just a few decades. The looming issue of planetary ecological disaster is a direct reflection of the state of human consciousness. The outer world mirrors the inner domain; you are the environment, and therefore you must evolve your awareness and value yourself, Earth, and your place in the multiverse. You are here on Earth to heal the wounds of trauma, fear, and separation that have accumulated in the human gene pool over the past five hundred thousand years.

As computers speed up and perform more functions by handling more data per second, they actually mimic neurological, cellular, and genetic developments simultaneously occurring within humankind. A blossoming is taking place in the minds and hearts of humanity, and you are called upon to recognize your place in the great scheme of creation by expanding your awareness and exploring the unusual and unlimited spiritual opportunities that distinguish these times. Your contributions are required. Establish a firm and clear foundation of moral excellence, and strive for the highest of ethical principles and virtues. You can make a worthwhile contribution to the planet by opening your heart and mind and using your inherent gifts to create a safe, loving, and peaceful world, where all life is valued and treasured. Every act of kindness and consideration changes and enhances the course of life, so live with a deeper passion for who you are and accord yourself and others the respect you all deserve.

An integrated, well-balanced mind vibrates at a frequency that is immune to negative influences.

The cosmic mind is built on a generosity that allows you to choose the experience of creation or destruction, integration or fragmentation. Creator or victim, the choice is yours. A benevolent higher power supports and sustains your world; it is a nameless source of energy that requires no worship or sacrifice or killing to share its power with you. A much larger plan is unfolding in the cosmos, and the seeds have been planted by everyone on Earth. Even though your human brain wave technology is naturally equipped for enhanced awareness, you must choose to use it. An integrated, well-balanced mind vibrates at a frequency that is immune to negative influences. The purveyors of tyranny play a noteworthy role in the game; they are shaking your reality to its core and gifting you with a loud wake-up call. By threatening your security and survival, the empire of the day acts as a stimulus to compel you to create new frequencies of self-empowerment. A new civil disobedience is steadily stirring the realm of the human mind, and being that necessity is the mother of invention, the results of this great awakening can catapult the human spirit into the vast and gracious horizons of compassion, creativity, and illustrious spiritual growth. Once again the choice is yours.

The more you choose the staple of spiritual power, the greater your contribution is toward stabilizing the planet. The purpose of our intersection with your reality is to direct you toward your own internal power, a force that has been overshadowed, ignored, distrusted, imprisoned, and even faulted for being evil. Your inner power exists as an inalienable right of consciousness; it is a tool for living and affecting the world you encounter. Any spiritual awakening is challenging because a reinterpretation of reality is always involved. You must summon your courage in order to emerge from denial, for only then will you know and realize how inner-connected you are. As you take charge of your life energies, consider the following proclamation with great care, for these words exemplify the concept of conditioning your life with an attitude of cultivated trust:

"I am a creator. I am here to create a safe and bountiful life. By vibration and frequency, I choose to be healthy, productive, and wise. I have great gratitude for my abilities to recognize that thoughts produce frequencies, and I can create a frequency that supports the safe, probable world I live in by directing my energy toward what I want to experience. I walk through life with clear, conscious intent to weave my energy, like a gossamer thread in a large and beautiful tapestry, throughout the world I encounter. I fully realize that a multitude of probabilities and belief systems exist side by side with mine. And in mine I am safe. In mine I am guided. In mine I love and trust my body. In mine I know my cells are precognitive and that I am a co-creator of the multiverse. I know I am a valuable being. I know that I will receive the impulses, the signs and signals and guidance that I require to always be in the right place at the right time, for my highest good and that of all those around me. All this I know, and for this I am most grateful."

By availing yourself of a greater sense of personal power, you will discover the exalted state of all power, which is the power to heal. Your greatest realizations to be carried over from this life into the next will invariably be about the healing power of love. In all its many splendors, the exultation of love is the ability to see the point, purpose, and significance of life's events, to willingly transcend and release old, worn-out patterns of perceptions and the beliefs that lock them in place. Once you come to a true understanding of the power of love, you can safely venture into areas of both physical and non-physical reality in need of cleansing and healing. Throughout the globe, areas that are dank and decayed and in need of rehabilitation are symbols of energy mirroring the inner world of feelings and beliefs, those areas within the genes that carry ancestral wounds of victimhood and despair. The cycle of consciousness involved in this healing along the lines of time encompasses the past half a million years in your terms, a time when an influx of energy changed the game plan of Earth. The game itself is an ancient cooperative venture, played to express a living art form of creativity; and as games and good dramas are enacted, antagonists and protagonists can be relied upon to provide plenty of mischievous action.

*O*nce you see a bigger picture of reality, you can release the feelings of powerlessness that hold you and your genetic line captive.

Many of your ancestors developed and used their abilities to see beyond the linear assumptions that modern people embrace as the only interpretation of time and space. Time is simultaneous, and many forms of intelligence view your "now" and interact with you and your world by focusing their attention in your direction. They are attracted to the nanosecond because times of accelerated energy hold the opportunity for the frequencies of disempowerment to be healed. Experiences can be reinterpreted and understood from a viewpoint outside of time, and once you really grasp that you are a multidimensional creator, you will see that there is a point and purpose to life that ripples far beyond the current era. Once you are able to open to this knowledge, your new wisdom will bring out the best of your abilities. And, once you are able to see a bigger picture of reality, you can release the rigid thought-forms of victimhood and the feelings of powerlessness that hold you and your genetic line captive.

Your ancestors are also in the game playing from their own perspective, and many of them are in deep accord with your desire to expand your awareness into the realms of other realities. Many dimensions of consciousness are connecting to work together to free the human spirit. When the focus of your energy is mentally alert and trustingly heartfelt, great balance is established within your field. Even though living in trust requires a major shift in consciousness, you know that even seeming adversity offers opportunity to grow in spiritual awareness. And when you develop deep gratitude for life, then you really move forward in the game.

You will also realize that through you, others play the game as well. We have come to Earth to play the game that is played throughout existence. As time unfolds and the plot thickens, the importance of each player will become more apparent. Eventually everyone may take a bow of acknowledgment for participating in the nanosecond, and for giving a stupendously memorable performance. Within the game the greatest victory and ultimate achievement is to feel the power of love within all creations by transcending fear without annihilating its purpose. To immerse yourself in physicality and to explore the depths of emotions; to at times feel wounded and powerless, and then to emerge from these feelings and engage your consciousness and see the point and purpose to the patterns of life; to recognize and apply your power to change reality—now that is playing the game!

At the dawn of the third millennium your place in the multiverse is still a great mystery. The choice to create a probability that is sustaining to your growth as a spiritual being is ever present and always awaiting your selection. To consciously create what you want, remember to relax, focus your attention on your intentions, and trust in your inner power. If you can remember to apply this teaching: intention, expectation, action, and results, you will be thought of many years hence as a pioneer of the third millennium—a pioneer of the power of love, a pioneer of consciousness, and ultimately as a pioneer of the people. In your era, your time on Earth is not about the building of massive monuments for posterity to ponder. The potential of your civilization's greatness lies with something much more ephemeral and esoteric; it has to do with using your mind to build frequencies of awareness that will dismantle the shroud of ignorance that controls humanity.

You are one human family desperately in need of peacemakers who have reverence for the sanctity of life.

You are one human family desperately in need of peace-makers who have reverence for the sanctity of life. Each thought and feeling carries its own unique vibrational signature, and to liberate yourself by exploring the depths of your emotional intelligence is an act that requires great courage and compassion. You are challenged to reconsider the story of Earth by elevating yourself out of ignorance, and by uniting with the people of Earth as they awaken from a long, solemn slumber. Peacefully applying your emotional intelligence toward respecting the intelligence of Earth, and accepting responsibility for becoming fully informed of humanity's legacy, are now of the utmost priority.

The awakening of conscious awareness is unstoppable. You must value the life you are living; you are highly adaptable and well prepared on many levels of reality to deal with your chosen probabilities. You must gather the courage to believe in your inner strength. Pay attention and focus your attention, and your mind, body, and the subatomic levels of your being will start to gather new intelligence. Remember the sounds, sights, and scents of nature create hemispheric balance between the right and left sides of the brain, allowing you to tune in to what is occurring with greater precision and clarity. When you balance your body, you can integrate the new fields of energy that carry codes of consciousness for navigating this huge transformation. You are here to restore dignity and full operability to the code-reading device that you call the human body. With everything speeding up, we remind you once again that everything is a dance of energy, a swirling sea of subatomic particles that can be differentiated to become symbols of energy used to qualify the field for creative expression. At whatever level you are playing this game, it is about learning how to swim in symbols used to explain, explore, and differentiate the field of existence in cooperation with other versions and interpretations of reality. And your species' development involves direct learning through your experience of nature. Ultimately, you are responsible for what you create.

When people pay more attention to nature and care for the Earth rather than obsessing on war and financial portfolios, you will know the transition to greater awareness has truly taken hold. The land must be loved into vitality, and nature must be recognized and cherished as an intelligently designed interactive system of information that connects you to layers upon layers of multidimensional realities. The use of poisons, explosives, and harmful frequencies to destroy what you do not understand is another stage of denial that disavows the inherent meaning of life. Plants and creatures are very cooperative once you learn to focus your attention and communicate with them.

Spend more of your time in nature; turn off the air-conditioning and open the windows, notice how the creatures keep the energy moving with their bustling activities. Immerse yourself in the sounds, sights, scents, and tastes that nature offers. Take long walks, sleep on the ground for a change, and gather with friends and loved ones to watch the stars. Slow down and sit with the trees, spend leisurely afternoons in the meadows or by the sea, climb mountains to meet the rarefied energies, swim in the waters, and savor the sweet sensations of nature's intelligence. Use your attention to focus on the dance of subtle energy; remember, when you do not focus your attention with your own volition, others will grab it for a roller-coaster ride through their own versions of reality. Each year the summer solstice sun takes you to the peak of perceptual attunement. Tune in by paying attention and then placing your attention in nature; new energy is coming in and you certainly do not want to miss the latest news from the sun! Use your power to create a safe and nurturing version of reality, calling forth a civilization that readily accepts responsibility for the spiritual duty to uphold the standards of decency.

Intend to keep yourself healthy, wealthy, and wise; be rested and rejuvenated, relaxed and personally responsible for your own well-being. The power to live well and prosper is yours for creating, so plant the seeds of heightened intelligence, creativity, courage, and gracious change in the garden of your mind. And when you feel your ancestors stirring in your blood, when propensities and programs of old that need healing appear in your reality, in dreams or musings, remember why you are here. Remember your decision to heal, and use your will and your clear intent to understand with compassion the perceptions and experiences that have been passed on to you. Respect other people's right to carry the pain they choose in order to find the truth of their sorrow. Every experience is based on a choice with a distinct purpose. This acknowledgment can set many, many beings free because it is judgment and fear that create the chains that bind you. And if you can understand that fears are for you to deal with and to heal, then the story of the nanosecond will later be told as a momentous mindful victory. Look to the magic of these times by understanding the history of your world in a new light. Question and question again, and then pay attention to see what patterns of behavior and beliefs come forward. And when you encounter a challenge that appears to be more than you can solve, turn your problem over to a higher power. And ask for guidance; ask for all the assistance you require. The cosmic mind sees and knows the way to many solutions, and when you acknowledge this aspect of your reality, you fling open the gates to the inner worlds of the higher mind.

Humanity is preparing to redefine the invisible world beyond the arguments and limitations of science and religion.

A vast intelligence, far beyond your current definitions of God, fills the invisible realms of existence. Cosmic Intelligence is watching and waiting for you to wake up to the new horizons of reality. Humanity is preparing to redefine the invisible world beyond the arguments and limitations of science and religion, and prior to the unveiling of this new insight, many cumbersome and worn-out structures must be refurbished or removed from the scene. Cosmic energies deliver blueprints of possibilities that penetrate your greater mind and seep into your cells to actualize and activate codes of knowledge deep inside your genetic patterns. Even though you cannot see the multitude of radio waves running through the air, you have come to rely on their presence because of the modern developments of technology. Similarly, intense cosmic waveforms, which occupy various subtle locations on the light-spectrum band, have a far more powerful effect on you and your world than all of your broadcast bands combined.

Energies from the Galactic Center are playing the most important role throughout these twenty-five years of human transformation. In December of 2012, the culmination of the nanosecond occurs with the winter solstice sun making an alignment with the center of the Milky Way Galaxy, which is over thirty thousand light-years from Earth. The sun will rise on December 21 to conjunct the intersection of the Milky Way and the plane of the ecliptic completing a twenty-six-thousand-year processional cycle. This event will be like a long-awaited home-coming, a reconnection to your deepest roots as a spiritual being. You will be recharged and revitalized with unbounded creativity from the Womb of the Mother, and you shall know the truth of your origins. And as the years unfold on the way to this auspicious reunion, your solar system will become increasingly active in preparation for the big event.

Once again, it is time to connect the dots. The answer to life's complexities is to be able to laugh; for when you can laugh, you free yourself from victimhood and the chains of disempowerment. When you laugh with good-hearted innocence at your own creations, you are free. It is also worth it to wonder, for wonder opens and unravels reality. Beliefs create reality; they are magical constructs created in your mind, energized in your imagination, and fueled by your feelings. Beliefs are the invisible building blocks, the conditions around which you agree to interact with reality. In this regard, your civilization, like every other, must learn to trace the subtle workings of how beliefs become reality in order to understand the mysteries of the multiverse. So what is your game plan? What will you do with your power to create the world? What will you choose to believe? Remember, how you see and interpret the events of your times will determine the version of the world in which you find yourself. It may appear that there is one version of the world, yet that too is an illusion. Probabilities are as common as grass on the ground; they spring forth from the decisions based on your thoughts, feelings, desires, and emotions. The reality you create may not be the same as that of your neighbor, even though you live on the same street. Reality is tricky and so is creating it, and power is trickiest of all. And power, dear friend, cannot be avoided; power is, and you and power are part of all that is, therefore you are power. The question is, how will you deal with your power? There are no limits to your creativity; your challenge is to overcome your fear of becoming a powerful being.

We are here to teach you how to navigate reality, to provide new metaphors for your evolving consciousness so that you can be effectively creative on the multidimensional game board of existence. We offer you a map for your spiritual development—one that will build confidence and personal empowerment—so you get the best miles-per-galaxy while living in these times. And when the nanosecond is over, you *cannot* look back and say: "I wish someone would have told me what was going on!" We are telling you now. The game of existence is the game of life, the game of awareness, the game of consciousness, the game of energy, and the game of freedom. Each version involves using your creativity to navigate the immense changes that the nanosecond provides. We salute your courage for choosing to live during this time of transformation. We ask you to look deep inside and discover your brilliance, for the indomitable human spirit is patiently awaiting your attention. We encourage you to go forward and to change your life with grace and ease. We advise you to take the risk to love and be loved, and as you build the version of the world you most desire, we extend our most sincerely sustaining support. We urge you to dream wisely to find the future you most desire, to anchor it into your heart, knowing the path is chosen.

Accepting responsibility for your life is your first and most essential act of empowerment.

Accepting responsibility for your life is your first and most essential act of empowerment; you cannot grow in awareness if you are full of conditions and reasons why you cannot attain whatever you desire. Developing a stance of personal responsibility will open all the doors to healing old wounds and energies that have blocked the flow of human development. There are many ways of perceiving life; and how you interpret the world depends, of course, on what you choose to believe. As new truths unravel, ask questions! Your task is to activate the higher mind, to liberate yourself from the tyranny of fear, and to value and understand your human sensitivities. Remember, when everyone is staring off in the same direction, be sure to turn around and glance over your shoulder to see what else is happening. Using your abilities to create a new probable world is the name of the game! All realities are occurring—destruction or regeneration is a choice. You can have whatever you want; your thoughts, dreams, and intentions alter the structure of reality, so which program do you choose to create?

As always, it is with great pleasure that we create the opportunity to share ideas and energies with you and your world, to bring you a bit of inspiration and upliftment in these times of stupendous transformation. Dear friend, this is a time of great choosing in thought, word, and deed, and for our final words of wisdom, we advise you to choose your probability wisely and to stand by your dream. May your path of choice always lead to very pleasant journeys.

ABOUT THE AUTHOR

BARBARA MARCINIAK is an internationally acclaimed trance channel, inspirational speaker, and best-selling author of *Bringers of the Dawn, Earth,* and *Family of Light,* which collectively have been translated into more than twenty languages and have sold over five hundred thousand U.S. copies. She has a BA in social science, and is also the publisher and editor of the quarterly newsletter *The Pleiadian Times.* Her extensive worldwide travels, astrological studies, and a lifetime of alternative free-thinking augment her personal understanding of the material she channels.

The Pleiadians are a collective of multidimensional spirit beings from the Pleiades star system, and have been speaking through Barbara Marciniak since May of 1988. The Pleiadians are here to assist humanity with the process of spiritual transformation in the years leading up to December 2012. Their distinctive style blends wit and wisdom, common sense and cosmic knowledge in teachings that encourage expansive thinking and personal empowerment, and which have been compared to native shamanism.

For information on *The Pleiadian Times*, audio tapes, classes, workshops, and sacred-site tours, visit Barbara's Web site: www.pleiadians.com, or send a self-addressed stamped envelope (foreign inquires please include an international postal coupon) to:

Bold Connections Unlimited
P.O. Box 782
Apex, NC 27502